LINCOLN LIBRARY
October 2013    909

# AMERICAN DREAMERS

OPTIMISTS, MAVERICKS, AND MAD INVENTORS
SHARE THEIR DREAMS FOR BRIGHTER FUTURES

SHARP/STUFF
W+K TOMORROW

©2012 Sharp Stuff

All rights reserved.
No part of this book may be used or reproduced in any matter, including but not limited to websites and other digital media, without prior written permission from the publisher.

*American Dreamers*
Edited by: Nick Barham, Jake Dockter, Mark Searcy, Matt Brown, Tiffani Bryant and Chelsea Bauch.
With support by Matt Keppel and Adam Lucas.
Design by: Mark Searcy

ISBN: 978-0-9886039-0-5

Sharp Stuff
224 NW 13th Ave.
Portland, OR 97209
www.makesharpstuff.com

To explore more American dreams and to learn more about Sharp Stuff visit makesharpstuff.com or talk with us on Twitter at @MakeSharpStuff

Portions of this book have appeared previously and were reprinted with permission by the rightsholder.

Portion of *Reset* by Kurt Andersen. First published in 2009 by Random House. Reprinted with permission of the author.

Portions of Yul Kwon's entry were published as, "The Rebirth of American Manufacturing," on Huffingtonpost.com (May, 1st 2012). Reprinted with permission of the author.

Chris Anderson's entry was given as a speech at the graduation of Harvard Graduate School of Design, class of 2011. Reprinted with permission of the author.

Portions of Claire L. Evan's entry were published as, "On Curiosity and its Shadows," and "Footprints on the Moon" at Scienceblogs.com/universe (August 6/August 26, 2012). Reprinted with permission of the author.

*The views presented within do not necessarily represent the views of Sharp Stuff or the other contributors. They are the views of the contributor and theirs alone. Sharp Stuff takes no responsibility for the opinions of the contributor.*

www.makesharpstuff.com

"My new American Dream is the hope that my old American dream—the one that I was lucky enough to live myself—will continue to expand and be available to all who seek it."

— ARIANNA HUFFINGTON

# FOREWORD

Nostalgia kick-started this project.

It felt that, as a country, as people, we had forgotten how to dream. When we looked back at earlier decades, we saw ambitious, shiny dreams full of rocket packs, equality, and cloud cities. Social progress met technological evolution, supercharged by optimism and the belief that a better tomorrow for future generations was being created.

We wondered how we could regain that optimism.

We wondered if there were still dreamers out there.

And while the American Dream might have taken a hit, we found plenty of American dreamers.

In the place of one dream that guides us all, we discovered many: created by inventors and prophets, designers and poets, artists and entrepreneurs who believe in brighter futures. *American Dreamers* brings these visionaries together: Dr. Zubrin reminds us why humans must travel to Mars; Cindy Gallop offers a real world alternative to porn; Stan Lee calls for heroes; and Arianna Huffington banishes old media gods. From cooking to space travel, from sex to running, this is a mixture of projects, schemes and blueprints for tomorrow.

This collection of over fifty dreams is just the start. We're continuing to talk to dreamers and collect dreams. If you find some in here that inspire you, let us know. If you know other dreamers who should be here, tell us their name. And of course, share your dreams with us.

Those cloud cities and rocket packs aren't as far away as they might seem.

"One never knows what will change the world."

—STAN LEE

# DREAMERS

| | | | |
|---|---|---|---|
| 2 | Ed Finn | 194 | Rae Bryant |
| 7 | Yul Kwon | 202 | Creston Davis |
| 13 | Arianna Huffington | 207 | Kurt Andersen |
| 18 | Jane Kim | 214 | Dr. Robert Zubrin |
| 24 | Israel Bayer | 227 | Amber Case |
| 32 | K. Michael Merrill | 234 | John Zogby |
| 36 | John Hockenberry | 241 | Ani Zonneveld |
| 43 | Claire L. Evans | 248 | Ross Borden |
| 51 | Susan McKee Reese | 255 | Natalie Bailey |
| 55 | Charles Bradley | 261 | Panthea Lee & Zack Brisson |
| 63 | SoulPancake featuring Rainn Wilson | 271 | Jon Friedman |
| 68 | Stan Lee | 274 | Nader Tehrani |
| 71 | Shannon Galpin | 286 | Ellen Dunham-Jones |
| 83 | Jamie Hyneman & Adam Savage | 300 | Alexander Rose |
| 93 | Nirvan Mullick | 309 | Hideshi Hamaguchi |
| 104 | Dr. Cameron M. Smith | 315 | John Maeda |
| 118 | Michael Brennan | 319 | Leslie Bradshaw |
| 122 | Michelle Rowley | 325 | Aaron Koblin |
| 126 | Ann Friedman | 332 | Richard Saul Wurman |
| 132 | Danny Kennedy | 340 | Matthew Matthew |
| 141 | Curtis Kulig | 347 | Baratunde Thurston |
| 147 | Jennifer Lee | 354 | Ji Lee |
| 152 | Cindy Gallop | 362 | Wayne White |
| 159 | Justin, Travis & Griffin McElroy | 370 | Nisha Chittal |
| 164 | Tim Wise | 378 | Jason Pollock |
| 176 | Melissa Hanna | 385 | Naomi Pomeroy |
| 179 | Richard Nash | 391 | Jessie Zapotechne |
| 184 | Matthew Dickman | 398 | Chris Anderson |

# ED FINN

---

*Ed Finn is the founding director of the Center for Science and the Imagination at Arizona State University.*

us.tomorrow-projects.com

## AMERICAN DREAMERS: SHARING THE FIRE

Why are we talking about American dreamers, anyway? How did we stake our claim to be the land of opportunity, the global leader for incurable optimism? When Thomas Jefferson wrote about the American imagination, he chose the metaphor of fire. Ideas should flow like light in the darkness, "as he who lights his taper at mine, receives light without darkening me." Jefferson was one of the original American dreamers, a man with many faults but also an explosive mix of creativity and ambition. His passions ranged from gardening and architecture to the framing of constitutions, and he doubled as our first patent officer and secretary of state.

Jefferson and the other founding fathers knew that the new republic needed to balance optimism and pragmatism if the experiment was going to last. The separation of powers and the Declaration of Independence toe a line between human folly and human progress: a belief that the world can become better, but that its improvement and its stewardship depend on us.

You might say that the spirit of thoughtful optimism has infused some of our greatest achievements. The Internet and the Apollo missions were born out of nuclear anxieties and Cold War paranoia but transformed those impulses into startling victories for the species. Living out Jefferson's language, they lit up the globe, igniting the imaginations of billions.

In recent years, the spirit of thoughtful optimism has struggled to overcome the challenges of political infighting and cultural malaise. When we do contemplate big thinking today, it's almost never something to take on personally. Instead, we rely on well-funded entrepreneurs and major corporations to do our dreaming for us, content to wait for the new update or the latest sequel to appear and make us marginally happier, for a while. That kind of thinking has gotten us a world obsessed with incremental improvements in a few key areas while we ignore entire systems that are stagnating, crumbling, or just destructively churning along. We have spent untold billions in researching a few high profile diseases while hardly bothering to invest in new antibiotics or basic preventive medicine—drugs that actually work aren't as profitable as those that merely treat the symptoms. We agonize over gas mileage improvements while hundreds of new coal-fired power plants open around the world. The people who are changing the world either invest massive amounts of their own capital, like Bill Gates, or they perform end runs around existing social structures in order to achieve specific goals, like the X PRIZE Foundation. It's not that we've forgotten how to change the world. Barack Obama did it in 2008. Mark Zuckerberg did it when he founded Facebook in 2004. This year NASA landed a one-ton machine on Mars with automatic piloting. But what we're missing is a sense

> WHAT WE'RE MISSING IS A SENSE OF COLLECTIVE AGENCY, A SHARED NARRATIVE OF THE AMERICAN DREAMER. WE NEED TO RECOGNIZE THAT NOBODY IS GOING TO BUILD THE WORLD WE WANT BUT US.

of collective agency, a shared narrative of the American dreamer. We need to recognize that nobody is going to build the world we want but us.

Reigniting the tapers, rekindling our thoughtful optimism—that's the core mission of the Center for Science and the Imagination. We launched in the fall of 2012 at Arizona State University with a remit to get people everywhere thinking more creatively and ambitiously about the future. We are bringing artists, writers, humanists, and designers together with researchers and engineers to think big and do big things. We are building a global network to incubate moonshot ideas and a cultural engine for thoughtful optimism among faculty, students, and our communities. We know that to change the world, you have to start with better stories. We think thoughtful optimism means recognizing that putting a man on the moon and building better social systems here on Earth are equally challenging and equally important. It means better stories about sustainability and justice as well as artificial intelligence and space vehicles. When we say imagination, we don't just mean that initial spark of a new idea—we're talking about the human engine that keeps at the problem, adapting tools and creativity to build complete solutions.

We're not interested in "somebody should invent that..." but rather, "we can do this better."

We're building our own engine for thoughtful optimism by starting in the same place Jefferson did: recognizing the power of a good story to spread ideas like wildfire and light up the world. With the Hieroglyph project, we are partnering some of the world's great science fiction writers with leading scientists and engineers and asking them to imagine techno-optimistic stories set in the near future.

We are also hosting Tomorrow Project USA, a collaboration with Intel and the Society for Science & the

Public intended to spark fact-based conversations about the futures we want and what we should avoid. Our inaugural competition, Green Dreams, is open to college students everywhere and asks contributors to craft ambitious, science-based narratives about futures powered by renewable energy and sustainable living.

Last but not least, we are celebrating thoughtful optimism at Emerge, a three-day performance, exhibition, conference, and collective conversation about how art, science, and the humanities can help us think differently about the future. Emerge will take on the future of truth: the shared stories and the competing narratives that make up "fact" and "fiction" in the world today. It will be a collective experiment in thoughtful optimism (best performed, as always, with healthy doses of skepticism and humor) worked out in a series of iterative performances, conversations, and beautiful lies. Artists, engineers, designers, futurists, scientists, humanists, and makers will gather for a festival of cognitive dissonance that explores our own complex entanglements with truth, reason, and meaning. And that, my friends, is year one.

As we keep building this thoughtful optimism engine and extending our network of creative thinkers around the world, we want to start a new school of American dreamers. What we believe in, the fire that we want to share, is the knowledge that we need better dreams to build better futures. Won't you join us?

6   AMERICAN DREAMERS

# YUL KWON

*Yul Kwon is an American television host. He was the winner of* Survivor: Cook Islands *in 2006. He recently hosted* America Revealed *on PBS, exploring the industry and passion that makes America what it is.*

pbs.org/america-revealed

## MADE IN THE USA

Everyone knows that American manufacturing is dying. It's the industrial equivalent of a dead man walking. I thought so too before I spent eighteen months exploring the vast systems that support the American way of life. My journey was captured in a series called *America Revealed*, which aired on PBS earlier this year. Like a lot of people, I had come to accept the conventional wisdom that America doesn't make anything anymore and that all our manufacturing jobs have gone overseas.

Over the course of my cross-country odyssey examining different industries, I gained a far more nuanced perspective on American manufacturing. What I discovered is that the prevailing narrative of decline and decay is overly simplistic and in some ways flat out wrong. It turns out that America still makes lots of things. In fact, we manufacture more products today than at any other time in our history. But how we make things and what we make has changed—in some cases, dramatically.

Our manufacturing base used to be concentrated in a handful of large cities that were largely defined by what they produced. Detroit cranked out cars, while Pittsburgh was all about steel (hence, the name Pittsburgh Steelers). Many smaller cities were company towns where one firm supplied lifelong jobs to much of the community. Today, American manufacturing is more geographically diversified, less labor-intensive, and radically more efficient.

> TODAY, AMERICAN MANUFACTURING IS MORE GEOGRAPHICALLY DIVERSIFIED, LESS LABOR-INTENSIVE, AND RADICALLY MORE EFFICIENT.

For example, in Newport News, Virginia, I saw the construction of what will soon be the most advanced and powerful ship ever created—the U.S.S. Gerald Ford. It's a ten billion dollar nuclear-powered aircraft carrier whose construction demands a level of skill, sophistication, and resources that no other nation on earth could match. Parts and equipment are being sourced from nearly every state in the country, presenting huge logistical challenges. Yet the builders are using new manufacturing techniques and a virtual design blueprint system to accelerate the construction process while significantly reducing errors.

In Charlotte, North Carolina, I found a steelmaker that was experiencing record growth even as many of its competitors wilted from international competition. Nucor Corporation realized that traditional ways of making steel in America simply could not compete with low-cost suppliers overseas, so it decided to invest in groundbreaking manufacturing approaches such as using electric furnaces instead of conventional furnaces and recycling scrap metal instead of mining iron ore. Today, Nucor is America's most profitable steel-maker.

In Nazareth, Pennsylvania, the iconic guitar-maker, Martin Guitars, discovered that innovation in the manufacture of guitars didn't necessarily mean replacing people. Quite the contrary, they learned that there are some things you can't replace, like highly skilled human expertise. When they tried to automate and outsource too much, they began losing the very thing that made their products unique. So today, they've figured out how to automate the low value-added parts of the manufacturing chain while applying the skills of their employees towards the areas that require a uniquely human touch.

> THERE ARE SOME THINGS YOU CAN'T REPLACE, LIKE HIGHLY SKILLED HUMAN EXPERTISE.

I learned that the term, "Made in America," is itself evolving. American manufacturers nowadays often have foreign names. Over the last twenty years, the majority of the new auto plants in America have been built by foreign companies like Honda, Toyota, BMW, and Nissan. Together, these companies have put about forty-four billion dollars of new investment in the U.S., and they now employ about eighty thousand Americans. Why have so many foreign companies decided to build manufacturing plants here? As one expert I interviewed explained, "The United States is still a good place to build stuff, especially low added-value added stuff."

Nothing illustrates this point better than America's newest auto factory in Chattanooga, Tennessee, which is owned by Volkswagen and cost one billion dollars to build. Here, American workers are being taught the latest manufacturing principles. They're being encouraged to generate ideas on how to improve processes rather than simply build widgets mechanically. They also work closely with an army of robots that have taken over the most labor-intensive and repetitive tasks, leaving the humans to focus on more complex challenges.

Due to the ingenuity and resilience of companies like the ones I met on my journey, the value of what American workers manufacture today is nearly twice what it was in 1990. We make more than 1.7 trillion dollars' worth of goods each year—more than China, Germany, Japan or any other nation on earth. As surprising as it may seem, America is still the world's number one manufacturing country. Domestically, manufacturing still accounts for 12 percent of the U.S. economy, employs about eleven million Americans, and generates countless spin-off jobs.

Of course, one inevitable consequence of automation and other advances is that while our productivity has increased, we often need fewer people to make them. Combined with the outsourcing of lower value-added jobs overseas, the resulting loss of jobs in certain industries has been devastating to many American communities, especially those that grew up around large industrial cities and company towns. Too often, I saw the decaying hulks of a bygone era—abandoned warehouses and shuttered factories—still dotting the American landscape.

But if you look beyond the narrow parameters of manufacturing as it's traditionally been conceived and consider what kinds of things are being created in twenty-first century America, the picture looks quite a bit different. American engineers used to make things that you could see and touch. But increasingly, what they make now is less tangible but more valuable. The Internet has not only revolutionized the way products are manufactured, it's created a new information-based economy in which the raw materials are ideas. Silicon Valley and other technology clusters have become powerful engines of economic and job growth, even though many tech companies don't sell a product you can hold in your hand. Take Facebook. The concept of an online social network hardly existed not too long ago. Today, Facebook is one of the most valuable and influential companies in the world, with more users than the population of every country outside of China and India. It's also created a new software platform that allows anyone to

**THE JOBS ARE THERE, BUT THE PEOPLE WHO NEED THEM DON'T HAVE THE SKILLS TO FILL THEM.**

launch a business online, something that's already resulted in thousands of new companies and billions in revenue.

American companies dominate this new economy, yet despite their constantly-rising need for talented engineers, we're not producing enough workers to meet demand. The jobs are there, but the people who need them don't have the skills to fill them. So the larger questions loom—how can we bridge the skills gap between our current workers and the jobs that are growing? How can we retrain workers who have lost traditional manufacturing jobs so that they can become employable in today's economy? How can we educate our children so that they have the tools and training they need not just to find jobs, but to continue the tradition of innovation that has made America the most productive nation in history?

There aren't any simple answers to these questions, but I nonetheless came away from my experiences with a newfound optimism that I hadn't expected to find. A revolution is unfolding in what and how America creates. Some of the changes have exacted a tragic cost on many Americans who have been dislocated in their wake. But there is no question in my mind that America is still the best place on Earth to build new things, and that our leadership in innovation will endure.

**A REVOLUTION IS UNFOLDING IN WHAT AND HOW AMERICA CREATES.**

**NOTE:** *Portions of this essay previously appeared in the Huffington Post article "The Rebirth of American Manufacturing," on May 1st, 2012.*

*12* AMERICAN DREAMERS

# ARIANNA HUFFINGTON

---

*Arianna Huffington is the president and editor-in-chief of the Huffington Post Media Group, a nationally syndicated columnist, and author of thirteen books. In May 2005, she launched* The Huffington Post, *a news and blog site that quickly became one of the most widely read, linked-to, and frequently cited media brands on the Internet. In 2012, the site won a Pulitzer Prize for national reporting. In 2006, and again in 2011, she was named to the* Time 100, Time *magazine's list of the world's one hundred most influential people.*

huffingtonpost.com

## NEW MEDIA GODS

### What kind of future do you dream of?

I dream of a future where the fundamental promise of America—that our children will have the opportunity to do better than their parents—has been restored.

### What needs to be done to get there?

While we need to keep talking about our shortages—of jobs and revenue and good ideas coming from our leaders—we also need to start focusing much more on our surpluses—the creativity, ingenuity, wisdom, and inspiration that have the power to bring about the solutions we so desperately need. The civic activist John Gardner said it best: "What we have before us are some breathtaking opportunities disguised as insoluble problems."

> WE NEED TO START FOCUSING MUCH MORE ON OUR SURPLUSES—THE CREATIVITY, INGENUITY, WISDOM, AND INSPIRATION THAT HAVE THE POWER TO BRING ABOUT THE SOLUTIONS WE SO DESPERATELY NEED.

### *What is your new American Dream? How is it different from the old one?*

My new American Dream is the hope that my old American Dream—the one that I was lucky enough to live myself—will continue to expand and be available to all who seek it. In the preamble of the Constitution, we are told that we are constantly moving towards a more perfect union. But the American Dream that is at the heart of the founding of this country is, at the moment, at risk. America is now behind the Scandinavian countries in upward mobility, behind Spain, behind France. And being behind France in upward mobility is a little like France being behind us in croissants and afternoon sex.

### *How do we create optimism about tomorrow?*

By tapping into the barn-raising spirit that has always been part of the American DNA. We tried to do just that during the Republican and Democratic conventions, when *HuffPost* hosted panel discussions about job creation, moderated by Tom Brokaw. As a journalist and as a storyteller, in books like *The Greatest Generation* and *The Time of Our Lives*, Brokaw has chronicled the American experience in his own distinctive voice, and his work is a reminder that we can rekindle the American Dream, but to do so we need to summon the American spirit.

## What is the future or journalism?

It's a hybrid future, with traditional outlets adopting the tools of digital journalists—including speed, transparency, and engagement—and new media adopting the best practices of traditional journalism, including fact-checking, fairness, and accuracy. A future where the division between "old media" and "new media" is increasingly blurred.

## How are the current changes in journalism an opportunity for the future?

The current changes have led us to a Golden Age for engagement, for consumers who can access the best stories from around the world and be able to comment, interact, and form communities. The *HuffPost* community is an incredibly vibrant one—we're coming up on our two hundred millionth comment. Through this kind of platform, we are able to put the spotlight on voices that wouldn't otherwise be heard, telling the stories people care about most—and, just as important, helping them tell their stories themselves.

## How can more people share their stories; what is the opportunity for people in news and storytelling?

Our Golden Age of engagement means that, more than ever before, people are able to use technology to share their stories. The opportunity lies in the fact that, while the Internet's early years were defined by random searching, something new has emerged: a search for greater meaning.

## What will we write about in the future?

To begin with, the "we" has expanded. The days of the media gods, sitting up on Mt. Olympus and telling us how things

**THE DAYS OF THE MEDIA GODS, SITTING UP ON MT. OLYMPUS AND TELLING US HOW THINGS ARE, HAVE ENDED.** are, have ended. People are tired of being talked to; they want to be talked with. Ours is a global conversation, with millions of new people pulling up a seat at the table—indeed, nearly three billion people will join the Internet community. So, as new platforms have given voice to the voiceless, we've witnessed a shift from presentation to participation. Which means, more people now have the chance to write—and post photos, videos, podcasts, etc. etc. etc.—about what matters most to them.

17

# JANE KIM

Jane Kim began her art career early in life by obsessively painting flowers and bears on the walls of her bedroom. She loves the outdoors and brings the joy she gets from nature back to the studio. Recent commissions include the Amazon Aid Foundation, Yosemite National Park, The Cornell Lab of Ornithology, The Smithsonian, The Nature Conservancy, and the San Francisco Conservatory of Flowers.

ink-dwell.com

## MIGRATING MURALS

My true north is creating art that impacts the way people see, interact with, and think about the natural world we're surrounded by. Our planet is home to incredible and wondrous life, and I dream of a world where the earth is appreciated and protected. I feel most excited, both visually and intellectually, in nature. Combining that with my passion for art gives me unrefined excitement. Sharing even a fraction of that with the rest of the world is the best gift that I know how to give. If I can spark curiosity about wildlife and the natural world in others through art, then my dreams are contagious. And shared dreams are really powerful.

In 2011, I founded INK-DWELL, a studio that creates art to inspire love, appreciation, and protection of the natural world. I've dedicated more than two years to creating a public art and conservation installation called *The Migrating Mural*: a series of murals that showcases—-in towns, cities, and along major highways—-endangered migratory species and the need to protect them. Each mural is a monument to these animals.

In the summer of 2010, I lived in Yosemite National Park where I learned about a very special animal, the Sierra Nevada bighorn sheep. The Sierra Nevada bighorn sheep is a distinct subspecies and exists only in the eastern range of California's Sierra Nevada. At one time, they numbered in the thousands. In the nineties, there were so few sheep they could be identified as individuals in the field. Today, it is considered one of the rarest large animals in North America.

It became an obsession of mine to see a Sierra Nevada bighorn sheep. It's hard, really hard. I contacted a biologist who has devoted his whole life to studying and restoring the Sierra bighorns and I finally saw them! I even helped collect sheep poop, and once poop's involved, you know you're in deep. It was then that I decided I would make the Sierra Nevada bighorn sheep the first animal of *The Migrating Mural*.

*The Migrating Mural: Chapter One: Sierra Bighorns* is a year-long project during which I'll paint a series of four murals about the life of Sierra Nevada bighorn sheep along US Highway 395, to bring attention to this very special megafauna. The murals begin in Olancha, CA and end in Lee Vining, CA, a distance of about 145 miles. Each mural corresponds with a herd unit occupying that area and shares some of their biology, such as the growth stages of a ram. I'm very excited to make this animal the first subject of

> OUR PLANET IS HOME TO INCREDIBLE AND WONDROUS LIFE, AND I DREAM OF A WORLD WHERE THE EARTH IS APPRECIATED AND PROTECTED.

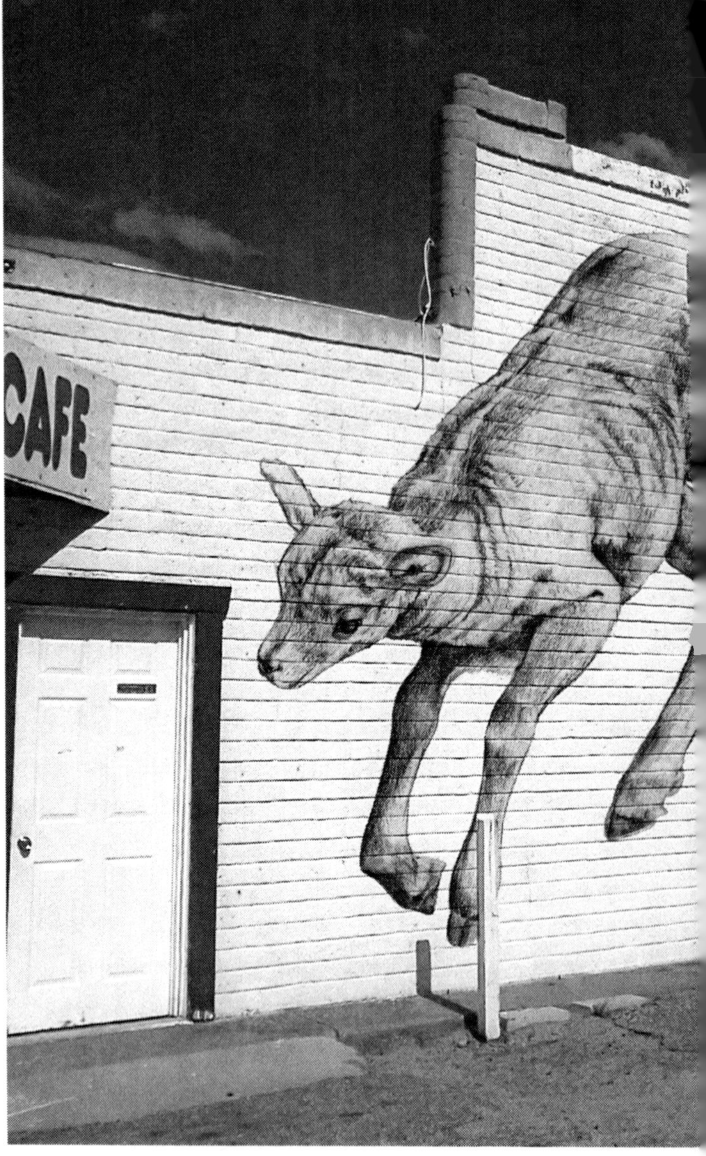
CAFE

*Courtesy of Jane Kim*

*The Migrating Mural* and committed to being a steward for wildlife through art.

My dream for *The Migrating Mural* is for it to become global in scope and scale. It could become a program for key environmental and public and private sectors to partner with. We'll identify an animal, region, and series of mural sites, then offer grants for artists to paint each one. The migration route of North Pacific blue whales runs from Baja to Alaska, so a panel of judges would choose an artist in each town along this route to paint a mural. It's a beautiful way to connect many different places with one project, one animal, and one goal.

To launch this project, I used Kickstarter to try and raise enough money to fund the first mural. It was awesome. Within one week, the $20,000 goal was met. For me, the most incredible part was that the project was made a reality by people from all over the world. Kickstarter was a built-in advertisement for *The Migrating Mural* and that is exactly what projects like this need to have an impact. The more people know and believe in *The Migrating Mural*, the more the word will continue to spread. It becomes infectious and everyone wants to be a part of it.

It's a big win all around. The animals get attention, the locations gain beautiful art and a new economic driver, and everyone gets a ton of positive attention. Good work today can influence others to do the same, so public support is the first and most critical step towards great change. If we can get a variety of towns, people, and organizations around a common goal, we can build on that to continually generate public interest and participation. I think that it's all about spreading the word, getting involved, and popularizing the project. Small victories that empower us today impact and change the trends for the future. Let's get the world excited about this!

> GOOD WORK TODAY CAN INFLUENCE OTHERS TO DO THE SAME, SO PUBLIC SUPPORT IS THE FIRST AND MOST CRITICAL STEP TOWARDS GREAT CHANGE.

23

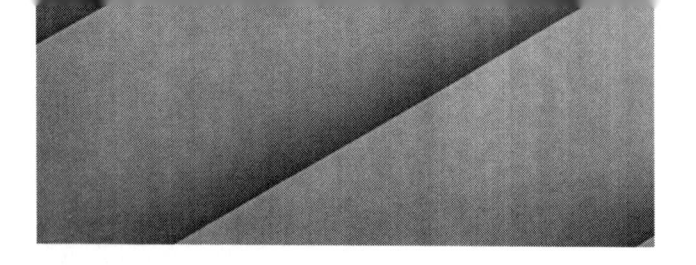

# ISRAEL BAYER

---

*Israel Bayer is the Executive Director of* Street Roots, *a street newspaper in Portland, Oregon. He is also a published poet, artist and photographer.*

streetroots.org | opensourcery.com

## THE NARRATIVE IS CHANGING

The narrative is changing.

The vast majority of the narrative about homelessness has been told through the eyes of great historians and novelists, professors and intellectuals, journalists and pundits. The actual voices of many of the people who have experienced poverty throughout history have been lost or forgotten.

That is all changing. The technological age is beginning to turn this storyline on its head.

The rapid pace of technological advances is allowing individuals in poverty the opportunity to tell their own narrative and to communicate with one another in new ways. It's also allowing grassroots organizations who operate in the trenches of poverty the ability to document and share the work they do, while giving voice to the people they serve. Imagine if social service workers and local governments used social media to document the experience of getting people into housing. The systems level approach to social service work that is so hard to communicate to the broader public would be boiled down to stories and images of people's difficulties and successes. It could change public opinion.

It makes more sense to Tweet one hundred pictures of people getting an apartment with a key in hand, over the course of six months, than trying to explain to the public in one shot, why one million dollars from taxpayers will house one hundred people they don't have any connection with. Communities that have no connection to urban or rural poverty would instantly feel more connected and want to help tackle the problem of homelessness and the work nonprofits do by understanding the experiences and struggles people face.

## STREET NEWSPAPERS AS EXAMPLE

I've worked directly with people experiencing poverty at street newspapers in Portland (*Street Roots*) and Seattle (*Real Change*) for nearly fifteen years. During that time, I've seen the power of media as a vehicle for empowerment and advocacy. More importantly still, I've seen the power of communication between individuals and the community at large. The street newspaper model is simple. People experiencing poverty sell newspapers in front of local establishments, mostly in urban environments to gain an income. It's a model that has deep roots in the print industry.

What makes the model unique and continue to work today, in an era of digital journalism, is the interpersonal relationship between people on the streets, local businesses and the community at large. When people are able to create genuine relationships and connections to one another, new storylines emerge. No longer is George, a street newspaper vendor, just another homeless person on the corner. Instead

street
$1 roots

Mayor Sam Adams

*Courtesy of Israel Bayer*

he becomes an individual woven into the community fabric. People learn that George loves to fish, and that he likes baseball. Possibly they learn that George is homeless because of a traumatic brain injury, or because of economic reasons. What they also understand is that George is a human being. George begins to gain self-worth, understanding that people in the community do care for his well-being and new friendships are formed. George begins to gain self-confidence knowing that he is working for his own income and offering people something they enjoy. George also has the opportunity to contribute towards solutions to problems he himself faces by having a voice.

Street newspaper readers, in turn, are able to connect with a broad range of issues surrounding poverty and culture through the newspaper, while building a relationship with someone across class lines. All of this is happening simultaneously with thousands of vendors selling street newspapers in cities around the globe.

Today, there are one hundred twenty street newspapers in forty countries and growing.

## WILL TECHNOLOGY SAVE THE POOR?

Over the past two decades, we've seen a movement toward the idea that if people had greater access to technology they may be able to end their poverty. That's simply not true. In certain instances technology may contribute to offering new opportunities, but it will not end poverty on a global scale. What technology can do is give people experiencing poverty more of a voice.

On one hand, I'm an optimist. I believe that with the right set of circumstances and opportunities, any human being can be successful. I'm also a realist and understand poverty itself is cruel and offers little opportunity for a large group of people without education and an adequate social safety net.

It's impossible to change deep-rooted public perception about the homeless or to develop new and innovative resources for the poor without having local conversations. In order to have new conversations, the voice of people experiencing poverty has to be present.

## A NEW WORLD

We live in a world where the media landscape is rapidly changing. Due to the lack of resource development and a changing technological environment, no longer will newsrooms, book and magazine publishers, photojournalists, and universities have exclusive rights to how the stories of the poor are told and viewed in the world we live. Knowing that it's harder and harder for these institutions to secure the resources to deliver the story of people experiencing poverty, we must find a way to offer an income and train the poor to deliver the stories themselves.

Imagine if museums were not only able to reflect on art, history, and culture, but were able to bring the voices of different communities experiencing poverty to life (real time) through highlighting people's lives through their own lenses using multi-media platforms? What if universities required courses in a range of subject matters that engaged the individuals and communities they were studying through new technologies? Why shouldn't news organizations embrace citizen journalism, incorporating the voices of people in poverty to reflect the subject matters they are covering?

The list goes on.

In many ways all of this is already happening peer-to-peer and by a younger generation that is choosing to access information in new ways. Open source technology, social media, and new inventions will continue to elevate the role

> IN ORDER TO HAVE NEW CONVERSATIONS, THE VOICE OF PEOPLE EXPERIENCING POVERTY HAS TO BE PRESENT.

poor people have in their own narratives. The next steps require real investments and leadership from nonprofits, foundations, and the private sector to elevate the stories of poor people into broader platforms for institutions to access and improve on. The future narrative of people experiencing homelessness and poverty is an open book. If we listen closely and plan accordingly, the horizons are limitless.

31

# K. MICHAEL MERRILL

---

K. Michael Merrill is the world's only publicly traded person. He works on projects in various forms with many people, all guided by the gentle hand of his shareholders who have invested their money and time to add accountability and expertise.

kmikeym.com

## THE FUTURE IS OKAY

> THE FUTURE IS SLAPPING AT THE WINDOWS AND SEEPING IN TO FLOOD THE BASEMENT.

All people think their time is the worst, with social changes wrought by man and the end always being near. We have less reason to think this now than previous generations, and more reason than others. But it's not a pissing match to see who lives in the darkest days of humanity. In fact, it's sort of the opposite. Are there fucked up things happening all across the world? Yes, there still are. Is this the greatest time to ever be alive? Yes, until tomorrow. Present a list of all the flaws in the world and I'll reply, "Great, now we know what we need to fix." It's an opportunity not a problem.

The future is no longer a dream. It's here. The future is slapping at the windows and seeping in to flood the basement. We have bacteriophage that can be used to deliver DNA messages, we have intelligent information systems automatically detecting threats and recognizing criminal behavior, we have headsets that read brainwaves and allow us hands-free control of computers. We are on the cusp of normalcy for kids printing physical objects at home, we have wallpaper that selectively blocks radio frequencies to limit wifi or cell phone usage. This is happening right now.

Of course some people find rapid change horrific. They imagine the worst of these changes wreaking havoc. There is a sliver of pessimism, but that is a symptom. The disease is fear. We retreat to nostalgic ideas of the idyllic past, attempting to recreate a world that is more under our control. As kids we imagined the future to escape the present and now as adults we imagine the past to escape the future. The most pessimistic thing I've come to realize is that optimism is not a choice.

> AS KIDS WE IMAGINED THE FUTURE TO ESCAPE THE PRESENT AND NOW AS ADULTS WE IMAGINE THE PAST TO ESCAPE THE FUTURE.

## *What social changes excite you the most and make you hopeful for tomorrow?*

The Internet. How could there be any other answer? Maybe it's too generic an answer? But how else do we talk about it? It's not the technology. The way the Internet works has become mostly invisible. It just exists. A global communication network. It's not perfect, but it's pretty close! I just registered a new domain this morning. My new domain is as easy to get to as the biggest sites that exist: Google, Facebook, Twitter, and Wikipedia. It is just a URL. Easy to start and cheap to run. What did you make today?

That's the part that I find the most exciting. As much as we try to create an audience on the web there is a spirit in the way it was built that calls people to create instead of consume. Start a blog, post on Facebook, make a video for YouTube, jump into a random live video chat, sell your shit to strangers, put ads on your blog: sell them some t-shirts and a coffee mug, quit your day job, interview your heroes, and eventually get interviewed by those that think of you as their hero. Fuck, that's exciting. That happens every day!

## What steps can we be taking now to change the future?

**PARTICIPATE. STOP FOLLOWING AND LIKING AND WATCHING AND READING AND START MAKING AND POSTING AND DOING. MAKE THE WEIRDEST PARTS OF YOUR LIFE BORING. JUMP INTO THINGS YOU FEAR YOU WON'T UNDERSTAND.**

Participate. There is but one step. Stop following and liking and watching and reading and start making and posting and doing. Talk about the things you love, the more obscure the better, and find your community of like-minded weirdos. Blur the line so far between your Internet life and your off-line life that you find the term IRL to be offensive. Become best friends with a person you've never met. Tell them incredibly personal shit. Start a business with them. Never meet them in person and feel normal about it.

The future is only exciting because it hasn't happened. As soon as it happens we adjust to it and it's normal. Boring even. So get out and make the weirdest parts of your life boring. Push yourself harder. Be weirder. Make it more normal. We will destroy the concept of normalcy by making everything normal. Once it's ubiquitous it no longer exists.

Jump into things you fear you won't understand. Reprogram your car. Implant an RFID in your body. We can facilitate the future by participation. Don't wait for it to be boring. Get in on the future while it's still weird! We can't change the future, but we can embrace it and help it happen.

35

# JOHN HOCKENBERRY

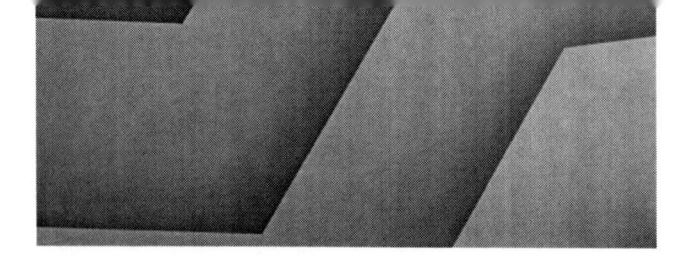

*John Hockenberry is a journalist, author, and presenter. He is the founding host of the public radio program* The Takeaway, *and has worked in network television, documentary films, and new media.*

## IMAGINE THERE'S NO COUNTRY, IT'S EASY IF YOU TRY (IN 2012)

John Lennon's catchy 1971 lyrics notwithstanding, America's dream state began and ended with a single memorable phrase almost exactly ten years earlier. "Ask not what your country can do for you. Ask what you can do for your country." This communal notion of a government and its people in collaboration inaugurated John F. Kennedy's foreshortened presidency and was almost immediately set aside. The government would do a lot for people in the ensuing years. The imperatives of the Johnson Great Society programs, Nixon's government expansion, and the huge Reagan-era enlargement of the Pentagon would deliver help to the poor and elderly, deregulation and prosperity to politically savvy interests, and a sense of military supremacy and security for all.

**OUR CIVIC ENGAGEMENT IS EITHER AS DONORS OR RECIPIENTS OF TAX REVENUES.**

In 2012 this is all breaking down. In an unsustainable spiral of inflated commitments and deflated political will, that eloquent bit of JFK oratory has become a strident and uninspiring argument over entitlements versus taxes. We are a binary nation divided according to rich and poor. Our civic engagement is either as donors or recipients of tax revenues. For more than a generation we have been voting on the basis of impulses that come from the familiar question, "Are you better off today than you were four years ago?" or statements like: "Government doesn't solve problems; government is the problem." The quality of national life relates to little more than individual prosperity and individual security with government at the specific service of groups who can mobilize to get it to enhance their individual interests. All questions of civic engagement relate to quantity rather than quality in our time. The magnitude of political contributions, rates of taxation, and voter turnout tell us nothing about the quality of life in America or how we might define a mission to seek a brighter future.

Did JFK understand back in 1961 that we would eventually get to this?

"Ask not if you are better off than you were four years ago, ask if you are more engaged in creating the conditions for you and those around you to survive and thrive."

This is no political sound bite. It is at best a lyric resisting a melody. It is a thoughtful upgrade of the JFK sentiments that is also a lament born out of the anxious gray uncertainties of the twenty-first century. As political systems and traditional institutions lose their language and bearings and find themselves unable to reassure or mobilize their constituents we need fundamentally new ways of calling people to action. Changing circumstances and a suddenly unwelcome national narcissism has hopelessly outdated the American Dream. We must dream beyond this malaise with something tangible.

> **THE MAGNITUDE OF POLITICAL CONTRIBUTIONS, RATES OF TAXATION, AND VOTER TURNOUT TELL US NOTHING ABOUT THE QUALITY OF LIFE IN AMERICA OR HOW WE MIGHT DEFINE A MISSION TO SEEK A BRIGHTER FUTURE.**

The great irony is that we have mechanisms to dream of a more meaningful future with many pathways to get there and we have learned to overlook them all in our degraded politics.

We tell people to dream and reach for the stars. Do we really mean it? Are our relentless "follow your dreams" messages in children's books and TV shows accompanied by any suggestions on how to get there? I suggest that these invocations to dream and aim high are nothing more than some opiated ploy for improving short-term self-esteem. I think they lead directly to the bluster, rage, and ignorant passions of the Tea Party and other contemporary political zealots. We see them in passionate extremes on cable news shows and in Super-Pac financed photo-op rallies trying to take back the country. They, and their skilled media surrogates, are engaged in politics as though it is some redemption window and they are trying to get recompense for a smudged dream ticket they have been clutching since childhood. These are the outcomes of our dreams today.

> WE VALUE THE IMPULSE TO REACH FOR THE STARS BUT HAVE NO PATIENCE FOR THE WORK IT TAKES TO GET THERE.

We don't really believe in our dreamers. We encourage their imagination but don't think they can actually succeed beyond a hope of winning something like a lottery. We value the impulse to reach for the stars but have no patience for the work it takes to get there. America's collective lottery of achievement and success is the principle venture of the tribe-of-one individualism that characterizes our national ethos today. Our dreams should be the product of a collective vision with organized teams of communities dedicated to get there. Outside of the question of "Are we better off?", the welfare of our communities is not something we have any intuitive feel for anymore. Endless empathy for fetuses, burning flags, "the middle class," something called "traditional marriage," and arguments over "legitimate rape" are only more evidence that we have no way of speaking about the real communities we live in and defer to these conceptual communities of dogmatic values and narrow issues.

The very concept of the nation-state and our politics are so challenged because the groupings and communities that define our elections seem to have little relevance to our lives. Either they can't accomplish anything, or their purpose is so at odds with anything that we individually might want, our public institutions find themselves stymied with division and inertia. By contrast, the impromptu communities formed in social media and in other digitally enabled purpose driven campaigns seem vital and all about relevance, they can't exist without a sustained reminder of their relevance. Once upon a time, people would come together to fight city hall or elect a candidate or build a new water system as only an extraordinary occurrence, an occasional timeout from the normal communities of place. Now, people are increasingly involved in movements, gatherings, and communities that exist in a communication space where geography is an afterthought. Urgency fills a vast range from communities that track everything from the trivialities of where pop star Nicki Minaj is eating lunch to the life or death casualty count and military siege in Aleppo, Syria. In these communities, the only organizing principle is collective relevance to the membership, and that relevance may trump mere longevity, a real challenge to venerable institutions, and political units with tenured bragging rights, like Fairfax County (established in 1742) or the State of Nebraska (established in 1867).

We are entering what I call a new spirit of 1776. It is the growth of a collective yearning for civic democracy to evolve away from these geographic designations. People are disgusted with systems of accidental organization that can be gamed and distorted to produce outcomes no one trusts and meet few people's needs. The persistent suspense of "battleground state" driven Electoral College campaign

WE INHABIT A NATION LIVE BLOGGING ITS OWN CAR WRECK IN SUPER SLOW MOTION.

strategies ensure that those who voted for the loser will dismiss as illegitimate, the result of any national election in the United States. It insures that the media, well paid in campaign dollars for their efforts, can tell us day after day, "It all comes down to Ohio, or Florida, or Iowa." The anti-democratic logic of such statements is ignored in deference to the engaging narrative that begins to look more and more like a nation live blogging its own car wreck in super slow motion.

The isolating pop-psychology of cheering on the dreamers and their long-shots, the clinging to unsustainable success measures like "the number of billionaires in Orange County," the behavior of celebrities, achievements of sports teams, or people who follow Oprah out of some presumptive ghetto of poverty, these all postpone the day when we will grasp our real strengths. When we will find a civic identity that transcends these borders and jettisons these trivial ambitions and allows people to move on to the business of actually designing and building the lives they can realistically imagine.

> THE LONGER TRADITIONAL INSTITUTIONS STAND IN THE WAY OF THAT TRANSFORMATION THE CLOSER WE GET TO THEIR DEMISE.

The longer traditional institutions stand in the way of that transformation the closer we get to their demise, the easier it is to associate them with a twenty-first century Bastille. History tells us that we should embrace even a challenging and radical Spirit of 1776 before it becomes an inevitable catastrophe and uncivilized Slaughter of 1787. To play with dates one last time; in less than two years it will be 2014. We will be one hundred years removed from the Great War that extinguished the hope of a new century, assured the world that the scars and damage from centuries of outmoded Roman, Slavic, and Napoleonic identities were alive and well and would have a last stand in Europe. That showdown in a technological age that had moved beyond the destructive scale of the petty motives of the combatants nearly destroyed civilization. It would be good to reflect on how far we've come since 1914. And so my new Spirit of 1776 is better seen as the Spirit of 2014. Might it be an earnest effort to see how the potentially destructive scale of our presence on the planet requires a degree of unity and leadership beyond the capacity of our petty and stalled institutions?

"Imagine there's no country and ask only what we might collectively do for ourselves as citizens of the world." These words do not immediately lend themselves to a melody, but we should quickly learn how to start singing something close to it.

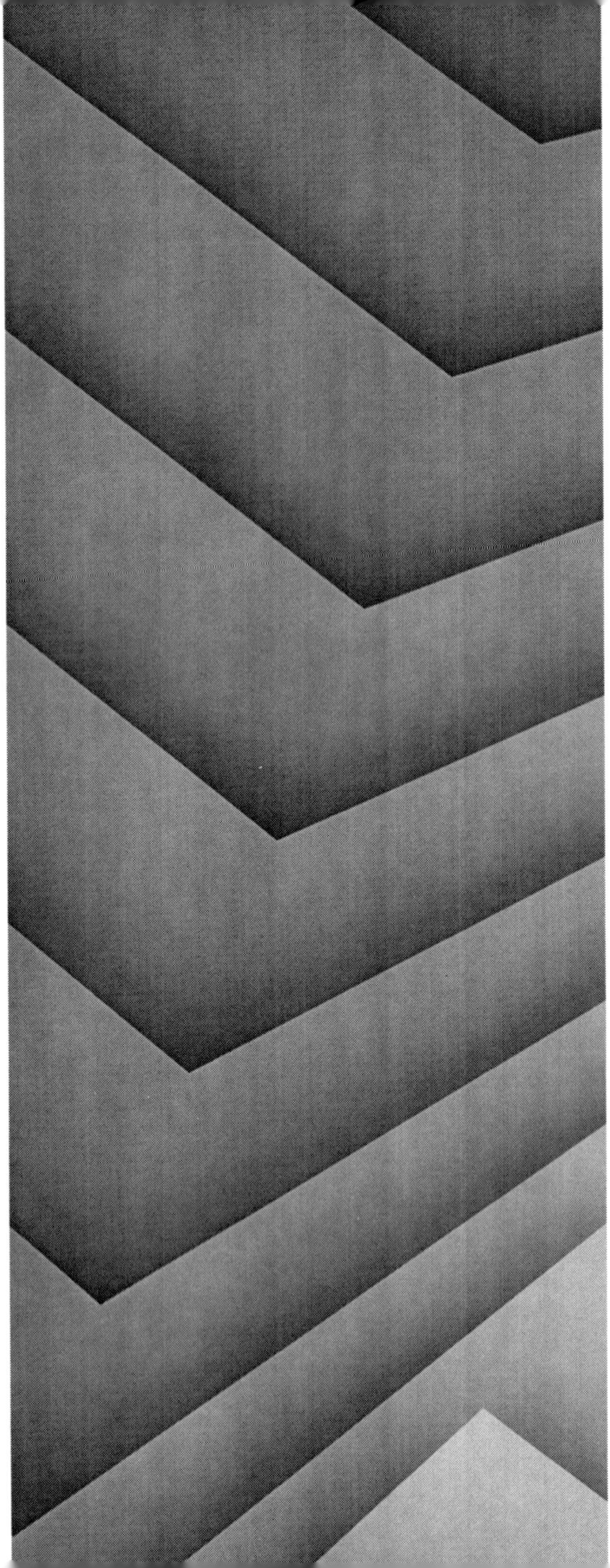

# CLAIRE L. EVANS

---

*Claire L. Evans is a writer and artist working in Los Angeles. In addition to performing in the conceptual pop group YACHT, she works as a science journalist and pens a blog,* Universe, *which addresses the synchronies among art, science, technology, and the cultural world at large. Her work was recently anthologized in* The Best Science Writing Online 2012.

clairelevans.com

## CURIOSITY'S SHADOW

This year, we lost Neil Armstrong, an accidental hero, thrust by fate onto a rock in the sky. Many dreamt of walking on the Moon before he did, and a few men did after him. He happened to be the first. Hopefully many more men, and women too, will echo his iconic footsteps in the future. Perhaps even future space tourists will huddle around Tranquility Base, laying nostalgic 1960s filters over their high resolution snapshots of an upended American flag from a long-ago mission.

In the meantime, we have NASA's Curiosity rover to take candid pictures of the worlds beyond our reach. When Curiosity landed on Mars, those of us who tuned in vicariously via NASA's live coverage watched the roomful of tense engineers explode with pent-up excitement, and heard their disembodied voices whispering through the control room, "Holy shit! We did it!" Their headsets fell askew, they glad-handed one another, falling across their desks, before being immobilized by a sudden hush as the news spread, "We've got thumbnails."

Thumbnails. We all watched as a tiny image formed, transmuted across the void of space and into the room. It was black and white, an indistinguishable gesture of light in a blur of dark pixels. The engineers cheered and held one another as they gazed upon this small, inauspicious sight. One man sobbed at his desk. Then another image came down the line, this time more resolved. We began to see the grain of the dust, the pebbles, the outline of the rover itself, 352 million miles and fourteen minutes of delay away, struck against the Martian soil.

And so, as with so many missions before it, the narrative of discovery began with an acknowledgment of its own shadow. NASA's older Martian rovers, Spirit and Opportunity, were both avid amateur photographers of their own shadows as well. In fact, such images have been part and parcel of the visual language of space history since the Soviet Union developed and launched the Venera probes in the early 1960s; which, beginning with Venera 9, were the first landers to send back images of another planet. Those pictures too, taken before the cameras were undone by the very atmosphere they hoped to document, were of light and shadows cast on rocks. Rocks that looked for all the world like our rocks, light like our light, and shadows like our shadows, only cast on an alien world.

These mobile laboratories, the fragile accretions of countless engineers, so distant from Earth, are not astronauts. Not quite. I'm not necessarily sentimental about manned missions to space; I know it's a messy business, limiting, and often more trouble than it's worth. The human explorer defecates, sweats, needs sleep, and is afraid. But exploring the Moon, for example, wasn't just a matter of rock samples and spectrographs; the real laboratory was the human mind. It's not without reason that the things we remember most about the Apollo program are its words and gestures, the famous "first step" and the steps which followed, the proclamations, then, later, the reflections.

The real triumph of the Apollo program was its unforeseen shift in tone, driven by a desire to objectively beat the Soviets down to the wire. Most Americans don't know the unmanned Russian craft Luna 15 was beginning its descent just as Armstrong and Aldrin were tromping about the Moon's surface. Neil Armstrong said a great many beautiful things about his experiences. Most astronauts did; going to the Moon has a tendency to turn test pilots into poets. That matter of cortex-shifting is called the Overview Effect. Neil Armstrong articulated it with his characteristic clipped decorum:

> GOING TO THE MOON HAS A TENDENCY TO TURN TEST PILOTS INTO POETS.

*"It suddenly struck me that that tiny pea, pretty and blue, was the Earth. I put up my thumb and shut one eye, and my thumb blotted out the planet Earth. I didn't feel like a giant. I felt very, very small."*

Did you know NASA accidentally erased the original Moon landing footage during routine magnetic tape re-use in the 1980s? The footage the world saw on television that July day in 1969 was actually taken from a slow-scan television monitor and re-broadcast, picture quality reduced. The space between the primacy of that moment and its place in the narrative of the twentieth century is obscured by a layer of irretrievable analog decay, time, and distance. Now death, too.

We lose heroes from the space age and the temptation is to eulogize an era, not a person. Neil Armstrong's death does not signify the dwindling hopes of a different America. Today we have a completely new approach to space, from which we'll learn a great deal. Maybe not from humans coming home and struggling their whole lives to convey the gravitas of their experiences in words, from astronauts whose dreams at night are forever colored by dusty panoramas and pea-sized Earths. Rather, from smart machines serving as our eyes and ears. Instead of famous footprints, we now leave tread marks.

> WE SHOULD INVENT POETRY ENGINES, ROVERS EQUIPPED WITH ALGORITHMS THAT CAN TURN VAPORIZED SOIL SAMPLES INTO POIGNANT INSIGHTS.

NASA's Curiosity rover is wonderful and has already proven a robot's capacity to ignite the global imagination, but it cannot perform the simple acts of grace that can be the lasting effects of a mission to space. We should invent poetry engines, rovers equipped with algorithms that can turn vaporized soil samples into poignant insights.

For now, unmanned space exploration can tell us everything, but not how the dust feels under its boots, nor that giant loping strides and kangaroo jumps are the quickest way across the surface. It can't, like Buzz Aldrin, privately take communion before stepping out onto the lunar surface, or quote Psalms in its final broadcast before splashdown ("What is man that Thou art mindful of him?"). It has no thumb to blot out planet Earth, no heart to feel very small, and it can't retire from the space program to live the rest of its life on a farm in Ohio, like Neil Armstrong, who was forever mindful of his position as only an incidental figurehead for an effort of thousands of people.

The current moment in space exploration is not defined by loss, however. Rather, it's a paradigm shift, one that will be seamlessly adopted by the generations born long, long after the ghostly black and-white footage of men on the Moon first beamed down to Earth. The science fiction writer William

Gibson put it this way: that the moment we began sensing and recording with technology, our extended communal nervous system, the "absolute limits of the experiential world" were "in a very real and literal way... profoundly and amazingly altered, extended, changed." We no longer relied on the limited capacities of our individual memories, nor did we quite fully trust the bounded senses of our apparatus; free to back ourselves up and reach ourselves further outward, we extended our reach. We also loosened the definition of "we," allowing our tools to become part of us in subtle ways. Now, closer and closer to the machine, we share a "largely invisible, all-encompassing embrace."

**WE CAN LOOK AT CURIOSITY'S SHADOW AND UNDERSTAND, WITHOUT HESITATION, THAT IT'S OUR OWN.**

We can't cleave these machines from ourselves; they are our eyes and ears. They are us. I can't go to Mars and see what it looks like for myself. Nobody can—although perhaps the future Neil Armstrong of Mars lives among us today. I might not live to see that historic step into red dust. Instead, though, I have seen a robot, a laboratory, a sentry of extended sense organs for the human race, roll forward. I find it profoundly moving, not only because with

Curiosity, something technically inconceivable has been accomplished, but because we—that room full of high-fiving tinkerers, and us plebeians too—can look at Curiosity's shadow and understand, without hesitation, that it's our own.

**NOTE:** *Portions of this essay previously appeared as, "On Curiosity and its Shadows," and "Footprints on the Moon" at Scienceblogs.com/universe (August 6/August 26, 2012).*

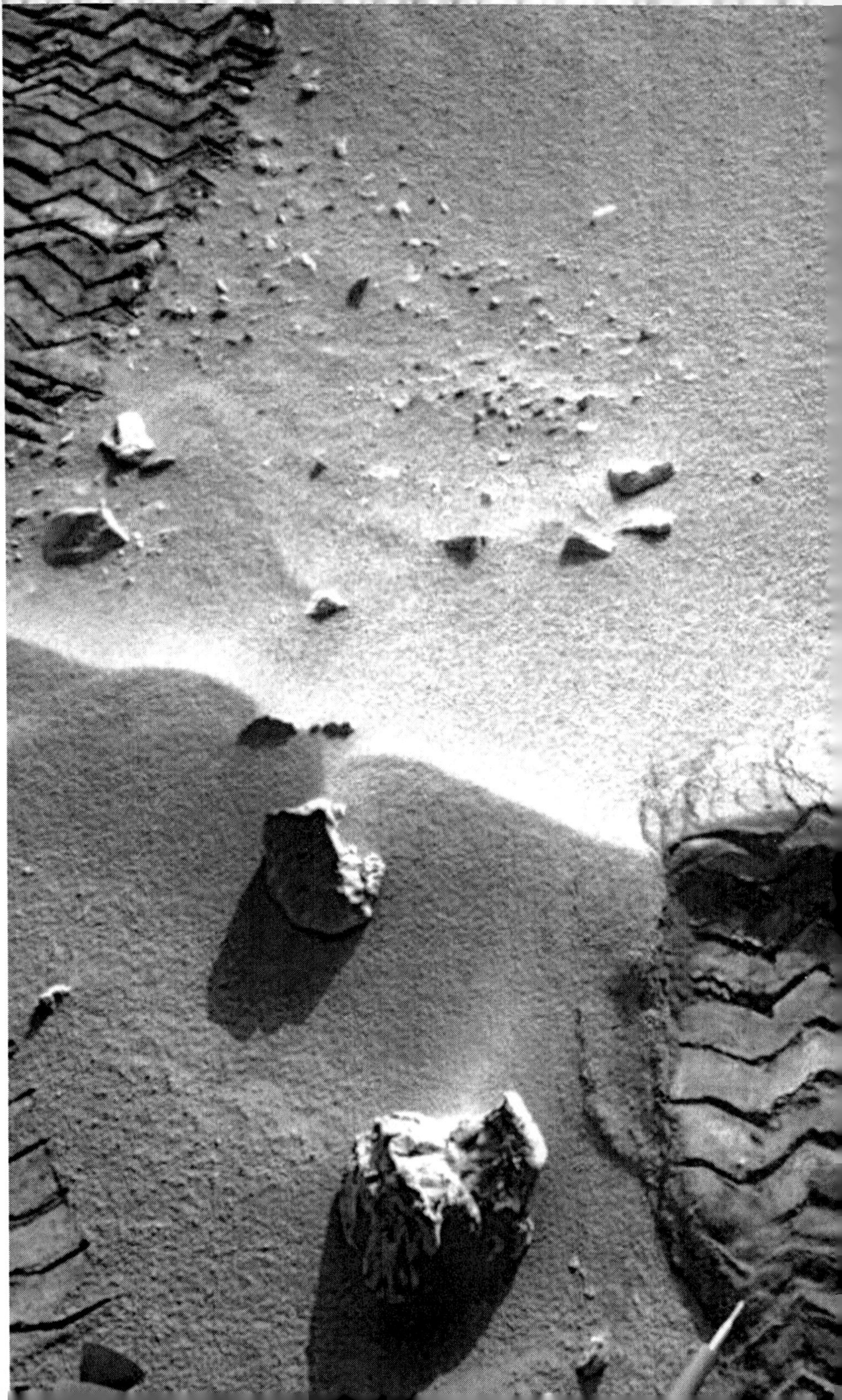

*Courtesy NASA/JPL-Caltech*

50 AMERICAN DREAMERS

# SUSAN McKEE REESE

---

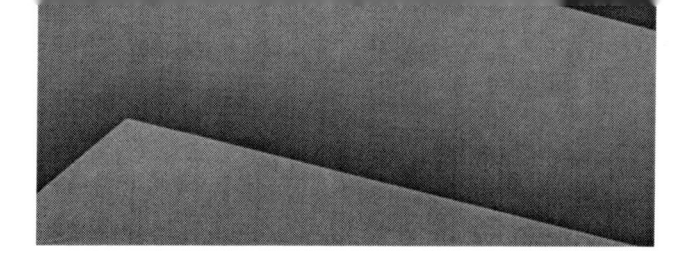

*Susan McKee Reese teaches literature and writing in the Department of English at Portland State University with a particular passion for Irish Literature, Magic Realist Fiction, and the healing power of writing, especially poetry.*

## HOPE FROM FICTION, LAKES, AND DAUGHTERS

My dream for the future is that it is one as lovely as our past and present here in Portland, Oregon, in 2012. I dream that we will somehow move away from islands of plastic choking our oceans, from all things that endanger the health of our planet and ourselves and that freedom from fear in all its forms is possible for every living person.

What gives me hope? My twenty seven-year-old daughter gives me hope. Young people give me hope. Old people give me hope. People in between give me hope. I am a teacher and fortunate to work with students of all ages, of all genders, of all ethnicities, and I see this wonderful microcosm thriving as we engage in deep discussion of all that is important in our lives. We read works that provide insight into our human dilemma, works which are really maps toward understanding. Never underestimate what you can learn from: Don Quixote, Mrs. Ramsay, Gregor Samsa, Pierre, Anna, a giant whale, an obsessed man with a ship and a harpoon, Oscar Wao, Jane Eyre, Cheryl Strayed on the Pacific Crest Trail, Pete Fromm in the Bitterroot Mountains, or all those other glorious characters and works from which we have to choose.

I take great hope from the fact that we are all still writing, still creating, and sharing stories around continually changing forms of a campfire, creating ourselves in our world as we go along, aware that it is possible to revise again and again.

I take hope from the fact that Mary Oliver tells me in "Wild Geese" that I "do not have to be good, do not have to crawl on my knees through the desert," but "just have to let the soft animal of my body love what it loves." William Stafford reminds me that, "There is a lake somewhere/ so blue and far nobody owns it./That lake stays blue and free; it goes/ on and on./And I know where it is." I, too, know such a lake. I carry Naomi Shihab Nye's words from "Jerusalem" close to my heart that "It's late but everything comes next."

> I TAKE HOPE FROM THE FACT THAT WHEN I WAS YOUNG, THE END OF THE WORLD WAS PREDICTED...AND IT DIDN'T HAPPEN.

I take hope from the fact that when I was young the end of the world was predicted, specifically, at least once a year and it didn't happen.

I take hope from trees, lakes, rivers, streams, mountains, bear, moose, chipmunks, herons, owls, eagles, cats, and dogs, to name a few. I find hope in a glass of cold, Oregon water, or jumping into a cool stream on a hot day. I am hopeful that no matter what humans seem to do, we continue to be trumped by the universe and its volcanoes, earthquakes, tsunamis, and winds. I find it hopeful that we are really not in charge. Never have been. Never will be. So I try to enjoy this great gift.

And I read a lot.

And I write.

And I am filled with hope.

# CHARLES BRADLEY

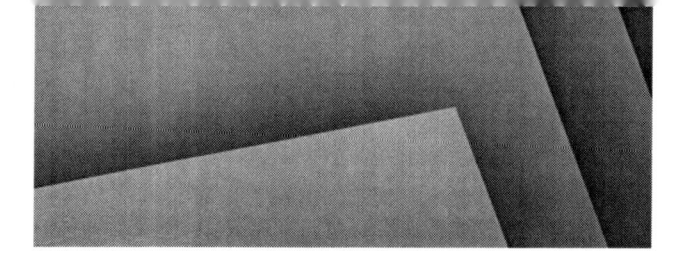

---

*Charles Bradley, also known as "The Screaming Eagle of Soul," has travelled all over America, singing soul, and working as a James Brown impersonator. In 2011, Charles released* No Time For Dreaming, *an album of his own songs, becoming an instant star. A film about Charles, called* Soul of America, *was released in 2012.*

thecharlesbradley.com

## WHY IS IT SO HARD TO MAKE IT IN AMERICA?

### How can we regain a sense of optimism for the future?

They always say, "To get the dreams of America you have to work hard and give all you have to give." But it is getting harder than it ever was before. My mother used to say, "Son, when you do something put your heart into it," but when I did, people in control tried to break me down. All I am trying to do is give them the best of me. Now, people don't want you to be the best that you are. They want you to follow them and they want to keep you in distress. They will take your job and you need a job to keep a roof over your head, pay rent, and pay bills. When they take those from you where else can you go? Back to the streets again. I used to just grit my teeth, keep my mouth quiet, and do what they said. They were the ones who wrote the check. Sometimes it is hard just to maintain, to keep on with where you are at.

I say that God is my strength, my witness, and my salvation. That is what kept me strong all through the years when I was falling on my face trying to get back up again. I was going all around the country trying to find a place, trying to find my space. I was begging for an opportunity. How we are going to change this world is by being the person who we are. We need to work hard and hope the right person will see it. I hope people understand that I am doing the best I can, that I am doing it with honesty and respect for my fellow man.

> WE NEED TO WORK HARD AND HOPE THE RIGHT PERSON WILL SEE IT.

For five years I was homeless and living in abandoned buildings. Then I was in the projects until they called me and I got my record out. Now, I am getting ready to move out and it is scary because now I am getting another chance with my music. I have got to come forward, full force, and let the world know that all I have been asking for is an opportunity. I am still a little afraid to speak out and tell you how I feel because I am scared someone might pull the rug out from under me. I don't want to get out of the projects and end up on the streets again. I don't want to go to a shelter. I know how that feels. I'm not begging, just give me an opportunity. I will put my heart into the job and work to the best of my ability.

I take the hurt and things people do to me and move forward with open arms. There was a show in Texas where it started raining. There were a lot of people there but they postponed the show. Those people said, "No. We want to see Charles Bradley." So, they moved me to a different stage but it was still raining and the circuit breakers went off. Everyone said, "Charles, you are going to get electrocuted." But I wasn't worrying about that. I said, "Those people are standing out there in the rain to see me? I can't leave." Then the lights came back on and I saw the people out there in the rain and mud. I said, "No, we are not gonna have this." So I jumped off the stage, went in the mud with them, and we were having a ball. I got all up in the mud. It was all over my face. The crowd grabbed me and they were saying, "Man, we don't see any other artists with mud on them." I said, "I am just one of you. I wanted to have the opportunity to show how grateful and happy I am, to thank you for this opportunity. " I cried. It was the most beautiful, joyful, tearful, and loving moment. That rain was tears from heaven; that is how I look at it. Only in rain like that can people share the love.

I learned about racial separation as I grew but I never carried it inside of me. All I carried was the honesty of my heart. When Martin Luther King got killed I started learning and thought, "What is this? Why can't we share?" All I look at now that I have grown up is if someone has a good heart. If you have loved me as a person, I do not care what color you are. I feel their heart.

## And what do you think it is about soul music that communicates that?

Soul is in anything. If you got a clean heart and a clean mind and you have been abused, used, and refused—that is soul. If you know you've been hurt and the world is doing you so wrong but you keep a clean heart—that is soul. Soul is a spirit. It can be in country and western and it can be in rock. It can be in anything. It is when the soul and heart and the mind are clean.

The reason I like soul and funky music is because of how they play it and get their spirit into it. They pump it out. I can look at the music and the way they are playing it and feel my past. They way they play lets my spirit open and tune into the spirit world. When I feel the spirit world and they are playing

*Courtesy of Kisha Bari*

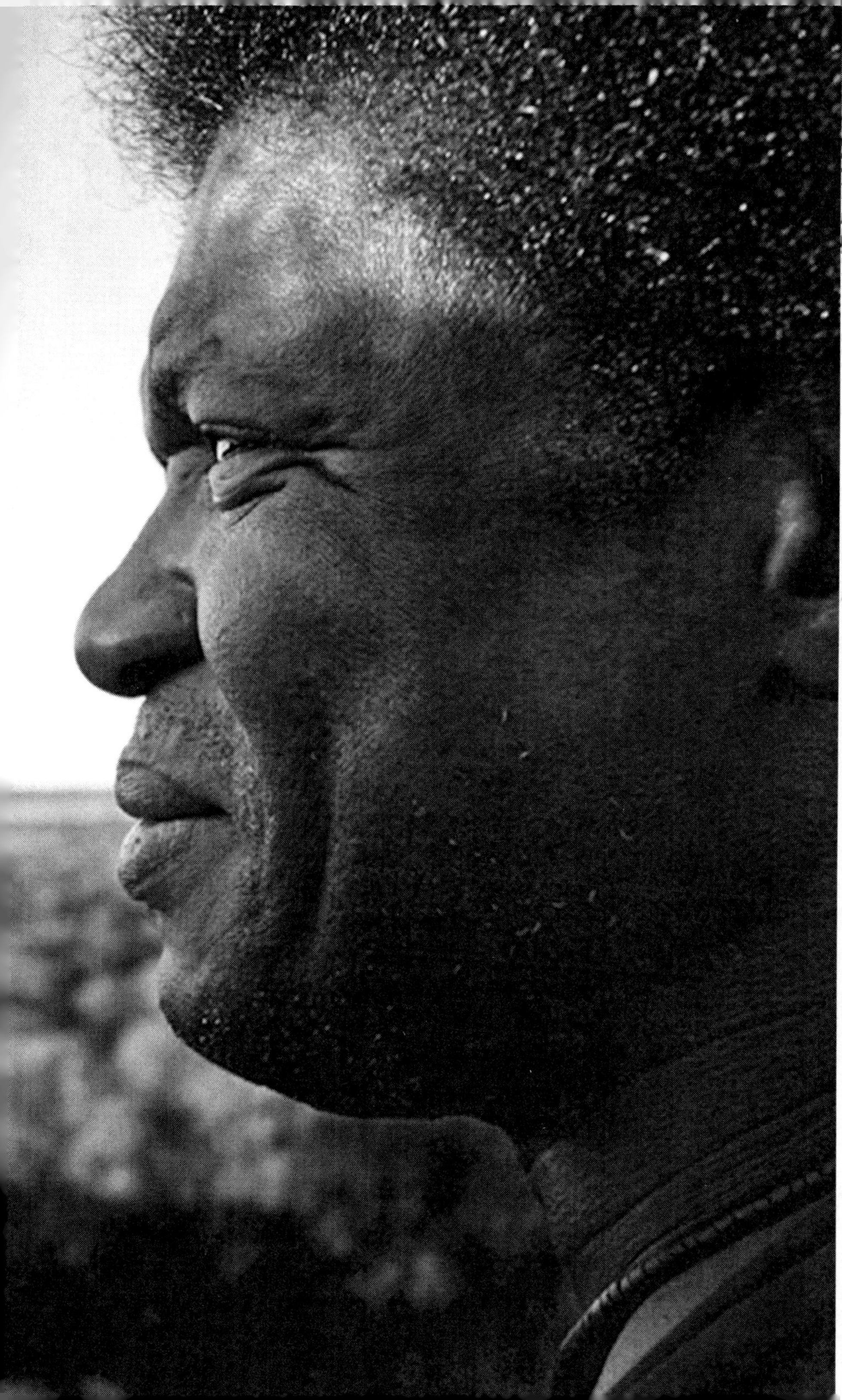

> **WHEN I FEEL THE SPIRIT WORLD AND THEY ARE PLAYING IT THAT WAY, OH, YOU ARE GOING TO GET A SHOW! YOU ARE GOING TO GET SOME FUNKY MUSIC AND EVERYONE IS GOING TO FEEL THAT RHYTHM AND FEEL THAT SOUL.**

it that way, Oh, you are going to get a show! You are going to get some funky music and everyone is going to feel that rhythm and feel that soul. It is coming from the spirit world and that is the deepest you can go. You can go on the surface of yourself, go on stage and sing beautiful words, but if you are not in the spirit—you ain't got nothing. All you are doing is singing words to the music, making sounds. But when you can go past that and go into the spirit world, that is where all your energy is. Everything you do on this planet is in the spirit and that is why I believe in it. That is where you find so much soul.

## Can soul music save the world?

One way we can save this world is if each person knew when they were wrong. Don't keep your wrongness and carry it your whole life. Don't think you are getting away with it. If you keep it and bring offspring into this world, that offspring is going to make those same mistakes. We don't get away with things. When you know in your heart that you did something wrong and you don't confront it, that same pattern will keep coming over and over again. All we can teach humanity is to know your wrongness. Correct yourself and then the world will change. All these material things are gonna use you. They aren't loving you. They are loving what you got. Yes, I want nice things but I want somebody to love me. When I am not sure of who I am, and not loving all those the Spirit asks me to love, life is hard.

My mom said all the time, "Son, be of good cheer, do good to those who do you wrong. Later on in life you will see what you learned." My pastors said, "Son, keep pressed in your way." Pressed in your way means making it through corruption and keeping that love. When they try to change you, you keep pressing. Know that God is somewhere watching you and pressing your way through all of this.

I have been to my deathbed and back and seen so much in this life. You need to keep going and that is why I am doing this music, living on the road, playing all these shows. I am letting the people know who I am. I want to open my soul and my heart. I want them to look at me and then ask themselves if they have done anyone wrong. We need to open our hearts to open minds. We need to stay open, not closed up.

**WE NEED TO OPEN OUR HEARTS TO OPEN MINDS. WE NEED TO STAY OPEN, NOT CLOSED UP.**

*62* AMERICAN DREAMERS

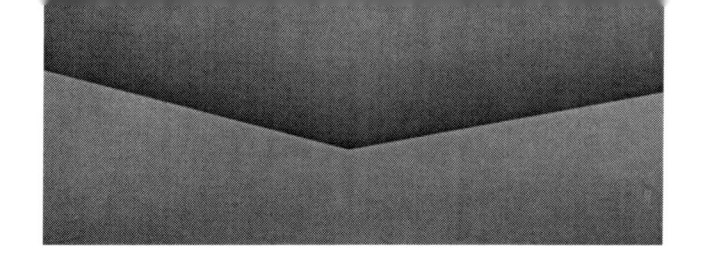

# SOULPANCAKE FEATURING RAINN WILSON

---

*SoulPancake was originally founded by actor Rainn Wilson of* The Office *and his friends Joshua Homnick and Devon Gundry in 2007. SoulPancake offers discussions, blog posts, questions, creative activities, writing exercises, polls, interviews, columns, videos, and original art by up-and-coming artists.*

soulpancake.com

## TALKING ABOUT FAITH

### *What kind of future do you dream of and what needs to be done to get there?*

We dream of a future where people are excited to collaborate, communicate, and unleash their creativity in order to make the world a kinder, more beautiful place. To get to this future, we need open minds, and moreover, open hearts. We need to let go of our fears and simply learn to love each other more.

Our dream is to give people everywhere a voice and a purpose for their lives. We want everyone to have the freedom to express themselves. We dream of a world where we can create and collaborate together and continually inspire each other to do our very best.

### How do we create optimism about tomorrow?

> THE VIEWS FROM THE TOP OF THE MOUNTAIN ARE GOING TO BE MAGICAL.

Creating optimism means understanding that things are not always going to be easy. If there is what seems like an insurmountable mountain ahead, we can either give up, or we can accept that even though it will be a hard climb, the views from the top of the mountain are going to be magical.

### Why is it important to talk about issues of faith, and spirituality? How does SoulPancake go about encouraging dialogue without dogma?

Spirituality is such a loaded word. For some people, it means chakras and crystals. For others, it's a direct expression to a higher power. Some even see art as an expression of spirituality. Whatever it is, we believe it's one of those fundamental human concepts that we often avoid talking about. And yet, it's important to explore your own personal beliefs around the topic. So at SoulPancake, we strongly encourage talking about issues of faith and spirituality while always having an open mind. SoulPancake isn't a place to force your opinions on someone else. It's not a place to tell someone they are wrong. We try to create a safe environment for people to share their ideas and learn from one another.

SoulPancake seeks to create opportunities for people to explore who they are, to open their hearts, and catalyze their creativity. In that world, we would be more compassionate towards one another and better equipped to solve problems. We become stronger because we have a unified whole made up of very diverse parts.

Discussion is the first step. That dialogue must then lead to action, otherwise it's useless.

## Does the future need more soul, or do we eventually become more and more disconnected?

We're at an interesting moment in our evolution, where technology is simultaneously connecting and disconnecting us. The only way to make the connections that mean something, however, is if we inject something more soulful into those interactions.

## How do we create stories, narratives, and spirituality that serve humanity instead of dividing it?

The DNA of what we create has to be that of open-mindedness, acceptance, and respect. Exploring ideas is not about asserting our opinions; it's about learning and exploring. The foundation of what we create is to speak to the hearts of people, as opposed to their heads. If you tell stories that open hearts and stir the soul, then you have the power to bring people together and move humanity forward instead of dividing it.

## Can we celebrate religion?

The only way to come together and celebrate religion is if we eliminate all trace of judgment. The minute one group feels judged by another, there is conflict. It takes an extreme amount of humility to recognize that what you believe may only be right for you.

> THE ONLY WAY TO COME TOGETHER AND CELEBRATE RELIGION IS IF WE ELIMINATE ALL TRACE OF JUDGMENT.

***What does the future of American faith look like; what things are happening now that excite you about it?***

I think there are two processes happening simultaneously in America: a divergence from blind faith and dogma and a resurgence of spirituality and greatness in the world. What is exciting about this is that it puts us all in a position to see ourselves as spiritual beings. This is a concept that all religions teach, and with that as a basis, we can then work together.

***A rabbi, an atheist, a Christian, a Buddhist, a Muslim, a Universalist, a Baha'i, an explorer and, a _____, all walk into the future; is it one where they can all get along?***

Yes, it is. But only if they seek to connect through their hearts first.

67

# STAN LEE

---

*Stan "The Man" Lee's influence over comic books is incalculable. His co-creations, Spider-Man™, X-Men™, and The Avengers™ have been monster movie hits, helping make Marvel Comics the leader of the comic book industry. Some of Stan's other great co-creations, such as Fantastic Four™ and Daredevil™ are now in development, while Iron Man™, Thor™, and The Avengers™ have sequels on the way. In 2008, President Bush presented Stan with a Medal of the Arts, lauding his amazing career.*

therealstanlee.com

## NEW AMERICAN HEROES

In the past, because of World War II, the Vietnam War, the Korea War, and the Cuban missile crisis, America needed patriotic heroes. While a hero should always be patriotic, our focus has changed. Today's heroes battle terrorism, injustice, and super criminals. I don't think the basic structure of the hero ever really changes. Whether it's today or decades ago, a hero fights anyone who threatens the safety of his fellow man.

Comics are no longer just for kids. They're read by people of all ages. As for changing the world, one never knows what will change the world. A brilliant comic book story probably has as much chance of changing the world as a brilliant novel or movie or anything else.

**ONE NEVER KNOWS WHAT WILL CHANGE THE WORLD.**

*Courtesy of POW! Entertainment*

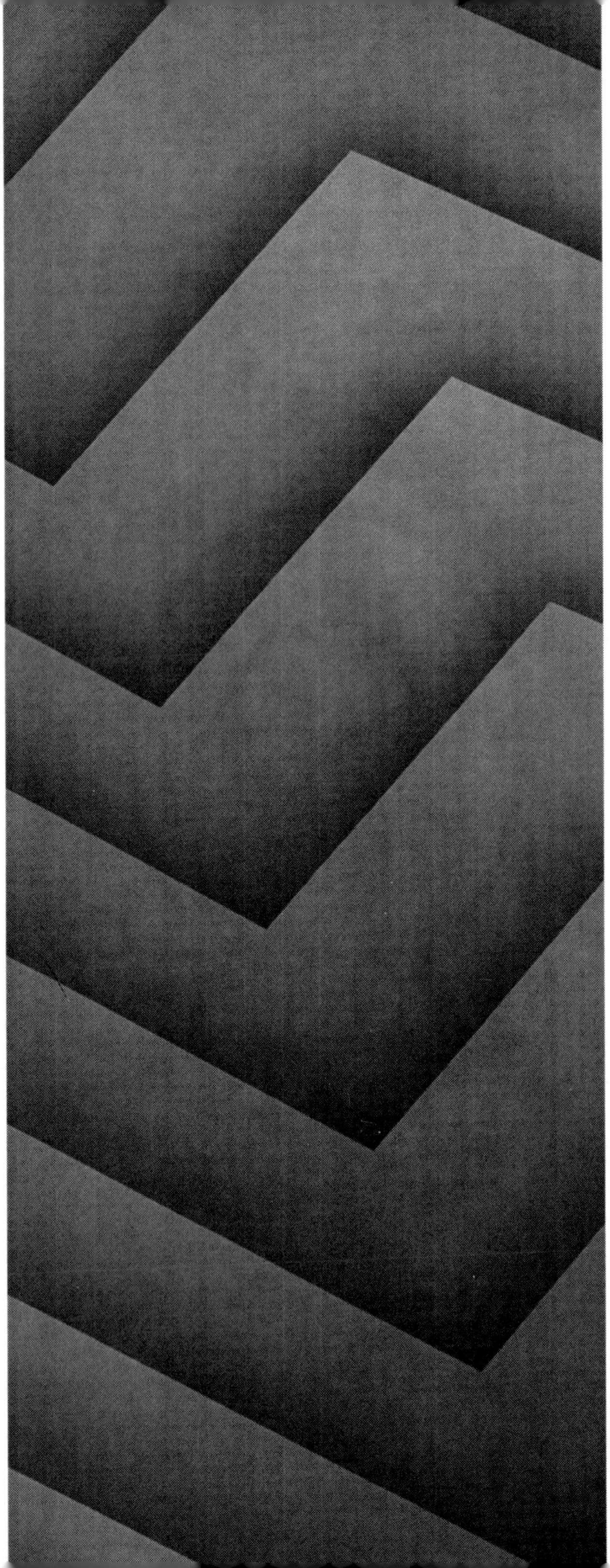

# SHANNON GALPIN

---

*Shannon Galpin founded Mountain2Mountain in November 2006. A rape survivor and mother, she realized she couldn't just stand on the sidelines, watching women and girls denied basic human rights. Shannon writes regularly for* Huffington Post *and* Matador Network, *and is currently authoring her first book. She has been featured on* Dateline NBC, Today Show, Huffington Post *and* Outside Magazine. *Shannon was nominated for Adventurer of the Year by National Geographic.*

mountain2mountain.org

## GIVING WOMEN A VOICE ONE BIKE AT A TIME

I was the first woman to mountain bike in Afghanistan. That really came from the fact that Afghanistan is a country where women cannot ride bikes, but as a foreign woman I am allowed to push on gender roles in a way that is more risky for Afghan women. I can challenge the gender roles as a mountain biker and a woman that lives in Colorado. I look at Afghanistan in the way it was viewed back in the 1950s and 1960s, a tourist destination and a country that is rich in natural beauty. It would be an adventure travel paradise if it was not dealing with the instability of ongoing violence and war. I hoped to look at the area as a region and country that is more than what we see in the news and to show another side of the humanity and region many turn their eyes from. We need to see that it is worth our attention and at the same time confront gender barriers and raise the discussion of women's rights in Afghanistan. I hoped to start this by simply riding a bike and using the bike as a symbol for social justice. It is used in Southeast Asia and Africa as a tool to increase accessibility to education, keep women safe by providing transportation, and even serve as an ambulance in rural areas. When we realized we could not use the bike in those ways, because women were not allowed to ride bikes, I decided to push on that barrier and serve both sides. To show the difference of how we see Afghanistan through American eyes and how we see gender barriers in Afghanistan. The bike is transformative.

I founded Mountain2Mountain in 2006 to focus on developing a voice for women and girls in conflict. For the past five years, I have predominantly been working in Afghanistan and have been focused on building schools and clinics, and looking at ways we can increase access to education and health. We are also looking at the layer that supports all of that—the layer that is about discovering voice and creating value and encouraging young women to use their voice and to have confidence to work for access, especially in countries like Afghanistan. Half the time it is a matter of convincing or fighting others to gain access to basic education much less equal rights.

We do these things in several ways. One of our more alternative programs has been through graffiti art. With young students at the University of Kabul's Contemporary Art program we looked at the power of street art and public art to give voice to the youth, the next generation. We support young musicians and collaborate with programs that support the burgeoning modern music scene. We also work with young female activists willing to march in the streets and fight for their equal rights and representation in government. Some of the more traditional ways have been in building a school for the deaf in Kabul, training midwives, and training teachers.

Our next trip to Afghanistan is about the *Streets of Afghanistan*: a photography exhibition with larger than life images. It is a collaboration between Afghan and western photographers that has developed over the last few years and shown in the United States. The purpose is to showcase a different side of Afghanistan, to break stereotypes we see in the media. We want to show a rich and beautiful country that is gorgeous and has spirit, and show it in a way that many have never seen. We will hopefully humanize Afghanistan so that we can gain more support for the projects that go on there.

In the future, after four years of working in Afghanistan, we are taking a lot of the lessons of working in conflict zones and applying it to young women who live in United States conflict zones. We are launching our first domestic program working with young women at risk and victims of gender violence in a program we are calling Strength in Numbers. The program uses the vehicle of a bicycle to create strength, empower voice, and build camaraderie between women who have been victims to change that perception and label. The women who come through these week-long camps bond, develop, and find their voice through the power of a bike. We then work with them as they come out of the program and back into their communities to become

*Image by Travis Beard, Courtesy of Mountain2Mountain*

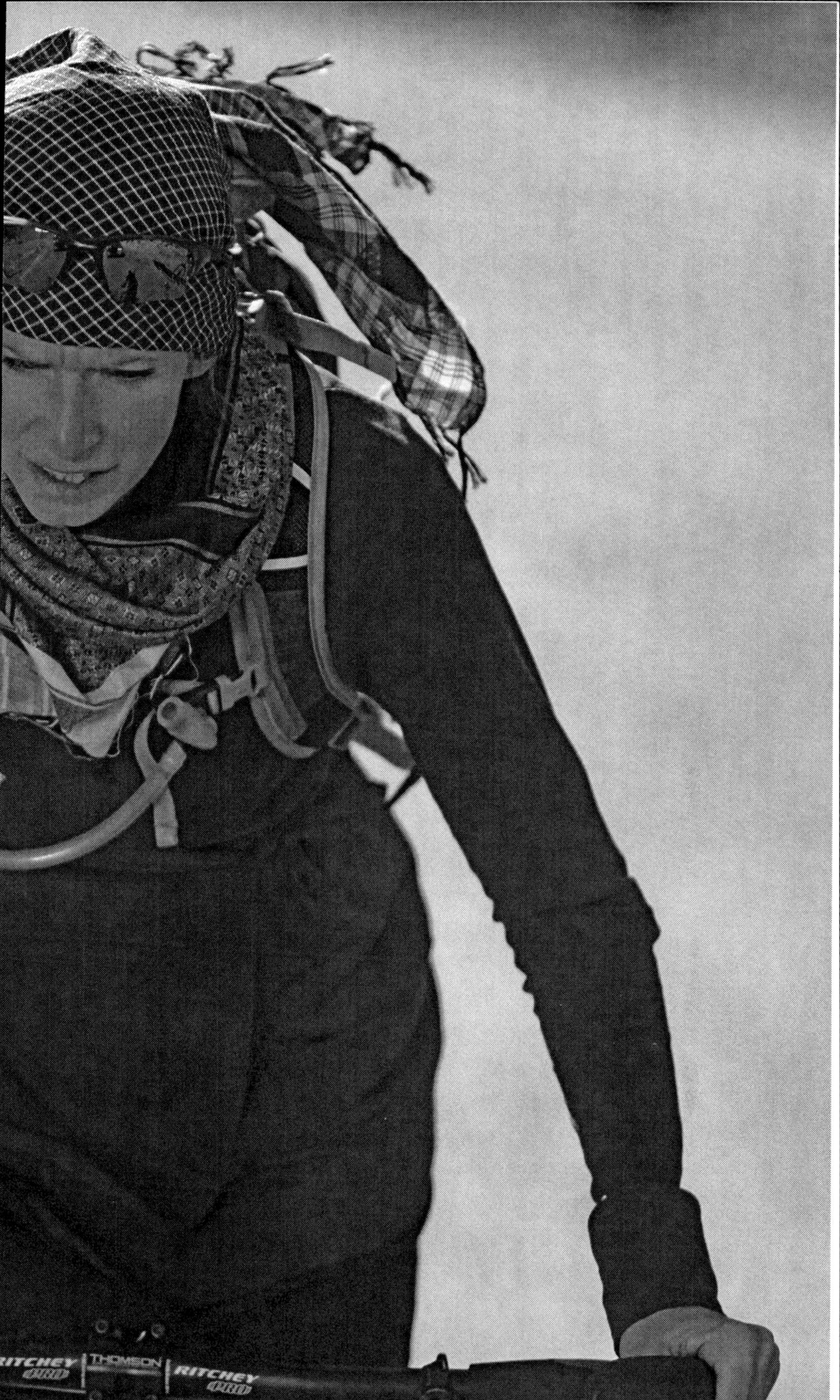
RITCHEY
PRO
THOMSON
RITCHEY
PRO

involved and create a ripple of change. The bike becomes a metaphor not only to build their individual strength but to look at how they use the strength they build. We bring in guest speakers, watch films like *The Invisible War* and *Miss Representation,* and look at the role of women and the role of victims, and we look at how changemakers make the leap. We explore the idea that it is not the role of government or NGOs to change many of these ideas but the responsibility of individuals. We want to develop citizen engagement in these women so that the change sparked in the program ripples out into their communities. Over time, we look to work with these women and girls to help support ideas and programs that they want to launch and to work them into our international programs. We hope to bridge the international and domestic programs with peer mentorship. The reason we use a bicycle as a tool for this program is that it has played a role in the development and narrative of Mountain2Mountain.

## *Bringing all of this into one vision, what do you dream the future looks like?*

This is all about the power of voice in a Pygmalion sort of way. It all comes back to expression. When you have a voice that gives you power over your own story you can take it outside of your walls, community, and country. That is the catalyst for change. Too often what you see is a victim mentality, either as individuals or over an entire country. When you look at someone as a "victim" you have a different response. You pity those people; we pity those women. Pity is not an empowering emotion. It does not help you invest in those people or that country. Pity is a very disempowering emotion.

In my own narrative I could be called a victim. I was raped and nearly killed when I was eighteen. My sister was raped. I have been there. I know how I could be viewed versus how I want to be viewed if I had a different geography or family. I could pity myself, and others could see me that way and treat me that way. I feel that you can take the mentality and change it. Look at the fact that those who endure great suffering, who have been victimized, also have a very deep well of strength. There is an almost unbreakable backbone when you can access that. You have empowered people to be incredibly fearless and strong. But it takes a shift in how we treat them and how they treat themselves.

When we talk about victims, whether they are half the world away in Afghanistan or victims of rape or human trafficking in the United States, there are young women who could be future leaders. They could be changemakers in their community. They have already endured the worst of the worst. Nothing can hurt them anymore; they know that they can survive and when you know you can survive, a great resolve that comes. There is great strength. All of the programming we have done comes from that idea. If we can change the perception of victimhood, we can create an "army" of women that can change the world.

> IF WE CAN CHANGE THE PERCEPTION OF VICTIMHOOD, WE CAN CREATE AN "ARMY" OF WOMEN THAT CAN CHANGE THE WORLD.

### *So let's assume your dreams come true, what would that world look like? How do these empowered women create a better tomorrow?*

It comes back to the basics of human rights. Everyone in a democratic society, and in a peaceful world, has to have a voice and a say in the decisions that are made, whether that is in your home, community, or country. When you have huge populations that are disempowered simply due to gender it is impossible to imagine a world that is just for all. You cannot have a world that is based on the tenets of human rights and peace and compassion if half of the world is treated differently based on gender.

> IN AFGHANISTAN, A WOMAN'S VOICE IN A COURT OF LAW IS WORTH TWO-THIRDS OF A MAN'S VOICE. WHEN A WOMAN IS RAPED, IT IS HER WORD AGAINST HER ATTACKER.

In this utopian world where everyone has a voice and everyone is viewed as equal regardless of gender, you have an equal playing field where decisions are made on a global scale. Everyone is treated as a human and that resonates through ethnicity, race, sexual preferences, as well as gender. None of these indicators have any role to play in how we make our decisions. Instead, our decisions are made on what is best as humans and what is best for our communities. But in many places, and even the United States, women's rights are still something to be fought for. They are still dictated unequally. Everyone should have the same access, respect and voice. In Afghanistan, a woman's voice in a court of law is worth two-thirds of a man's voice. When a woman is raped, it is her word against her attacker. If her attacker says, "I did not do it," her voice is always worth two-thirds of his. That is a very tangible way to talk about voice that truly does matter.

***How does all of this play out in your life? Is all of this work, both domestic and international, really just a way to ensure a better world for your own daughter?***

When I first started, I operated from a sense of self. "What do I need?" But soon you look to your family. My parents had two daughters. Both of us were violently raped. So I ask what will happen to my daughter and that plays into the start of Mountain2Mountain. However, I am very cognizant that it is not just about me or her, or about what we need. If you look at the opportunities that I have had and the opportunities my daughter will have based on being born in America, that ensures a higher level of safety (despite what I know to be true in terms of violence). We have a higher level of safety, a guaranteed education through grade twelve, a chance at post-education, a right to vote, and in general a right to pursue whatever dream we have. That is huge. That is the American Dream. That is why people choose to come to this country.

We launched Mountain2Mountain in Afghanistan because it has been repeatedly ranked the worst place in the world to be a woman. Looking at the young women there, my daughter's counterparts, they don't deserve less than what my daughter and I have in terms of opportunity just because they are from a different ethnicity, border, or geography. I have had girls in Afghanistan ask, "How did you find us? Why do you care? Why are you here?" My response is always the same, "You deserve to have the same opportunities that my daughter has."

If all your stories and reporting and sources are focusing on the war instead of humanizing stories set along the backdrop, it becomes a different thing. You have extreme poverty in Africa but that is not the story, that is the backdrop. The stories are the amazing individuals living their lives as musicians and artists, doctors, lawyers, and fighters who make change in their communities. If we continue to focus on the poverty and famine but don't look at those living there we will never feel the power to get involved other than the dependency aid drops. That does not empower.

Why don't we look at female rap artists in Afghanistan? One performed live in Kabul last week as part of a Central Asian rock music festival, not in an embassy but among the Afghan youth. Imagine it: musicians from all over Afghanistan and Central Asia performing live for an Afghan audience with their own music, rap, hip-hop, heavy metal, grunge, and rock. That story epitomizes what is possible in a country like Afghanistan, where ten years ago one would be beheaded for performing like that. That is a ten-year shift and is major news. So changing the news story is essential.

> YOU HAVE EXTREME POVERTY IN AFRICA BUT THAT IS NOT THE STORY, THAT IS THE BACKDROP.

### *What's the best way to get involved?*

For most people the first step is the hardest; it is the fear of the unknown and failure. I have failed more times that I could tell. You will fail, everyone does. You have to be willing to fall flat on your face in order to accomplish anything. Be willing to take that risk. The apathy stops you from being willing to take those first steps. The fear of failure stops people from taking that first step. The thought that you have to be Gandhi to make a difference stops people from taking that first step.

My dream for America is that we realize that en masse we have the capacity to achieve great things. We have to use our voice, work one step at a time, and be willing to make mistakes. It is the big steps and the little steps. It is just like voting. When you look at a vote and think of yourself as an individual voter, it is easy to be apathetic. "Why does it matter if I stand in line and cast a vote? My one vote has absolutely no bearing. It is literally a drop in the bucket. It is just one vote. Nobody will miss it." It is so easy to think of it that way. But we vote not because of the individual vote but because you believe everyone else is voting with you. We believe that en masse we do have the power to affect change.

It is the same with humanitarian aid. My work is a drop in the bucket and creates very little change but I believe that others are adding their drops in the bucket.

Things seem bigger also when they are half the world away. We tackle issues in Afghanistan but we can also tackle them in Colorado, New York, or Chicago. An issue like the environment is huge but are you engaged with fracking or dams? Are you passionate about food deserts or urban farming? There are so many niches where you can connect. There are even niches within those niches. It is everyone being willing to put their drop in

> MY DREAM FOR AMERICA IS THAT WE REALIZE THAT EN MASSE WE HAVE THE CAPACITY TO ACHIEVE GREAT THINGS.

the bucket, and being okay with it being a drop, because when everyone else is putting their drop in the same bucket, that creates waves.

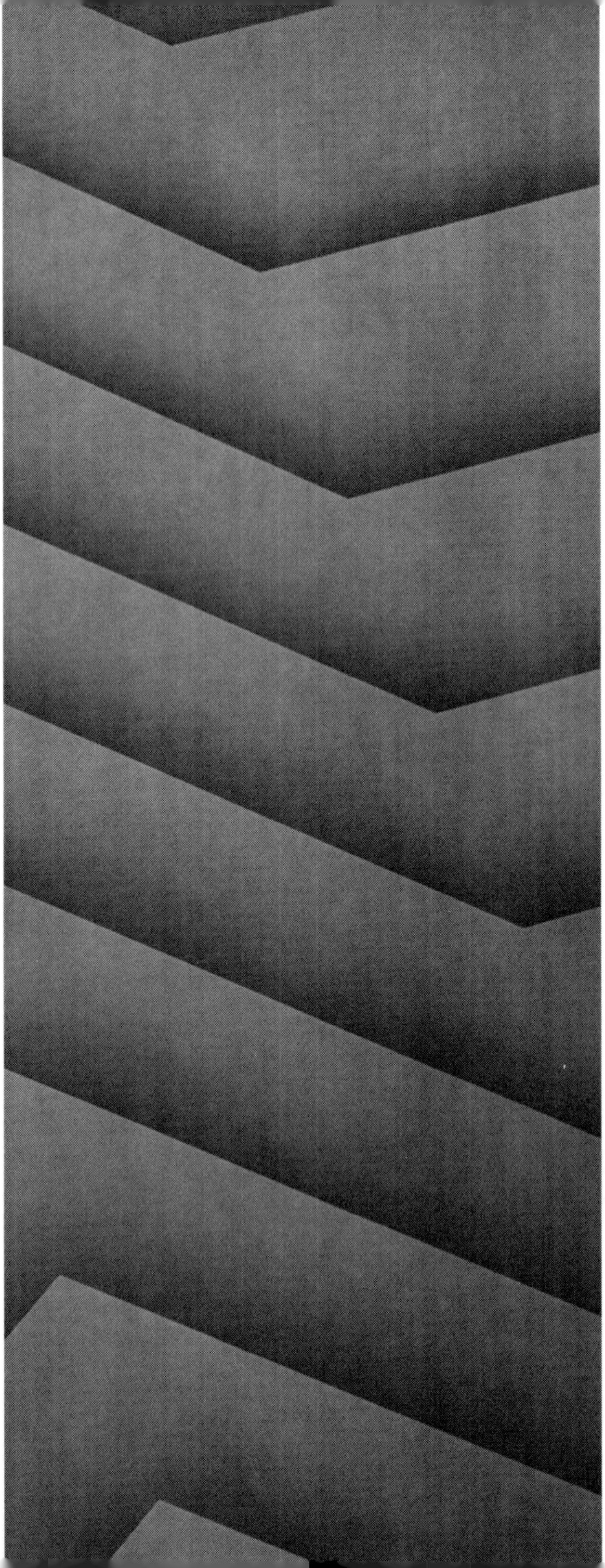

# ADAM SAVAGE & JAMIE HYNEMAN

---

*Jamie and Adam are the hosts of* Discovery's *hit show* MythBusters. *They have years of experience in special effects and are masters of elbow grease and process. Adam writes for* WIRED *and attends every Maker Faire. Jamie holds a degree in Russian Linguistics and is the creator of* Blendo, *one of the most dangerous robots in the world.*

## TINKERING WITH THE AMERICAN DREAM

### What is the value of making?

**ADAM**: For me, making things is a deeply important meditation. It the primary language by which I interact with the world, through my hands. The act of building has to happen in my head before it happens anywhere else. It is in that action, in my head, where I find the meditation really invigorating. In order to build something I have to understand it in my head. I build the whole thing mentally before I build it physically. I enjoy that process so much I seek it out wherever I can. I sit in theaters and look around, walking myself through the manufacturing process of everything I see; the lights, the cables, the fabric, the truss work, the sets, the furniture, and the carpet.

## How can hacking create a more optimistic future?

**JAMIE:** We work under the premise that science is not just for scientists. We are the poster children for that. We are not trained scientists, yet somehow, we end up doing a lot of science on our show. The reason is that we aren't coming at it as trained scientists, but we do want to do a good job. We have a passion for experimentation and building new things. To satisfy that passion and hunger to build and experiment we have to do a good job. We can't screw around (although there are benefits to doing that), we have to be methodical about our work if we want to move ahead and come to understand the problems that we find ourselves against.

That's all science is. Science isn't just for guys in lab coats. It is for anyone that simply wants to understand something and do a good job. The more methodical, diligent, and careful you are about your work, the more you write it down and are organized about it, the better chance you will have of being successful and coming up with particular solutions and answers.

That's what we do. It's a pretty profound thing. When we plan an episode, we don't come into the room and say, "Let's go do some science!" We just start thinking in an organized way. That's a very positive note for people at large, simply do a good job at thinking about things. In our modern world, things change with all these different inputs all the time, the rate of change is increasing. To keep up with it or to behave appropriately with our world, we need to do a good job. That means being methodical which means doing some sort of science.

**ADAM:** The key phrase is breaking down the steps. After fifteen years in the special effects industry, working on movies like *Star Wars*, I thought that I came to *MythBusters* with skills. But I didn't know anything when I started. The skills I have received since doing this show easily doubled or tripled anything I learned before. That is about taking a problem, process, or concept that I have never had experience with and learning enough to do a viable episode. That always involves breaking it down into understandable chunks. Take a problem that seems insurmountable and break it into pieces. Then attack each piece.

If you are talking about social movements, the key aspect there is community. Jamie and I are a weird lesson in community. I can't say we don't get along because we do, we are very productive together, but neither of us really enjoys the process. That process of working together. We drive each other nuts, but in that we have a fidelity to the best solution, not what solution happens to be the one we are invested in. We take it as a point of pride to be able to turn on a dime and change direction.

One of the great impedances to human progress, and when I think progress I think the elimination of human misery, is bias. People are unwilling to see what is in front of them or to look at viable ways to change what is in front of them. Those are things that we have to work together to achieve.

But when half of the people in this country think Earth is six thousand years old; half the people think global warming is total fiction; or people aren't sure if President Obama was born in our country, we clearly have a problem of people not listening to each other.

> ONE OF THE GREAT IMPEDANCES TO HUMAN PROGRESS IS BIAS.

JAMIE: One of the primary things that we've learned is that the most difficult part is right at the beginning where you have to be very clear about the questions you're trying to answer. What is the problem? What is it that you're actually facing? Once you do that and are very clear about what you're asking, finding out the answer is just like filling in the blanks. It is pretty much done for you. Now you just need to go through the motions methodically. We've often found that when we start off on a project, we get pulled in all different directions. We end up floundering in the brier, not knowing how to deal with something when it's not working. We've shown it on *MythBusters*, and we've seen it for ourselves. Often all it takes is to stop for a second to look at what you've been doing and then clarify what it is you're actually after. Once you do that, everything becomes very clear and you can move ahead.

The first thing we do is stop ourselves and say, "This is a myth." We ask, "Is there more than one thing involved in this myth?" Often, there is. Do we need to deal with them separately? Perhaps. Now, if you go in and start trying to define the questions that you want to answer, it can all be broken down into bite-size chunks in an orderly fashion. Before you know it, you're done. That same approach can apply to building a house. If you are going to build a house, you're going to want to know all about what the functions of the house are supposed to be. What problem is it going to address? What are all the different components? Well, you break it all down into little chunks. You buy the materials. You start to assemble them but you have a plan. If you don't have a plan and haven't been methodical about what you are going to do with that house, then you're not going to have a very nice house or you're going to take a long time to build it. It applies to everything from your daily life to doing science to building things, or even farming.

**JUST STARTING IS ONE OF THE MOST POWERFUL MOJOS THERE IS.**

If you want to do a good job, you need to be very careful about what you define as your goals—all the little pieces that you need to put together to come to an end result. Then, go pick them off one after the other in a methodical way. Before you know it, you've accomplished your task.

## *It is easy to get overwhelmed. How do we work on huge problems?*

**ADAM**: Just starting is one of the most powerful mojos there is. I always liken it to a very messy room. You wake up and look at the room that needs to be cleaned and it is overwhelming. There are too many things out of place, too many things gathered on one surface, and too many different categories. You clean the room by picking up one object. If you sat and mapped all the paths of the objects you would feel totally overwhelmed by the number of trips upstairs and downstairs and to the closet. If you just started doing it you will make a big dent quickly.

Early on in *MythBusters* we needed a special kind of firefighting pump that pumps fifteen hundred gallons a minute but no one would lend us one. Our producer said, "You will just have to build one."

I said, "I don't think we can do that."

"You are going to have to figure it out," he said. "That is the only option open."

We figured out how to do it and the pump we built pumps two thousand gallons a minute.

I think the thing that overwhelms people is the decision of when they want to get it done. They look at it and worry about how long it will take. We can't see reasonable progress. Give yourself a deadline. A deadline is a very powerful tool.

**GIVE YOURSELF A DEADLINE. A DEADLINE IS A VERY POWERFUL TOOL.**

## When you look to the future, what are you hopeful for and excited about?

**JAMIE:** There is definitely a rapidity of change. The rate of increased knowledge about our world as a result of new technologies, genetics, artificial intelligence, computer-aided design, and the Internet allows us to move forward much more rapidly. When it comes to challenges like global warming, one can hope that even though it took us a long time to damage the planet to where it is now, we're speeding up. I have hope that we'll be able to use that speed to figure out solutions to dig ourselves out of the hole that we have dug. For almost any of the pitfalls in modern society there is a glimmer of light that has increased. It comes from access to information, increased access to new technology that makes it easier to understand and manipulate our world and is something that allows us to hope. There is a chance that we might not destroy ourselves. There is a chance we can do things like solve common problems or cure cancer. At some point, there is a solution out there for whatever bad thing is killing a lot of people or whatever it is you want it to do. There is a technical solution that will most likely be reached to solve that problem and that possibility is accelerating. Even within my lifetime, looking at the things we have available to us versus when I was a child, the rate of change is really quite something. It will continue to accelerate as far as anything I understand.

## Who is getting it right?

**JAMIE:** I think the DIY mentality spurs a lot of innovation. There are people that are actually thinking about things. They ask how things work rather than just accepting that they work. As that carries through more of the culture, you are going to see more people like Elon Musk, Dean Kamen, and other innovators of our time having a wide impact.

I'm also delighted that we've been to the White House several times now. We were consulted by Obama and his people about how to expand interest in innovation because that kind of thing determines our future and the happiness of our offspring. If I were to pat one person on the back, it would be Obama.

## What have you found empowering in DIY that is not elsewhere?

**ADAM:** It took me a while but it became clear to me that our job is to be communicators. One of the messages I am committed to is a message of permission. It is okay to try things. It is okay to try things where you don't know what will happen. It is okay to try things and fail. It is okay to be a fool. It is okay to be obsessed. It is okay to be excited.

**JAMIE:** DIY culture allows people to internalize the things that they are dealing with. If you just read about something or leave something for somebody else to do, it can become just a pile of meaningless data on paper. Once you acquire actual physical experience with whatever that thing is, you start to be able to internalize it and get control over it. You get it in your head and it becomes an active ability versus a passive understanding.

That variability, especially if you take the point of view that science isn't just for scientists and engineering isn't just for engineers, is essential. If you want to do a good job at something, then everybody should have some level of confidence within anything that affects their lives so they can more appropriately deal with those same things. That internalization has to, by definition, have an active ability rather than a passive one. This means that you essentially start to apply those things to your life and you behave, if

> IT IS OKAY TO TRY THINGS. IT IS OKAY TO TRY THINGS WHERE YOU DON'T KNOW WHAT WILL HAPPEN. IT IS OKAY TO TRY THINGS AND FAIL. IT IS OKAY TO BE A FOOL. IT IS OKAY TO BE OBSESSED. IT IS OKAY TO BE EXCITED.

nothing else, more responsibly because you have internalized the things you are dealing with and realize, from your own experience, the implications of your actions.

A lot of these things are converging. The access that people and universities have to information via the Internet blurs the line between what one can learn on one's own and what one needs help to learn. Certainly the days of doing garage tinkering and coming up with something that saves the world are pretty much over. The advances to technology are going to be done on a molecular level using genetics or something that requires advanced technology. That requires very complicated and large institutions to help implement. At the same time, that kind of inquisitiveness is part and parcel of the DIY culture. The ability of an individual to problem solve is fundamental. Some of those people are actually in universities. I think we've only just begun to scratch the service. It's not a coincidence that the DIY culture started to develop around the same time that the Internet really started to rock and roll. The Internet is just sitting in front of you on your laptop or desktop machine. It allows people to build almost anything in the back of their garage as long as it doesn't require electron microscopes.

## *What is your American Dream?*

**ADAM**: It is not only okay to fail but it is necessary. I can't think of anything that goes to a deeper level for me. We all fail at things all the time. It is a universal truth. Being wrong, myopic, biased, and small-minded are all miniature failures. The hero is the one who knows when they have failed, to admit it and to move on. The villain is the one who has no idea that failure is happening around them. I try to follow Tom Robbins' advice and be the hero of my own movie. My heroes are willing to admit when they are wrong.

**IT IS NOT ONLY OKAY TO FAIL BUT IT IS NECESSARY.**

The Internet has made the world smaller but it has also served to make an endless number of communities. I am a liberal in the deepest sense of thinking it is our task as a community to take care of each other. Every time I want to figure out where I stand on a political issue I have a model town in my head with only fifty people in it. When you break complex socio-economic and political issues and down to a group of fifty people, things get simple really fast.

The dream I have for my kids is that they will find a community they belong to. Feeding the things you find you must do will bring the rewards you deserve. That will only happen if we take care of each other. It will not happen if we are all out for ourselves. It will not happen in Ayn Rand's universe (she is the ur-troll as far as I am concerned).

**JAMIE:** One of the things that I would like to see become more prominent is the idea that, as we move forward and resources become more limited, the luxury of not cooperating with the other people you share space and the environment with, will disappear. We don't have the luxury to do whatever we want or to expect that everything will be fine if we just look after ourselves. As the population continues to grow, or even if it stays the same, resources are going to be depleted. Society is going to see an increasing need to cooperate and collaborate. It requires people to set their sights on goals that are much more cooperative. The purely materialistic "get rich and consume as much as you possibly can" mentality is not going to be on the menu for very much longer.

> **AS WE MOVE FORWARD AND RESOURCES BECOME MORE LIMITED, THE LUXURY OF NOT COOPERATING WITH THE OTHER PEOPLE YOU SHARE SPACE AND THE ENVIRONMENT WITH, WILL DISAPPEAR.**

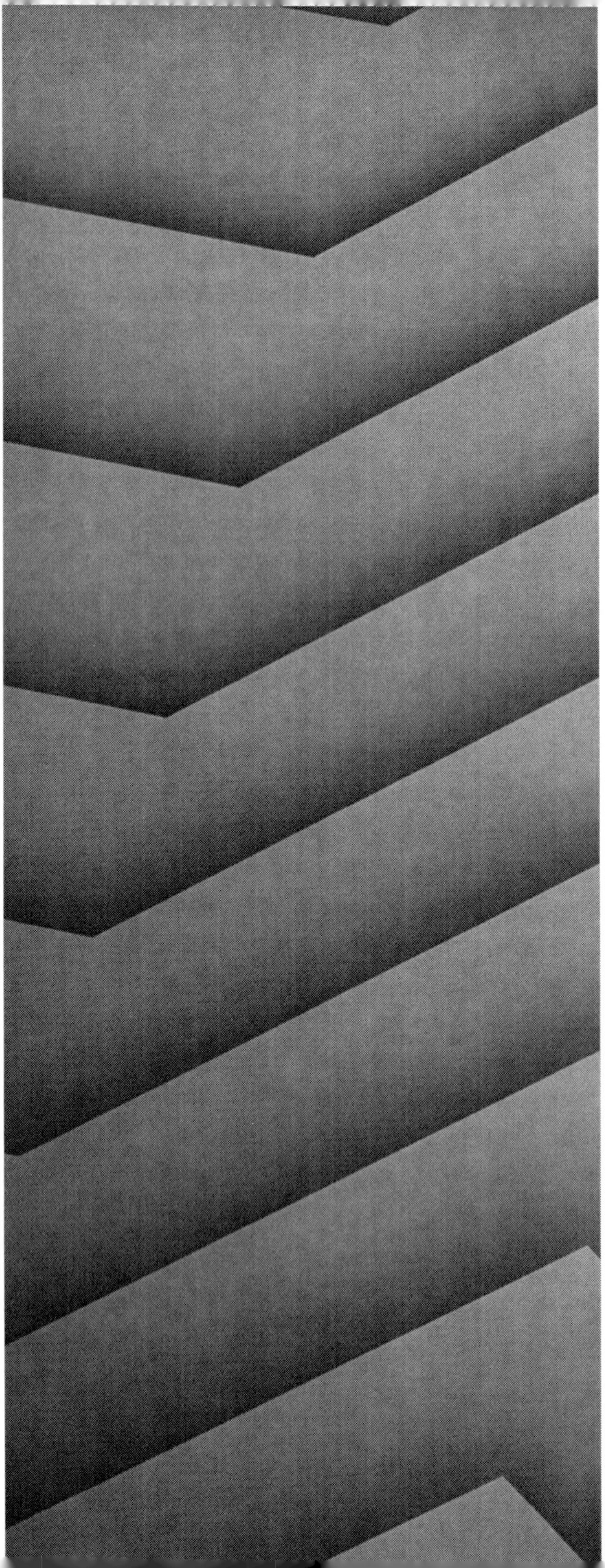

# NIRVAN MULLICK

---

*Nirvan Mullick is an LA based filmmaker, digital strategist, and creative consultant. In 2011, Nirvan co-founded Interconnected, an LA based creative agency, through which he directed* Caine's Arcade, *an 11-minute short film that has been viewed over six million times. They raised over $200,000 for a scholarship fund for a creative young boy, and launched a nonprofit called the Imagination Foundation to find, foster, and fund creativity and entrepreneurship in kids.*

cainesarcade.com

## CAINE'S ARCADE AND THE POWER OF CARDBOARD!

It all started with going to buy a door handle for my '96 Corolla. It was the last day of summer and I was in an industrial area of Los Angeles, where they sell used auto parts. I came across a random store, pulled in, and ended up meeting a nine-year-old boy named Caine who built a cardboard arcade using boxes from his dad's store. He asked me if I wanted to play and if I'd be interested in buying a fun pass to his arcade. It was a two-dollar pass that he had made which offered five hundred turns.

I bought the fun pass, and the rest grew from there.

It really started with Caine. Playing his games and seeing what he had made was very inspiring to me. It reminded me of my own childhood and the things that I used to make. I kept thinking about his arcade and I went back and asked his father if I could make a short film about his son's arcade. That's when his dad told me that I had been Caine's only customer, and I got to know more about how long Caine had been working on this. He spent the entire summer building his arcade and making it more functional and elaborate in preparation for customers, but he had yet to have any. The shop is in a very industrial area and they don't get a lot of foot traffic, and his dad started doing most of his business on Ebay selling auto parts, so Caine didn't really have a chance to have any customers for his arcade. The few people that did come by just bought their auto parts and left.

We crafted a plan to surprise Caine with customers. We organized a flash mob just to make his day. We put together a flash mob online, and invited anybody in Los Angeles to come out and make Caine's day and surprise him. Hundreds of people came out. So this little idea—this little Facebook invite—went kind of mini-viral. It made the front page of Reddit, and was featured on *Hidden LA*, which had about 230,000 Facebook fans at the time. Hundreds of people came out and we surprised Caine. That was the heart of the short film that I made. When I posted the film I invited people to chip in and try to raise a scholarship fund for Caine. The initial goal was a twenty-five thousand dollar scholarship fund. The first first day the film was posted, it got over a million views, raised over sixty thousand dollars for his scholarship, and just took off.

***How did you get from doing something really amazing for one kid and turn this into something else and can inspire others?***

It happened really quickly—the response was so immediate, and so universally positive. We got a report from Caine's dad that Yahoo had put the film on their homepage. They told Caine's dad that it was the most positively received story that had ever been on there. There was something very universal, and almost magical about it. It was making grown men cry and inspiring kids to start making things. Parents and teachers all around the world were writing us and letting us know that as soon as they showed the film to their kids, their kids would start making stuff. Kids would show it to their parents and their parents would start crying. We were getting tens of thousands of emails a day from people around the world. I didn't get much sleep. I didn't get any sleep for the first three days. After the first day his scholarship had reached sixty thousand dollars so we raised his scholarship goal to a hundred thousand dollars, and it cleared that the next day. After that we didn't want to raise it without knowing what we were doing.

I have a background working in the nonprofit space and it was clear by the response that there were so many other kids just like Caine out there. People were really responding to the positivity in Caine's story. It was trending on Twitter. It was giving people a lot of hope and making people smile. We started thinking about ways to help other kids like Caine. It was just serendipity that I met him. I have a feeling that there are so many other kids like Caine out there in every neighborhood, in every city, in every town, and they're making stuff, and maybe they're waiting for somebody to come. It didn't take much to really change Caine's life—it was just a small gesture. So the idea was to build a foundation

I HAVE A FEELING THAT THERE ARE SO MANY OTHER KIDS LIKE CAINE OUT THERE IN EVERY NEIGHBORHOOD, IN EVERY CITY, IN EVERY TOWN, AND THEY'RE MAKING STUFF, AND MAYBE THEY'RE WAITING FOR SOMEBODY TO COME.

that could find and foster the creativity and entrepreneurship of kids. That was the mission statement we put together three days after the film hit the Internet.

I got in touch with one of the foundations that I had worked with in the past called the Goldhirsh Foundation. Ben Goldhirsh started *GOOD* magazine, he's been involved in the nonprofit space and the for-profit space for a long time. I told him what was going on and he recognized that this was lightning in a bottle. This was an opportunity to try and do more with it, so he put up a very generous challenge grant of fifty-thousand dollars; for every dollar that went to Caine's scholarship fund, the Goldhirsh Foundation put up a dollar for the Imagination Foundation to get started. And at that point we raised the goal for Caine's scholarship fund from the one hundred thousand dollar mark to two hundred thousand. We have since raised two hundred and twenty thousand dollars.

The goals of the foundation are to promote creative thinking as a core social value. Beyond that, to give kids opportunities to create and make things built around their passions. Caine was making something that he loved and was learning a lot by doing it. This mirrors that idea and encourages kids to create and build things around what they're interested in. A lot of learning happens with project-based learning.

We started a school pilot program in the first two months, over a hundred schools in nine countries. We're using the short film, *Caine's Arcade*, and inviting kids to build cardboard arcades. A lot of the teachers and classes made math arcades or used it to teach social entrepreneurship. They used the arcades to raise money for their PE class, or for children's hospitals as well as the Imagination Foundation. It's gone beyond just arcades. Kids are making rocket ships and complex pinball machines with simple mechanics, movie theaters, puppet theaters, museums, and art galleries. Across the board, kids are using cardboard to make all kinds of amazing things.

## What are some examples you have seen of the ingenuity of kids?

I've skyped with a lot of kids. I've been taken into some of these games and machines. I met a young girl from Arizona who built an entire motorcycle out of cardboard. She had thought through all the different components. I saw a few kids who had made a movie theater that you could go inside, and they had a little screen and lights set up. I've seen cardboard vending machines with kids inside it who will serve you a beverage. One of my favorites is a cardboard photocopy machine (which is actually online, I put a little clip of it in the *Caine's Arcade 2* film). It's a cardboard box with a cardboard toilet seat lid. It's got cellophane where you lay down whatever your document is, and the kid gets in the box with a flashlight, draws whatever it is that you put on the photocopy machine and when he spits it out of the side, he makes all the "rrrrrrrrrr" sounds of the device.

> KIDS ARE MAKING ROCKET SHIPS AND COMPLEX PINBALL MACHINES WITH SIMPLE MECHANICS, MOVIE THEATERS, PUPPET THEATERS, MUSEUMS, AND ART GALLERIES. ACROSS THE BOARD, KIDS ARE USING CARDBOARD TO MAKE ALL KINDS OF AMAZING THINGS.

## What is the value of having kids building and playing with these things? What are they learning through allowing them to play?

They are learning simple engineering, problem solving, describing their creation to other kids or parents and adults. They are storytelling and working in groups. There are a million different things that they are learning through play, and there is also this level of community coming together to support what these kids are making, which is also a valuable part of the equation.

We did an interview in the follow-up film with Robert

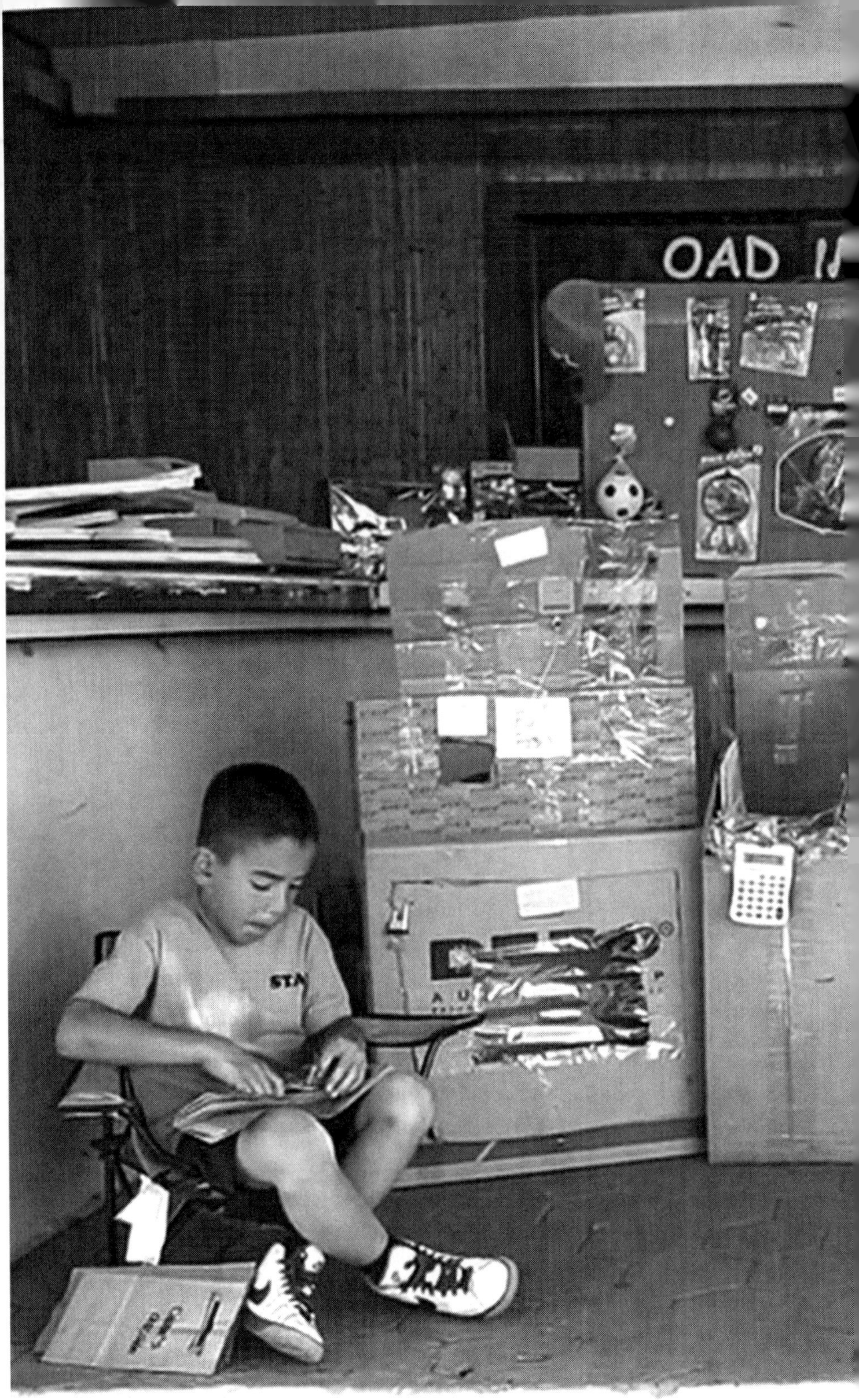

*Courtesy of Nirvan Mullick*

**THE WORLD IS CHANGING FASTER AND FASTER, AND THE ONLY WAY TO PREPARE FOR THAT UNCERTAIN WORLD IS TO HAVE CREATIVE MAKERS.**

Manning, who was the lead engineer from the Jet Propulsion Laboratory. When he was a kid, he built cardboard rockets and now he has helped build a real one that landed on Mars. There is definitely a connection between play, imagination, and innovation.

*If we get a whole generation of young people, like Caine, who are participating, what does the world look like when they grow up?*

The world is changing faster and faster, and the only way to prepare for that uncertain world is to have creative makers. Kids will grow up as creative problem solvers, able to adapt and transform resources that are around them, however limited those resources are, into new ideas and solutions.

When I first met Caine he wanted to join the SWAT team, and after the film came out he received encouragement and now he wants to be an engineer and a game designer. When people find their passion and they're encouraged to create and explore the things that they are interested in, you get people who are more engaged and more productive, and that's just a better future. I'm also really excited about collaboration with people who are working together to foster things like the Global Cardboard Challenge. It's happening on a local level and a global level. The idea of community is really crossing geographic boundaries. I think that's a really exciting trend that will inform the future as well.

Sometimes limitations can be the spark for innovation. And sometimes having less can create more. There's an environmental message in this, in what Caine created: reusing materials that are around you, finding new ways to use things, taking trash and turning it into a game or something that's fun, something that's useful. Problem solving skills are really at the heart of this, and there are certainly plenty of problems that need to be solved. Encouraging that kind of creativity and resourcefulness is going to help shape a brighter future.

*If a parent or a kid came up to you and asked, "How can I do something like this? How do I get started? How do I encourage my kid?" what would be your guide to building your own arcade?*

Start small with what you have, and do something that you actually care about. It doesn't have to be an arcade. In Caine's case it was an arcade because he loves arcades. He used the little basketball hoop because that was something that he had won at Shakey's Pizza. He didn't know what he was doing at first. He just kept building and improving as he went along. I think those are good lessons. Start with what you have, build as you go, and make sure you have fun.

*For those of us who can't go to Caine's Arcade, how can we get involved?*

Right now we're going into a strategic planning session since the Cardboard Challenge. The first six months were a total nonstop blur of activity where there was really this challenge of taking a viral moment of video and starting a foundation that would last. We started with the school pilot program and then we did the Global Cardboard Challenge which invited the world to play. We made a follow-up film about everything that had happened and had a call to action—people could go to the website and register to do a cardboard challenge, which is building anything that they wanted out of cardboard and imagination. We did this in a very short timespan. We had two hundred seventy events in forty countries on six continents registered, and tens of thousands of kids around the world building really incredible cardboard creations.

> I THINK WHEN PEOPLE FIND THEIR PASSION AND THEY'RE ENCOURAGED TO CREATE AND EXPLORE THE THINGS THAT THEY ARE INTERESTED IN, YOU GET PEOPLE THAT ARE MORE ENGAGED AND MORE PRODUCTIVE, AND THAT'S JUST A BETTER FUTURE.

On October 6th, 2012, the one year anniversary of the flash mob to make Caine's day, we had a global day of play where people could find cardboard challenge events around the world and go out to support the kids in their community. That was super fun and will be an annual event that we do through the Imagination Foundation. Every first weekend of October, people will be able to go and play at these events. People can sign up to do these events on the Imagination Foundation website. Other goals are for kids in underserved communities: giving kids the space to create, and to develop a more robust web platform that connects maker-kids with adults, teachers, parents. We want to create more community around making and also celebrate and share more stories of creative kids around the world who are doing awesome things like Caine.

Another thing we are moving towards, and are really excited about, is promoting and fostering social entrepreneurship at a young age. There are so many kids who have been using these cardboard creations to make little businesses, and raise money for different causes.

You always hear statistics about kids when they're young. They want to grow up to be artists, they want to grow up to be all these big things, but once they're in high school they've become way more practical just because those engaging and inspirational ideas get beaten out of them by the reality of life. I think we need to take a close look at the education system that we have in place, and think about the kinds of adults we're making in that system, and what makes sense in the new reality of our world.

> I THINK WE NEED TO TAKE A CLOSE LOOK AT THE EDUCATION SYSTEM THAT WE HAVE IN PLACE, AND THINK ABOUT THE KINDS OF ADULTS WE'RE MAKING IN THAT SYSTEM

# DR. CAMERON M. SMITH

---

*Dr. Smith works to bring an anthropological, human dimension to space exploration, and to cast space exploration as a natural continuation of human evolution. He teaches a wide variety of courses in human adaptation and evolution at Portland State University. He has recently published* Emigrating Beyond Earth: Human Adaptation and Space Colonization *and is currently writing* Principles of Space Anthropology: Building a Science of Adaptive Human Space Colonization.

cameronmsmith.com

## HOME-MADE SPACE SUITS

I am building a pressure suit in my apartment so that I can fly to fifty thousand feet in a balloon. As a child of the 1970s Space Age, I was sure that I would some day walk on Mars. Poor eyesight blocked me from the Astronaut Corps, but I am not quitting. I will build and fly my airship as far from the surface of the Earth as I can, and experience a view of the Earth from near-space conditions, where only my pressure suit will keep me alive. From programming an old Mac, to running a flight simulation, to building each valve and hose connection, I mean to do this with my own mind and resources, rather than relying on the government to get me there. The colonization of space is beginning now, and I mean to be a part of it, if only by showing that the technologies involved are not the exclusive province of NASA, but can be explored by a fulltime archaeologist and part-time astronaut.

In the 1930s, going to high altitude was done by balloon. Very interestingly, before World War II, it was not of strategic interest, they didn't think there could be anything done up there. The military didn't put money into it, so the pressure suits made in the 1930s were not military sponsored. They were in fact very low budget projects. Some were totally private, one man was a Spanish Air Force pilot but he did it entirely on his own. Wiley Post's suit was rubberized canvas with pigskin gloves. His shoes had simple laces working as the pressure restraint. I thought, if these guys could do that in the 1930s with their technology I could do it today with a diving suit, Russian helmet, and so on. After studying those guys I had the confidence to say I could go ahead and build a suit.

**THE COLONIZATION OF SPACE IS BEGINNING NOW, AND I MEAN TO BE A PART OF IT.**

## *How much does it cost to make a suit?*

I am always asked that and I just don't have a number. I have an envelope with all my receipts. I think it is much less than someone would spend on a very used car. It is far below five thousand dollars, closer to two thousand and 90 percent of that has been waste. I tried something out and the material didn't work, I cut it wrong, or the screw punctured something.

## *How did this all start? What got you dreaming about building your own suit?*

I had done expeditions to the Arctic for a few years, pulling a sled, and that was a very unearthly world. I went to Alaska and Iceland in winter many times. I loved that idea of

*Image courtesy of Dr. Cameron M. Smith*

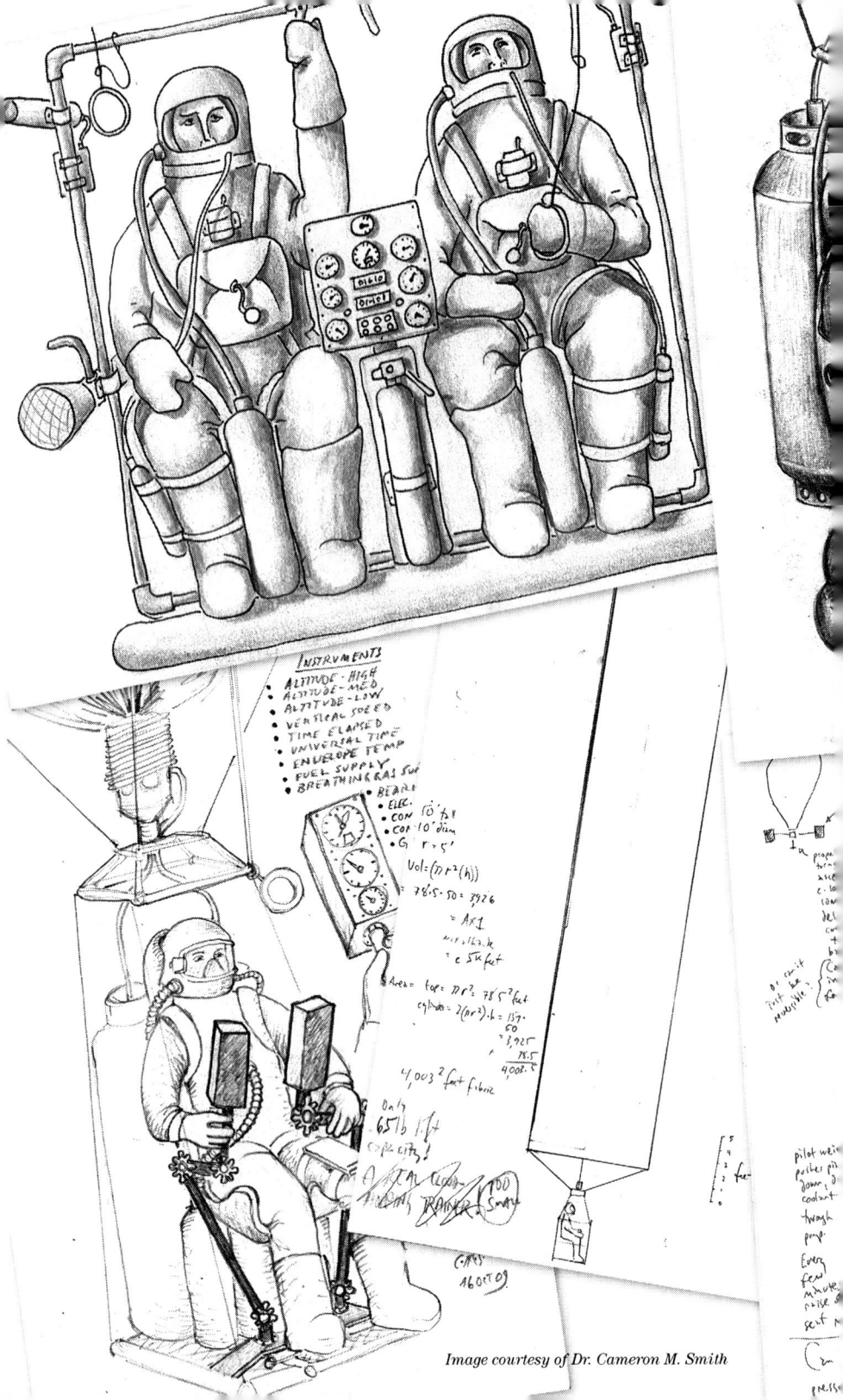

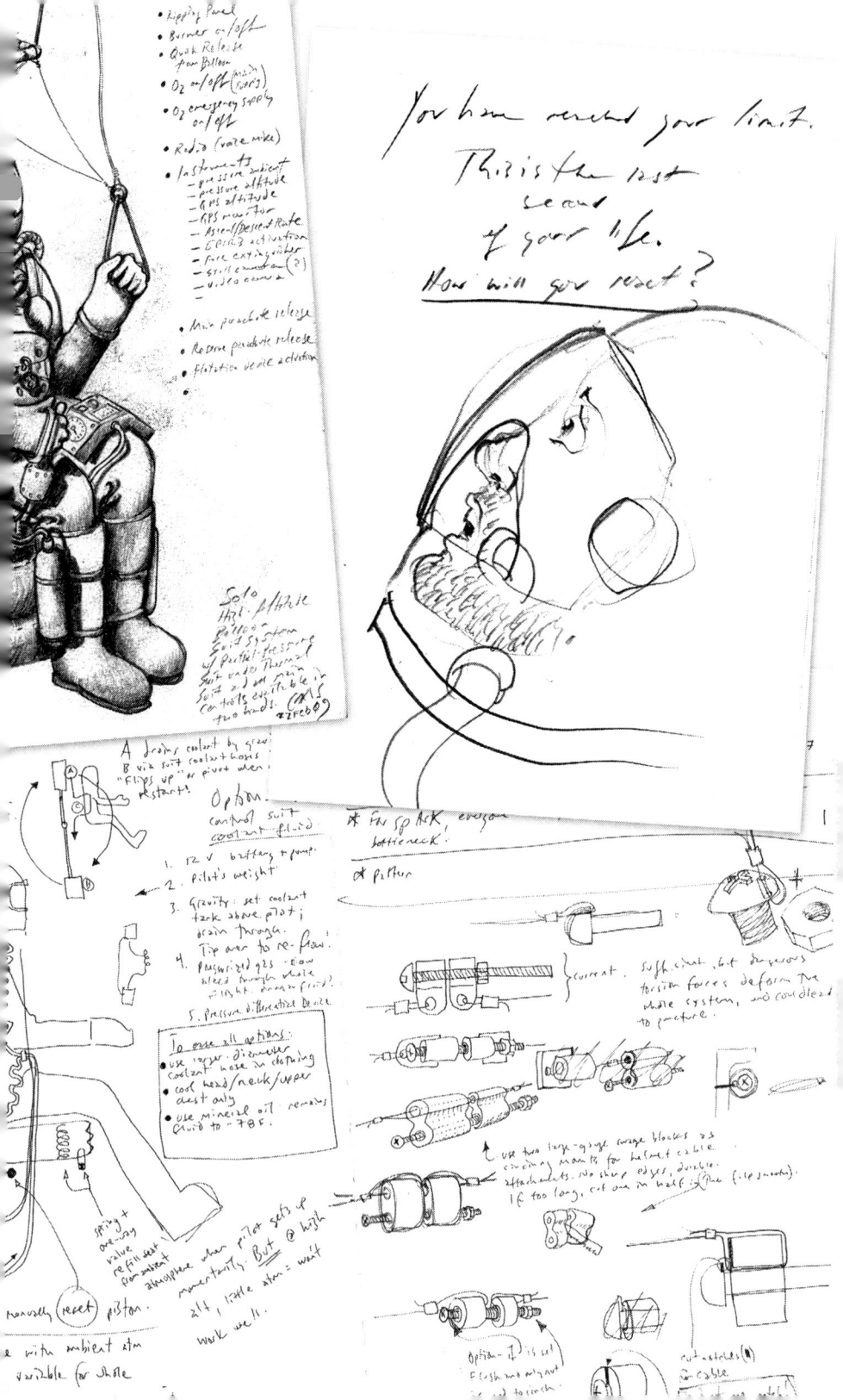

- Lighting Panel
- Burner on/off
- Quick Release from Balloon
- O2 on/off (main supply)
- O2 emergency supply on/off
- Radio (voice mike)
- Instruments
  — pressure ambient
  — pressure altitude
  — GPS altitude
  — GPS monitor
  — Ascent/Descent Rate
  — EPIRB activation
  — fire extinguisher
  — still camera (?)
  — video camera
- Main parachute release
- Reserve parachute release
- Flotation device activation

Solo High-Altitude Balloon Suit System w/ perfect pressure suit under thermal suit and own main controls available in two hands.

You have reached your limit.
This is the last second of your life.
How will you react?

A. drains coolant by gravity
B. via suit coolant hoses
"Flips up" to pivot when restart!

Options:
- control suit coolant fluid
1. 12 V battery + pump.
2. Pilot's weight
3. Gravity: set coolant tank above pilot; drain through.
   Tip over to re-flow.
4. Pressurized gas — slow bleed through valve + light stream front.
5. Pressure differential device

In over all options:
- use larger diameter coolant hose in clothing
- cool head/neck/upper chest only
- use mineral oil — remains fluid to -78°F.

spring + one-way valve refill self from ambient atmosphere when pilot sets to ambient atmosphere. But @ high altitude, little atm = wont work well.

manually reset piston

with ambient atm variable for altitude

* For spark, arcing = bottleneck.
* Pattern

current. Sufficient, but dangerous torsion forces deform the whole system, and could lead to puncture.

* use two large-gauge wedge blocks as securing mounts for helmet cable attachments. No sharp edges, durable. If too long, cut one in half. Then file smooth.

option - if it is cut flush and only need to cinch

> WHEN YOU ARE TEN YEARS OLD AND AN APOLLO GUY WRITES, "COME FLY WITH US," YOUR BRAIN PRETTY MUCH GOES ON FIRE.

an unearthly world. When I was a kid I had pictures from astronauts who wrote back to me. I would write to them and ask, "How do I go to space?" When you are ten years old and an Apollo guy writes, "Come fly with us," your brain pretty much goes on fire. But when I was a kid I also discovered my eyesight was poor and in those days the only way to space was through military aviation. You had to be a flyer and I wasn't. So that dream fell apart.

Then I got into climbing and mountaineering which led to the Arctic. That started to lead me to these places that were like the surface of another planet. I started thinking about space again. After those Arctic expeditions I learned how to fly a paraglider but the paraglider was very finicky. You need to have just the right air conditions, so I thought, "Maybe a balloon?" A balloon can go very high so maybe I could reconnect with that space dream again. Then I started looking into balloons and I wondered if I should build a capsule, though that's really complicated. I literally wondered how I would get it out the door of my apartment.

So what could I do?

I could build a pressure suit. I read about those guys from the 1930s who built pressure suits and went up in gondolas. If I could make a smaller thing, then I could disassemble it and transport it out the door to a flying site. High altitudes, one hundred thousand feet like Felix Baumgartner's jump, require a helium balloon and helium balloons are very expensive. I had done sponsored expeditions before but I really didn't want to go through all of that again. I could just do it myself. Those guys, like Wiley Post, did it themselves. There is a whole zeitgeist of do it yourself: I saw a guy online who open sourced his whole balloon construction. He lists every item and I got inspired by that. I will do it myself and not have to worry about sponsors or timelines. None of my heroes died in their suits, so I will try it myself.

## *Why is open sourcing it important?*

I want to show people that getting to space, and space access, should not be dependent on the federal government. It is great what they did with the Moon but to get large numbers of people moving, to eventually colonize space, you can't trickle them through. You need to have a lot of ideas and a lot of things happening again and again. NASA is a great research organization but there is so little money that they have to stay really focused. To get the costs down you need to have a lot of inventions. To get a lot of inventions you need to have a lot of people doing it.

When I got back into all this space stuff I wrote a book, *Emigrating Beyond Earth*. It connects anthropology and human evolution with space migration. It is not about robots, technology, or computers. It is about humans doing what we have been doing for millions of years, finding new places to live. A lot of people say, "Oh, we will just transport human problems off the Earth and mess up everything else." That is a pessimistic view and I take the optimistic view. We can better ourselves and I think we will have to.

The geologists, paleontologists, and astronomers all tell us that we will get hit by space debris someday. There will be another extinction event. There have already been five that have taken out the bulk of life on Earth. It is a numbers game. It is going to happen so do we want humanity to survive? I do. I want civilization to survive. It has all kinds of problems but I love it! We must find other places to live. I think it was Carl Sagan who said that we are a one planet species. Having all your eggs in one basket is a bad insurance policy. We know from ecology that species who get too tightly focused on one niche and can't adapt are out. Spreading out and diversifying is an evolutionary process.

I am too old to be able to go myself but I can try to get this idea out there. I hope to demystify it so it is made more

**SPREADING OUT AND DIVERSIFYING IS AN EVOLUTIONARY PROCESS.**

*Image courtesy of Nick Barham*

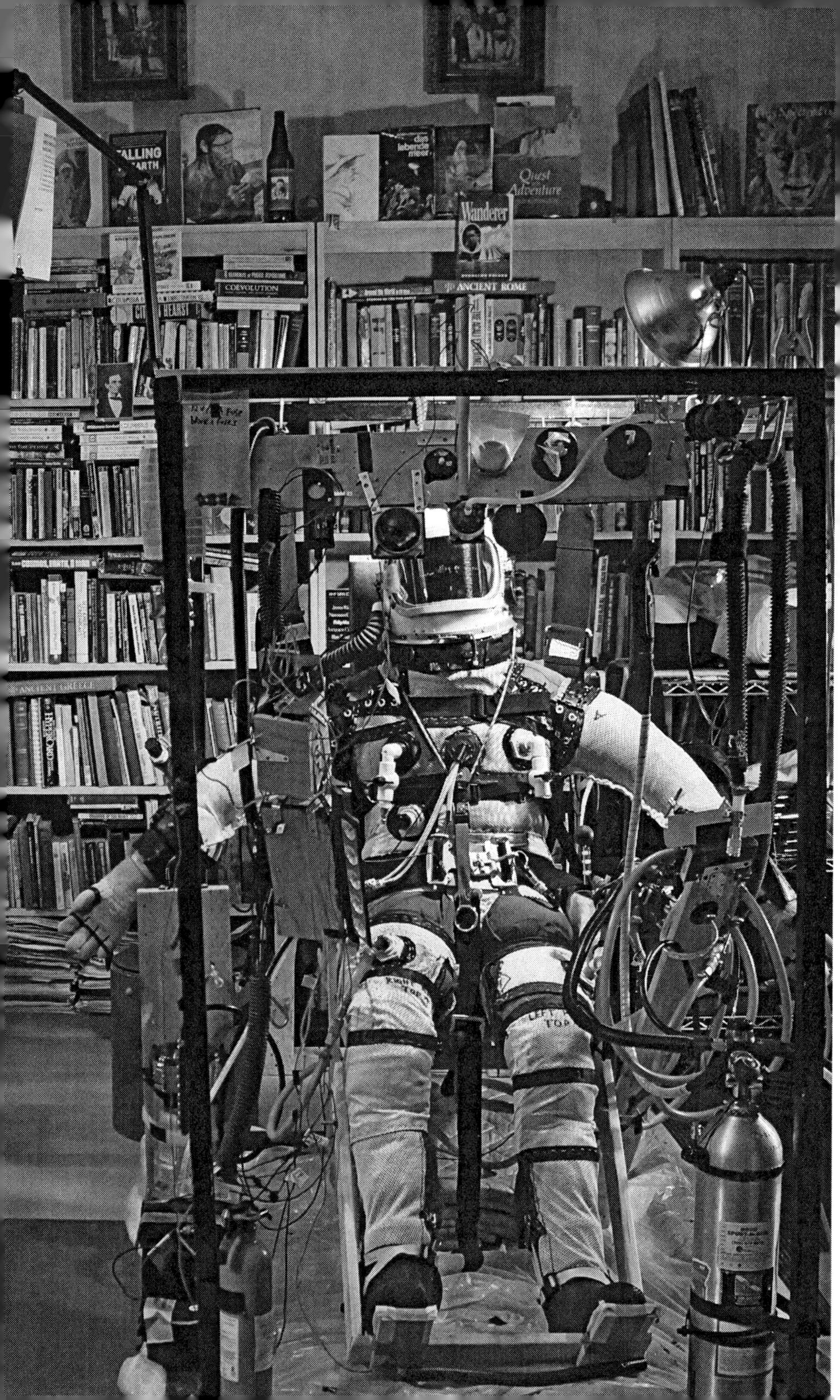

*Image courtesy of Nick Barham*

| File Edit Go Tools Objects Font Style

| **ALT** | 34756 | ALT ALARM |
| **FPM** ↑↓ | 764 | RATE ALARM |
| **FUEL** | 16 | FUEL ALARM |
| **OAT** | −37 | OAT ALARM |
| **BET** | 139 | BET ALARM |
| **OXY** | | OXY ALARM |
| **APSI** | 5.597 | APSI ALARM |

Seconds to Open Visor: 141

TTT  20 min

Altitude logged at 34472 feet

TTG  —

RESET  LAU

public and more people think, "Oh, yes. I could do that." I also want to put it into the context of human evolution. There is a chapter in my book that talks about shifting the way we think about it. For example, most people think about space exploration as missions but that gives a concrete end. After the mission you come back. I want to change space travel from a limited concept to unlimited. It is not an end but a beginning. That is a cognitive shift and that can be done by how we talk about it and how we even draw our images of space. We don't have to think of space just in pictures of people encased in technology but we should have pictures of people playing in space, space hotels where people are having sex, and living human lives.

> WE DON'T HAVE TO THINK OF SPACE JUST IN PICTURES OF PEOPLE ENCASED IN TECHNOLOGY BUT WE SHOULD HAVE PICTURES OF PEOPLE PLAYING IN SPACE, SPACE HOTELS WHERE PEOPLE ARE HAVING SEX, AND LIVING HUMAN LIVES.

I get angry and agitated when I think, "There is a whole universe out there. They just found a new planet a few light-years away. Why am I prevented from exploring the universe by one government?" That burns me up. The government is in the way. I love NASA, let them do research and continue sending rovers, but it is now time for more access to space.

I am talking to a couple of people who are developing a totally privately funded flight to Mars that is, in fact, one way. They do not mean to come back. It is a husband and wife team. They have been to the North Pole together. They walked to the South Pole together. They climbed Everest together. They are quite wealthy but don't have all the money they need so they are putting together money for a private space mission.

**What is the value in getting to the edge of space? Is the point to get to the edge and look out, or to look back at our planet?**

I want to look out. It is an almost tangible frustration for me that I can get that close and not go further. I want to go to the moon. I want to go to Mars. I want to explore out beyond. If you define space at about forty-five miles up from Earth, that is about most people's commute. If we just turned the axis of our commute up and got to that point; there is a whole universe out there! There is a universe of stuff to explore! That boggles my mind. It is right up there. If we can just get up there a little bit, it's like going through a door. Wow!

### And if this works, what are the next steps for your DIY space suit?

I think, "Well, if I am at fifty thousand feet what about one hundred thousand?" I think a hot air balloon maxes out at about seventy thousand feet. You could build a huge one but that gets out of the DIY. I am not really sure what I could do after that. I haven't thought too much about it. Right now, I want to make this a success and come back in good health.

All we ever see of the Moon is Neil Armstrong stepping off the ladder. But if you look at video from when they were five miles above the surface there are canyons, just wild terrain. We just see the footage they show every tenth anniversary, "One small step..."

**I WANT TO LOOK OUT. IT IS AN ALMOST TANGIBLE FRUSTRATION FOR ME THAT I CAN GET THAT CLOSE AND NOT GO FURTHER. I WANT TO GO TO THE MOON. I WANT TO GO TO MARS. I WANT TO EXPLORE OUT BEYOND.**

### Does looking back on Earth change how we see it?

I hope when people can look back at Earth and see, "My gosh! How incredible what we have is!" maybe then we will take better care of it. Historians have attributed the start of the environmental movement to those pictures of Earth from Apollo, the first earthrise. You could see the whole thing. It was, and is, surrounded by emptiness.

I hope that continues. The astronauts always say, "When you get up there you can never see borders. What is with these crazy wars we are always having?" I imagine we will always have conflict but maybe that perspective can be a game-changer. We have had big changes in our consciousness before: during the Medieval Era to the Renaissance. Maybe an increased awareness of space will do that.

117

# MICHAEL BRENNAN

---

*Michael Brennan is a technologist living in Philadelphia. He currently works for SecondMuse, where he is a global organizer for socially conscious tech initiatives such as Random Hacks of Kindness, the International Space Apps Challenge, and the Central America Domestic Violence Hackathon.*

mbrennan.net

## SOCIALLY CONSCIOUS GEEKS

How can a computer scientist make direct, tangible impact on the lives of individuals around the world? I don't mean through a fancier phone or a prettier video game. I mean for basic needs and emergencies: food, drought, shelter, jobs, health, hurricanes.

This question emerged for me as a young college student. I was earning a degree in computer science and running the college chapter of Amnesty International on the side. On one hand, I was programming late at night. On the other, I was writing letters in support of releasing political prisoners around the world. I loved both but, at the time, I saw no link between the two. This raised some concern, but I shrugged it off. I would figure it out later.

As the years went on, however, the question became more urgent. I returned to school in my mid-twenties to obtain a doctorate in the same field. "Figuring it out later" was no longer good enough. It caused me anxiety, even despair. The role of social consciousness in computer science wasn't taught in school. I knew I had to solve this issue or completely reexamine my future.

And through that search, I have found an answer that continues to evolve. This answer is the realization that tech geeks like me aren't just a resource to be tapped into for the sake of solutions created by others. No, we must be part of those solutions. Technology is at the heart of all challenges humanity faces, and the best solutions to those problems come from true collaboration between humanitarians, doctors, field workers, researchers, programmers, hackers, engineers, and geeks.

> TECH GEEKS LIKE ME AREN'T JUST A RESOURCE TO BE TAPPED INTO FOR THE SAKE OF SOLUTIONS CREATED BY OTHERS. NO, WE MUST BE PART OF THOSE SOLUTIONS.

The hacker can work with the food distribution specialist to realize the missing link in food access is a low-tech SMS system for identifying nearby farmers markets that accept food stamps. The programmer can work with the politician to lobby governments to release data on flood planes in a region so a city can better protect itself against seasonal flooding. The geek can team up with the homeless shelter coordinators to realize the ease of creating a low-cost solution to coordinating empty beds and ensuring more people have a safe, warm place to sleep at night.

There is more than that. The best part for me was the realization that it was we, the techies, who knew better than anyone how to collaborate via technology across borders and work with each other to use open source software and open data to tackle these problems. It was we, the hackers, who could put together something as unique as Random Hacks of Kindness—a global network of hackers who work with experts in every field under the sun to create free and open solutions to global human challenges. It was we, the programmers, who could volunteer for Code for America and change city government. We, the geeks, who could create software like the Tor Project that would be the backbone of communication for democratic revolutions around the world.

> WE ARE YOUR ALLY, AND YOU ARE OURS. WE UNDERSTAND THE TECHNOLOGY AND YOU UNDERSTAND THE PROBLEM.

This big picture is difficult to see for aspiring programmers working their way up through universities and corporations. Similarly, it is difficult for non-geeks to understand that they are capable of working side-by-side with technologists to create new kinds of change in the world. But the the message is spreading:

Hackers. Technologists. Programmers. Geeks. Whatever you want to call us. We are your ally, and you are ours. We understand the technology and you understand the problem. We must work together and co-create twenty-first century solutions to the problems humanity faces. And we can do it.

121

# MICHELLE ROWLEY

---

*Michelle Rowley is a software developer, community organizer, and entrepreneur. She's currently working to help women become part of the tech community through a program called Code Scouts.*

michellerowley.com

## HACK THE PLANET

I love shaking snow globes. I can't help myself. I'm enthralled by the snow swirling in the water, and bored when it's stuck motionless at the bottom.

When I look at the state of our nascent digital culture I see a snow globe begging to be shaken. Our technical capabilities as a species are increasing exponentially. The evolution of the Internet is measurable by the day. We are more connected to each other than ever before. But who's building it all?

The image of the stereotypical programmer is a nerdy white guy who likes computers and *Star Wars* (or *Star Trek*, but we don't even want to go down that road) and not much else. That may be a cheap caricature, but there's a hint of truth in it. Most computer programmers are white, male, and intellectually inclined. The snow in the globe fell a long time ago. Access to the knowledge, resources and connections required to be a creator in this space landed in the laps of a lucky few.

Even though I'm a woman, I made it into technology and became a professional programmer. I feel like I got lucky, and now I want to pass it on. My dream is to shake things up from the inside.

Fortunately, my field is ripe for disruption. Demand for programmers is exploding and the traditional education pipelines can't keep up. Self-taught programmers are making up the difference, and they're making a good living without much initial investment.

Here's a secret: programming isn't that hard. The idea that programming takes the brain of a genius steeped in years of mathematics is a myth. It's poisonous because it reinforces itself through a secondary consequence: it gives beginners a reason to interpret the normal frustration of learning, or plain lack of familiarity, as a sign that they're not cut out for programming, that they're just not smart enough, that they don't belong, and just like that, their potential withers before it has a chance to grow.

The antidote to this myth and its consequences is simple: community. All beginners need encouragement and help understanding frustrating concepts. They find comfort in the company of other beginners, in seeing that everyone struggles as they learn and grow.

I believe that by fostering learning communities for tech beginners, we can empower a much more diverse set of people to become the creators of the digital world. Just as writers of history shape the way we collectively understand our past, it's the programmers of today who are building the online world where all of us live. If that world reflects all the different perspectives of our diverse society, we will have succeeded.

> I BELIEVE THAT BY FOSTERING LEARNING COMMUNITIES FOR TECH BEGINNERS, WE CAN EMPOWER A MUCH MORE DIVERSE SET OF PEOPLE TO BECOME THE CREATORS OF THE DIGITAL WORLD.

We have an incredible opportunity to foster diversity among a new cast of creators and we owe it to ourselves, our children and the rest of humanity to ensure that we do.

125

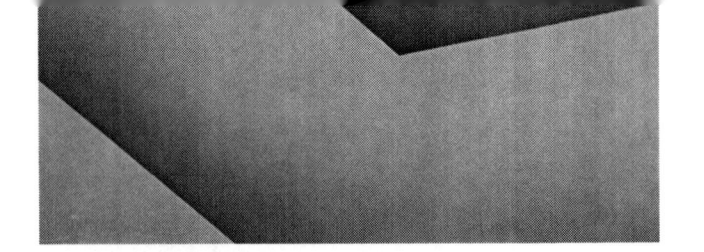

# ANN FRIEDMAN

---

*Ann Friedman is a columnist for* New York Magazine's *website and for the* Columbia Journalism Review. *The former executive editor of* GOOD *magazine, she and her colleagues produced a crowd-funded publication called* Tomorrow *after they were fired en masse.*

annfriedman.com

## ALL IN TOGETHER

I am really interested in which communities we claim as our own and which concentric circles we choose to invest in. We move from professional to creative to activism to family (actual family and the people that fill that role for us). Technology is making those connections less bound by time and geography. I'm super interested in that.

I'm by no means a techno-utopian who thinks that the Internet is a version of paradise where we don't have any of the same structural problems as we do in the real world. I don't believe that. I believe that it is a prism for the disadvantages and problems in the real world, but choose to look on the bright side, seeing the Internet as a way to visualize your friends, as a way of watching or following a piece of news that is important to you move through your friend group. We can see in this digital space how we connect in more organic offline ways. Seeing that reflect back to us can also strengthen us.

My core network of people, both special brain trusts and people that I know personally, are not all people who live where I live. I am a journalist in Los Angeles (which no one in their right mind would define as a hub for journalism) and I am a freelancer who works alone out of my house. Despite these facts, I have a really vibrant community of co-workers. Part of that is because of personal connections that exist offline. Part of that is because the digital world makes that possible. Part of that is because of our changing definition of who is a coworker and who is a colleague. I don't know if all of this is too abstract, but I think of "networks" as a sad dry word for things that are more exciting to me in the world. I'm a geek.

## *What's the difference between what you're envisioning and what we have now?*

We'll probably look back and see the tools we have to visualize and strengthen those networks as pretty rudimentary. I think the idea of posting a link, commenting on a link, and signing up for a service are going to feel pretty dated. Conceptually, we're headed in the right direction with the Google Circles idea. Using this notion that you interact with different parts of your life and have varying levels of openness and privacy with different people in your world both physical and digital is something we have yet to solve. A lot of networks have not figured out how to mimic that real world phenomenon of being more open with certain details with some people than with others. There are some things we want to share with the entire world. There are some things that we only want to share with a close group.

**THERE ARE SOME THINGS WE WANT TO SHARE WITH THE ENTIRE WORLD. THERE ARE SOME THINGS THAT WE ONLY WANT TO SHARE WITH A CLOSE GROUP.**

I think we are going to get a lot better at those things in the future. That's exciting to me.

We also need to pay attention to whether physical access points are truly becoming more accessible. Of course, this is a really old conversation about the digital divide, but I think it's going to get more and more relevant as we talk about whether your digital world will become more reflective of your personal one.

Everyone has people in their life. I have people that are my age that are just not part of the digital world at all. It's true that I'm not as close to them as I am with other people that I am constantly connected to in more digital ways from resourcing our friendships sometimes minute by minute. I think that it's an access question. Are those services built to be useful? Are they built so you can improve all sorts of social networks. Those are big questions. This idea of honesty, getting these digital connections to mimic all of the good things about how we organize ourselves in the real world. That's really the next step.

I don't read a lot of science fiction. I don't sit around thinking, "What if the Internet could..." Since I'm a journalist, I'm constantly reading how people are using technology. I'm interested in developing connections offline and on. Generally, I don't sit around in a proactive way thinking, "How would I do X, Y, or Z service as a platform?"

I have a friend right now who is studying biomimicry; the idea that in design, architecture, and engineering, we are taking phenomenon in the natural world and replicating them. In a more abstract way, if we apply it to how we communicate in real world interactions, how it is or isn't being applied in the digital world: what's the digital equivalent of happy hour? What's the digital equivalent to me taking a walk around the block? What's the digital equivalent of me bumping into a friend at the coffee shop? I'm not saying we need to have a digital analogue for everything in our lives, but I do think that is a line of questioning that is needed to sustain our cultural progress.

Like anything, there can be a positive and a negative. You can use the digital world to shrink your personal world view. You can also very easily use it to expand it. I was never a working journalist in the pre-digital era, so I don't really have a good comparison. For example, there is a broad assumption that Mitt Romney won the first Presidential debate. In the past, we would conduct focus groups. We would go to the local sports bar showing it in on the big screen, listen to people, or we would have a list of people that we would call and ask. Now we do a search for people's public Facebook posts. This is a really quick gut check of who is the perceived winner. On that level, it can be very worldly. We have more access to material, a more diverse set of people, people we've never met before, the opposite benefit of connecting with your existing network. You're more and more likely to do things from advertising to elections, to see things that are more and more like your own beliefs.

IF PEOPLE WANT TO USE THE INTERNET AS A PORTAL TO A WIDER WORLD, WHAT ARE THE TOOLS WE CAN GIVE THEM TO DO THAT?

If people want to use the Internet in that first way I described, as a portal to a wider world, what are the tools we can give them to do that? At the end of the day I'm an optimist. I think that the possibility of a broader world view and the possibility of stronger connections with the existing world far outweigh the negatives that are potentially associated with it. I'm also 100 percent certain that there is no going back, so why would you not choose to see the positive aspects of it?

***Do you think social networks have the potential to save the world?***

Connections between people are the things that have always changed the world and will change the world in the future. Maybe we call it a social network now, but I'm pretty sure that's not the phrase we will use far into the future. The fundamental idea of people making connections based on common interests and sometimes based on differences is the thing that has always changed the world. "Connect" has become this buzzy digital word. It's really how we interact with each other. If I had to write a headline, some type of "All in Together" would be the direction I would go.

131

# DANNY KENNEDY

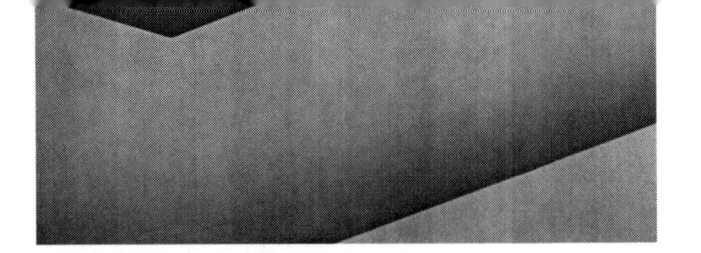

---

*A long-time social entrepreneur, Danny Kennedy has achieved global recognition as an environmental activist, spokesperson, and opinion leader. In 2001, he ran Greenpeace's California Clean Energy Campaign, the success of which helped lead to the current California Solar Initiative. Danny was the founder and first Executive Director of Project Underground and serves on several nonprofit boards.*

sungevity.com

## EVERYTHING WE NEED IS UP THERE

We've got more than enough sunlight. In one day, the sun produces more than we could use in a lifetime. So we're going to have to work out how to tap it. There lies the economic opportunity. That is the exciting thing. There are many more businesses like Sungevity to be built to do that work. And again it's American innovation that has made this a success story. The solar cell, this liberating technology that gives us electricity direct from the source, was invented in New Jersey in 1964, is an insanely efficient model. This is an innovation that we want to get out to the world. It will take decades. There's no pretense here. We're taking on the entrenched vested interests of the oil, coal, nuclear, and gas lobbies—these people run our government and have done so for decades.

## *Tell us about Sungevity: the model, the challenges and your greatest point of pride.*

What we've done is built an amazingly scalable business platform that makes it easy and affordable for homeowners to go solar. Our mission is about getting solar out there to the masses and building what we call the world's most energized network of people who power their lives with sunshine. To make that network happen we had to build a platform that addressed three core barriers to solar adoption. First, the cost, not so much the total cost but the upfront nature of costs. With other electricity you pay for it on a contract, with solar you pay for it upfront. It was really important to change that with our solar lease product, no down payments, pay as you go.

The second barrier was hassle. Change is hard for humans. We get electricity from the grid, we may not know from where or from whom. We may not like them much because they seem to raise the rates all the time. But what are the options? How do you do it differently? So we've made it as easy as possible by putting it online and turning it into a consumer experience—it's not yet as cool as Netflix, but almost.

The third barrier was trust and awareness that this is a real and viable solution. That's really built by social proof in the community. We've addressed that in our business with all sorts of partners, like nonprofits and companies like Lowes that refer us and validate the fact that we're an affordable and easy option for normal Americans to adopt.

Taking down the barriers to adoption is what we've done with the business. Our big challenges have been the usual startup story and then growth: the problem of getting stuck in front of headlights as you go through an exponential curve. We've been going for five years now and we've gone from zero people to 250 directly employed, hundreds more out there in our preferred installer network. We've got thousands of customers across the United States, we've got partners throughout the nonprofit and for-profit community, and we've got partner companies in other countries now. Trying to grow commensurate with that sigmoid curve of adoption is very challenging for small companies: we've had capital constraints, financing has been hard.

As for the greatest point of pride, I think that by doing and demonstrating that it's doable, I'm a big believer in deeds not words. The promise of solar power has been around for fifty years, it's a great American invention. I think seeing it come down to earth (literally, solar power was only for satellites until the last few decades) and taking it across suburbia with a simple online sunshine business model has really been a fun thing to do and something of which we're very proud. There are all sorts of absolute benefits there—we're saving thousands of families' money on their electricity bill, we're employing hundreds of people and feeding their families, and we're thumbing our noses at the powers that be and saying, "We don't need to do the dumb thing and dig it up from underground. We can get it free from the sky."

> **WE DON'T NEED TO DO THE DUMB THING AND DIG IT UP FROM UNDERGROUND. WE CAN GET IT FREE FROM THE SKY.**

### *How does solar power make America better?*

We're a job creation engine. All the politicians standing up and giving speeches on both sides of the aisle, talking about jobs, if you want jobs then get with this. That's the dream of full employment in this country and the dream of a meaningful career in our community. Solar delivers day in and day out, and amazingly even through the great recession. That's a big part of what we deliver as well as the benefits of lower costs for electricity, which everyone wants. We all need electricity but the fact that we can do it for less and do it better, cleaner, and faster than buying it from dirty fossil incumbent technologies. We're also involved in initiatives trying to spawn entrepreneurs here in Oakland, California, to provide job opportunities in this market, and through our work, we sponsor a nonprofit that puts solar into homes in Zambia for every solar lease we do here.

The ancillary benefit is spreading the American Dream. The tagline I like is, "Power is knowledge." Kids in remote parts of Zambia have no electricity and to experience electric light and to sit up at night, study, read a book, or even better, to access the Internet and all its benefits makes a huge difference. All this through the power of the solar system in their school. That's incredible. To give them the power to have that knowledge is really wonderful.

## *What's more effective in making change: activism or capitalism?*

There's myth in this country that it is great white men who make history. No, it's people, consumer, and political demand organized through the ballot box. It is through the back pocket and the hip pocket function of buying and choosing with our dollars and our feet as to where we turn up and vote on election day. Those forms of power go through cycles and stages—social movements have a process to them.

You need to prove there's a problem first, and then you need to prove there's a solution. That's the broad dynamic—that business as usual is going to do harm to the body politic, that the current power holders don't have our back and aren't trying to find true solutions. We do know what the solution is and we do have a path forward. The different roles required for the stages of the movement are different. Two hundred years of industrial revolution were great for a while but it

**TWO HUNDRED YEARS OF INDUSTRIAL REVOLUTION WERE GREAT FOR A WHILE BUT IT TURNS OUT THAT IT'S GOING TO KILL OUR KIDS.**

turns out that it's going to kill our kids.

We're addicted to fossil fuels, and as far as we've walked into the woods, we have to walk out. The people we will find on our return will more likely be businesses than nonprofits. Using the wheel of economic destruction that is entrepreneurial capital is a classic way to really radicalize something and change it up. That's what we're trying to do now and the solar industry is going to be the biggest remaking of the economy and policy this century. We're literally and figuratively, taking power and giving it to the people. We're putting it on their houses, rather than having it end up in some concentrated form of power far away in a regulated coal monopoly.

> WHEN THE HORSE AND BUGGY WERE DISPLACED BY THE AUTOMOBILE, A HUGE STATUS QUO WAS DISPLACED BY A MUCH BETTER BUSINESS, AND IT REDUCED THE HORSE SHIT IN THE STREETS AS WELL.

## Can America be energy independent? What does that mean for the world?

Absolutely. Through deployment and mass adoption we will create the new technologies we need, like nighttime power storage. When the horse and buggy were displaced by the automobile, a huge status quo was displaced by a much better business, and it reduced the horse shit in the streets as well.

We have the potential to do a lot with the technology we have. Through deployment we'll create more and more opportunities to harness the power of the sun that falls free from the sky. Individual homeowners and businesses who are going solar today are benefiting. They are energy independent and they love the freedom of it, the control over their own cost structure. As more and more of them do that the grid changes, the dynamics and economics of the utility industry changes. They're going to force business changes. They will start tapping into the no fuel model of providing electricity which is simply taking sunlight.

***When we talk about solar, it's usually about an environmental benefit, but you talk about it in human terms in that it gives economic freedom. Could solar also help with international conflicts and struggles over power? Could solar power lead to a more peaceful world?***

Fossil fuels have been the cause of tensions and conflicts for a century now and the book I wrote is forwarded by Gen. Wesley Clark. He'll be the first to admit that wars today are waged to protect fuel supplies. What's wonderful about sunshine is that we all have some. It's spread very evenly. At that level, the dynamic changes and everyone is allowed to have what is theirs by virtue of being on Earth. It spreads peace.

Moreover electricity is a very important service. It's a commodity service that gives us great benefits. The fact that we can make it better without all that conflict and tension in the supply chain and spread it thin like the resource itself, is one of the benefits of this tech set. I think we are talking about an upside beyond just the environmental benefits, which are many. We talk about climate change and air pollution: how many tens of thousands of kids in this country alone die from asthma caused by coal fired power plants? It's well known and understood, it's just an acceptable cost of doing business, which is crazy. We get rid of all that crap, and we move on to a model that puts power in the hands of people, literally on their roofs.

*We're big fans of companies like yours and Tesla, companies that are making the future, but the market remaines a niche. What will it take Sungevity or companies like Tesla to change America to being powered by sunlight?*

Solar still is very small, it's less than 1 percent of the energy supply in this country although in other countries like Germany, it's jumping up to 20 percent very quickly. Twenty years ago the landline telephony monopolies were saying, "Well, don't worry about that cell phone thing." Cell phones are a similar technology to solar: they're modular, silicone based devices that provide a better service for less.

Second, we should be aware that we're not just solving an environmental problem, we're also giving freedom of choice, we're giving independence and control. It's the smart thing to do. It makes sense. It's simply a better technological choice.

Another reason for change is water. It is becoming increasingly scarce in this new climate reality. We can't afford to boil off 39 percent of our water in steam boiling power plants. That's what we're doing right now. Clearly in 2025 we won't be doing that anymore. So what are we doing now? We're going straight to the stuff that falls out of the sky and cutting out the middleman. At the same time we're cutting out the industrial infrastructure we don't need and making a more efficient electricity supply. So we need to make people aware of that and we need to make them understand the independence the freedom and the control that comes from this decision that they're making. That's what Sungevity is about. We're trying to make it easy, affordable, and accessible to more people.

This country is a main global economic driver. You could say it's the belly of the beast, or you could say it's the heart of the machine. We have the potential to refashion America's grid with a solar solution, and by example help the world

> YOU COULD SAY IT'S THE BELLY OF THE BEAST, OR YOU COULD SAY IT'S THE HEART OF THE MACHINE.

go solar as well. American capital formations, American finance, and American government support will be critical to spreading solar globally as well.

## *If there was one thing that could make world better...*

It would be that the governments of the world stop squabbling about trade barriers, tariffs, and a trade war that's begun around solar. Instead, they need to decide to stand together and promote this revolution. It's inevitable, but it would be great if they got behind it now with a program of global commitment.

140　AMERICAN DREAMERS

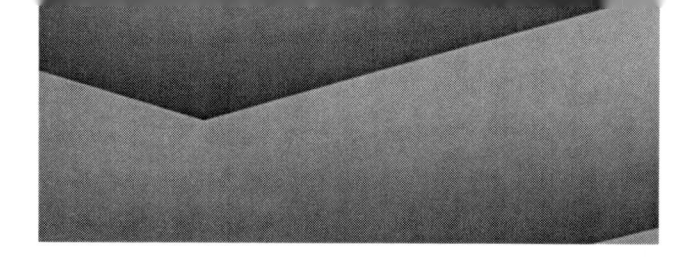

# CURTIS KULIG

---

*Curtis Kulig is a photographer, artist and illustrator who lives and works in New York City. He is best known for his* Love Me *campaign. Today, Kulig has become one of the fastest rising stars in both the art and commercial world, blurring the lines between pop art, typography and iconography at every turn.*

curtiskulig.com

## WE HAVE THE BLUEPRINT

**As an artist and communicator shaping the cultural landscape, what is your dream for the future?**

Rooftop vegetable gardens and parks on every building in NYC.

**How do you hope the role of public art will evolve in the future?**

It will be more important than it's ever been. With so much technology, we're losing our physical and emotional connections and public art provides something to engage with and gets people talking... not on Instagram or Twitter but face-to-face.

### How do you see the potential for the intersection of art and commerce in the future?

I hope that artists are acknowledged and paid fairly for their contributions. The greatest value is in the idea.

### What are your dreams for accessibility to art in general?

I want anyone to be able to walk into a gallery and feel comfortable inquiring about a piece, regardless of their knowledge or pocketbook. I want more cities to invest money in public art projects, ranging from painting and sculpture, to literature to filmmaking to music to comedy to theatre. And give more young artists opportunities.

### What innovations are you excited about, or make you feel hopeful for the future?

I'm excited about hybrids and biodiesel and a new way of thinking about energy. I saw a FedEx truck the other day that looked like a spaceship and I'm all for that.

### Who are some other innovators you think are changing things for the better?

Everything we ever wished for was already realized by Buckminster Fuller and Nikola Tesla decades ago. We have the blueprint, we just need to build.

### How do you envision the new American Dream?

I think it means saving Detroit first. It's about people helping each other, banding together, inspiring and supporting our friends. And being open to exchanging ideas to helping others succeed. Not accepting defeat, not feeling complacent, but

> EVERYTHING WE EVER WISHED FOR WAS ALREADY REALIZED BY BUCKMINSTER FULLER AND NIKOLA TESLA DECADES AGO. WE HAVE THE BLUEPRINT, WE JUST NEED TO BUILD.

making actionable changes towards a better life for everyone.

Less cubicles, more risk-takers, more dreamers, more believers, and most of all, more LOVE.

*144* AMERICAN DREAMERS

*Courtesy of Curtis Kulig*

146   AMERICAN DREAMERS

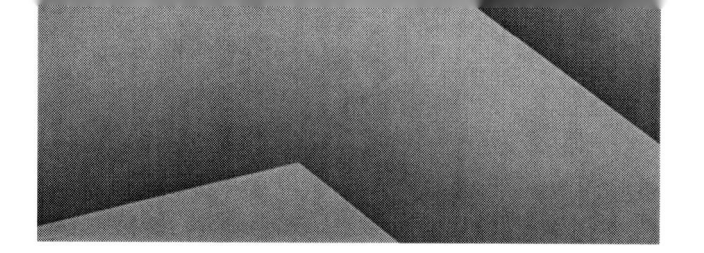

# JENNIFER LEE

---

*Jennifer Lee is a visual effects compositor and editor, digital intermediate editor, and an independent filmmaker. Her credits include* Beowulf, Enchanted, Vertical Limit, *and* Back To The Future 2. *Her current film,* Feminist: Stories from Women's Liberation *will be released in 2013.*

feministstories.com

## MY DAUGHTER CAN BE PRESIDENT

When I grew up, all the leaders were men. Presidential debates were always between men. The image of the presidents throughout American history was all men. The pages of a daily newspaper showed men making decisions while women were relegated to the style sections. My grandmother, born in 1910, often told me that it was "better to be a boy" because it was a "man's world." She wasn't being negative; she was imparting to me a fact in her world.

This was a long time ago, and we know that the world has changed tremendously for women and girls. Yet, many images remain the same. In the United States, women hold only 17 percent of our congressional seats, and we have never had a female president or vice president. The words "it's a man's world" may not be said to a girl directly, but the images tell her that men lead. These images shouldn't be a girl's "inheritance."

I've witnessed how these images have impacted girls time and time again. In 1987, my six-year-old sister said to my mother, "Women can't be president." My mother replied, "Just because we haven't had a woman president doesn't mean we will never have a woman president." My sister insisted her own point was right because she had never seen a woman as president. In 2008, the six-year-old daughter of a friend announced to her teenage sister that women couldn't be president because there had never been a woman as president. In 2010, a friend told me that his fourteen-year-old daughter told him she wanted to be a lawyer. After a brief pause she asked him, "Can women be lawyers?" Her father was astounded and asked me why she would ask such a question.

It is shocking that girls would say these things. After all, we all know that women can be lawyers and even president. So why are girls asking these questions? The answer is complex, and we might not know all the reasons at this time. However, there are steps we can take right now that will change her view of the world and of herself. A girl needs to know in her heart and mind that she can lead. She needs to see it. We can show her she can be a leader.

We can help create a world where women sit at the political power table equally with men. I take a step towards this future every day. I call it the "pathway to power" and in my home it is well-lit.

It won't be long before my daughter picks up the puzzle depicting the forty-four presidents of the United States and asks me, "Where are the women?" I dread this question. It means that the seed of limitation has been planted. If the girls you know are prepared, and you are willing to do the work, that image will not limit them. Would you give this puzzle to your daughter?

I show my daughter examples of female presidents often. Women are leading nations all over the world. Their pictures, interviews, and speeches are accessible through YouTube and international news websites. I show these women to my daughter. We listen to them speak. Ask yourself how different you would be if you grew up with this image on the walls of your elementary school classroom.

I make time to watch and listen to women politicians in the United States who are making news. I shut my partisan opinions in a cabinet, open my mind, listen, and discuss the policies presented. Sisterhood is an old term from the women's liberation movement of the mid-twentieth century. It means that solidarity between women is something to be honored. I have resurrected it in my home.

> SOLIDARITY BETWEEN WOMEN IS SOMETHING TO BE HONORED. I HAVE RESURRECTED IT IN MY HOME.

Cultural markers are images and stories from our society with which we shape our identities. American holidays like the Fourth of July tell us we fought for our freedom. Memorial Day tells us we honor the soldiers who fought in wars. Women and girls need cultural markers too. Even though there are no federal holidays named for women, that doesn't mean we can't celebrate women's achievements. All American women won the right to vote on August 26, 1920. It was named Women's Equality Day in 1971 by Congress at the urging of Congresswoman Bella Abzug. In my city on August 26th, I brought my daughter to march in a Women's Equality Day celebration at our City Hall. With a group of women all wearing white, we marched and honored the women who fought to get us the right to vote. These women are heroes, and one day we will have a federal holiday named for them. A girl will be able to see herself more easily as a leader when the phrase "American Hero" inspires an image of a woman in her mind. Marching with my daughter on this day was a unique experience. It was a first for me, but she likely assumed everyone celebrated Women's Equality Day. That's change.

When your daughter sits in a classroom, think about the effects of a simple history lesson. Don't let her teacher omit women. It was near Columbus Day when I was touring various elementary schools for my daughter. In every classroom there was a wall dedicated to world explorers. The explorers were all men. Now, it is true that Christopher Columbus and Sir Francis Drake were men, but it was the Queens and Kings who enabled their journeys. Queen Isabella of Spain and Queen Elizabeth of England were instrumental to exploration. There are also stories about women that have rarely been told. The explorer Marco Polo had a friendship with Princess Cocachin, the daughter of Kublai Kahn. Bring women into the picture. Increase your daughter's curiosity about women by talking about the women who shaped our world.

**DON'T LET HER TEACHER OMIT WOMEN.**

When President of Brazil Dilma Rousseff spoke at the United Nations General Assembly in 2011, she began, "For the first time in the history of the United Nations, a female voice opens the General Debate." She continued, "I share this feeling with over half of the human beings on this planet who, like myself, were born women and who, with tenacity, are occupying the place they deserve in the world. I am certain that this will be the century of women."

Electing a female president and making half of Congress female in the United States is important. Women are at least 50 percent of the population and we comprise 56 percent of voters. The pathway to the power table must be well-lit. There will be times when women's underrepresentation may seem too difficult to change, but don't give up. It is a very steep mountain to climb. However, a steep mountain is only one climb upward with one goal in front of us—the top.

151

# CINDY GALLOP

---

*Cindy Gallop is the founder of If We Ran the World and Make Love Not Porn. She speaks at events around the world and consults, describing her consultancy approach as: "I like to blow shit up. I am the Michael Bay of business."*

makelovenotporn.tv

## MAKE LOVE NOT PORN

I date younger men. I have for some time. They tend to be men predominantly in their twenties. And dating younger men, I encounter, very personally, what happens when you combine the extraordinary ubiquity and freedom of access to hardcore porn online with the total reluctance in our society to talk openly and honestly about sex. This results in porn becoming, by default, today's sex education.

When I realized this, I decided to do something about it. I put up a website called makelovenotporn.com that posts the myths of porn and balances them with the reality. The construct is porn world versus real world. This is what happens in the porn world and this is what actually happens in the real world.

There are a few important things about that site, which I think are relevant to why the response seems so extraordinary.

It's simple. It's very straightforward. It's very honest. It's nonjudgmental. And it's humorous. I didn't want the slightest whiff of "education" or public service announcement about it because that is a kiss of death. I wanted this to live in the world of hardcore porn. I wanted this to go viral in the way that hardcore porn goes viral. So, I made it funny. I wrote all the copy myself and I made it deliberately lighthearted to diffuse the awkwardness and embarrassment that exists around sex. Because makelovenotporn.com is a manifestation of me, it is everything that I am.

While I was building it, I got the opportunity to launch at TED, and I made a deliberate decision to be explicit in my TED talk because I knew that the audience would not get this issue unless I was extremely straightforward about it. So as a result, I think it's safe to say that everyone who was at TED 2009 remembers that talk. The talk went viral and that helped spread word of the site. In the three and a half years since I launched it, I have had zero time or money to spend on it. Nevertheless, with zero proactive promotion, makelovenotporn.com was getting an average of three thousand visitors per day. Anytime someone posted my TED Talk somewhere that would shoot up to ten to twelve thousand. This is a global issue. And without me doing anything about it, it went global. Makelovenotporn.com gets traffic from every single country in the world.

Every single day for the past three and a half years, I get emails about makelovenotporn.com. These emails come from every country in the world and they come from men and women, young and old, gay and straight. What blows people away is the simple fact that I stood on a stage in public and talked about something that everybody knows and nobody ever speaks about. As a result, people feel able to tell me anything. They pour their hearts out to me via email. They tell me things they've never told anybody about their sex life or their porn habits. Over time, these emails made me feel I had a huge personal responsibility to take makelovenotporn.com forward, to make it much more far reaching, helpful, and effective. I had to think long and hard about how to do this because this is a very difficult, very big, very complicated area.

> THE ISSUE I'M TACKLING IS NOT PORN. THE ISSUE I'M TACKLING IS THE TOTAL LACK OF A COUNTER POINT.

The issue I'm tackling is not porn. The issue I'm tackling is the total lack of a counter point. The total absence in our society of an open, healthy, honest discussion, and conversation around sex and porn. Perhaps if we had that, it would enable people to bring a real-world mindset to viewing what's essentially artificial entertainment.

If you broke the message of makelovenotporn.tv down to one thing, it would be purely and simply—talk about sex. The reason we should talk about it is because we get enormously vulnerable when we get naked. Sexual egos are very fragile. People find it bizarrely difficult to talk about sex with the people they are actually having it with, while they are actually having it, because we are terrified of hurting the other person's feelings, of derailing the entire encounter, derailing the entire relationship, but at the same time you really want to please your partner. So, you seize your cues on how to do that from anywhere you can and if the only cues you've ever had are from porn then those are the ones you'll take, to not very good effect.

I decided to find a way to embed what I'm doing in popular culture, to make it engaging, and entertaining, and compelling. While of course, being educational. If I want to counter the effects of porn as default sex education then I have to create something that has the potential to be as mass, as mainstream, and as all-pervasive in our society today as porn currently is. That's why I decided to turn makelovenotporn.tv into a business.

I believe that all businesses of the future should be about

doing good and making money simultaneously. I believe you can have a higher-order social agenda, and be enormously profitable. I decided to take everything dynamic that exists out there in social media currently and apply it to the one area that no social platform has ever gone or ever dared to go, which is sex. I want to socialize sex. I want to make real-world sex socially acceptable and therefore as socially sharable as anything else we share on Facebook, Twitter, Instagram, or Tumblr, I want to do with makelovenotporn.tv in the twenty-first century what Hugh Hefner managed with *Playboy* in the twentieth century, which is to bring sex out into the open.

I want to be the future of porn.

Porn is homogenizing real-world sex. I want to help bring the individuality, the creativity, and the self-expression back to real- world sex. And at the same time, I want to explode every piece of wisdom that exists out there about porn.

So, we've made makelovenotporn.tv a platform. We've put it out there and we invite anybody to submit and upload real-world sex. This is a wholly curated proposition. We haven't the faintest idea what's going to come back. You give people a platform, you see what they do with it.

It never fails to amaze me but I have no shortage of volunteers. When I talk about this concept, people say: "I want to be your first make love not porn star." Social media has lowered the barriers of shame and embarrassment everywhere. The time is right to do what I want to do now in a way it wouldn't have been even a few years ago. Like all user-generated content generally, makelovenotporn.tv is about creativity and self-expression, which porn is currently killing in sex. Every porn site currently out there has its drop down menu: *Anal, Asian, Hairy, Cream Pie,* whatever. We have our own version of that, but it's completely different.

Real-world sex is funny. If you can't laugh at yourselves

> I WANT TO SOCIALIZE SEX. I WANT TO MAKE REAL-WORLD SEX SOCIALLY ACCEPTABLE AND THEREFORE AS SOCIALLY SHARABLE AS ANYTHING ELSE WE SHARE ON FACEBOOK.

when you're having sex, when can you? Sex is loads of fun. In the porn world, sex is always deadly earnest. I want to reassure people that the same shit happens to all of us. Because we never hear that. So we end up going, "Oh my God, that was excruciatingly embarrassing. I can never sleep with anybody ever again."

For example, the total nightmare of putting the condom on. It's meant to go on like magic. As we all know, it does not happen like that. When it doesn't happen like that, things go soft, defenses go up, and encounters gets derailed. We want to capture the sex equivalent of *America's Funniest Home Videos*. You never see the outtakes.

Real-world sex is funny. Real sex is messy.

It always amazes me when people talk about porn as being dirty because porn sanitizes sex. In porn, nobody has hair. You never see anybody actually using lube even though they get through gallons of it. You never see these nice messy things that happen in real-world sex.

Real-world sex is responsible.

> **REAL-WORLD SEX IS FUNNY. REAL SEX IS MESSY.**

In porn, either there are no condoms, or all of a sudden the condom's on. Jump to: "We're fucking. Hey, where did that come from?" We invite the hottest, most arousing, real-world sex content to compete and eroticize condom usage. What's the most erotic way you can introduce a condom, put it on, take it off, and dispose of it? I have sex with condoms all the time and I want to watch my kind of sex. But I specifically want ideas for those awkward condom moments we all go through. If all of us had more creative ideas on how to make those awkward condom moments hot and arousing, there'd be a lot more safe sex happening, a lot fewer STDs and a lot less unwanted pregnancies.

People have reached out to me from everywhere saying they'd love to help. Including, much to my surprise when this first began happening, a lot of people in the porn industry, specifically Generation Y in porn. Because Gen Y porn is just like Gen Y anywhere else. They're entrepreneurial, they're ambitious, they're questioning and challenging the old-world order and want to be a part of the new. We have a category on makelovenotporn.tv where porn stars get to post the sex they have when they're off camera in the real world. Stars have real-world sex too, which is completely different from what they are doing in the porn world.

No matter how potentially controversial, offensive, or sensitive you find the whole idea of porn and sex, nobody can argue with what I'm doing. I want to make real-world sex socially acceptable to share. We're taking everything that makes Facebook, Twitter, and Instagram so addictive to people and applying it to the one area that those guys will never go. We are building a platform of tools which I call "sexual currency." We are discovering that the desire to do this lies a lot closer to the surface within many more people than you think. Given an excuse and given such facts and a social mission, people jump at the chance. Think about all of the celebrations of relationships that crop up in your Facebook timeline. Think about those engagement announcements, those wedding photographs, those displays of coupledom. All we're doing is providing a platform to celebrate that one last area of human relationships no other platform will allow you to. Our contributors are driven by exactly the same motivations. Our core proposition is that everyone wants to know what everyone else is really doing in bed and nobody does.

I had no real idea of the power and potential of what we're doing until I began watching our first content submissions. I've determined that real-world sex is more creative, more exciting, more surprising, more amazing, hotter, and more arousing than porn will ever be. It's phenomenal.

> NO MATTER HOW POTENTIALLY CONTROVERSIAL, OFFENSIVE, OR SENSITIVE YOU FIND THE WHOLE IDEA OF PORN AND SEX, NOBODY CAN ARGUE WITH WHAT I'M DOING.

*158* AMERICAN DREAMERS

# JUSTIN, TRAVIS & GRIFFIN McELROY

---

*The McElroy Brothers are real brothers. Justin, Travis and Griffin host the popular podcast,* My Brother, My Brother, and Me, *dispensing humor and advice (though they advise never to take it).*

## ON THE MAYAN APOCALYPSE AND ENDLESS SHRIMP

### *Is technology a force for good or for evil?*

**GRIFFIN:** Technology changes every day, and so does the answer to that question. Guns are a kind of technology, and those are usually pretty bad. But I can buy movie tickets on my phone, which is good. The Large Hadron Collider is definitely, definitely going to bring about the Mayan Apocalypse, which I don't fancy. However, the Game Boy Advance made me happier than any one thing or person ever has, or ever will again. Once, a person on the Internet said my neck was thicker than normal, and I was sad for four days. On the other hand, machines make medicine, which nearly cancels that last point out.

**JUSTIN:** I think what Griffin has stumbled onto here is that we need good technology to cancel out the bad technology. Sometimes technology can be isolating, creating virtual embryos that detach us from society. In those times, it's lucky we have social networking to reconnect with friends and loved ones. Other times, technology can become sentient and gain the ability to look like Robert Patrick as it ruthlessly hunts humanity's future savior. In those moments, I feel really grateful for the slightly less advanced cyborg assassins that we can reprogram to protect us.

> I FEEL REALLY GRATEFUL FOR THE SLIGHTLY LESS ADVANCED CYBORG ASSASSINS THAT WE CAN REPROGRAM TO PROTECT US.

Still, in other moments, technology like the Internet Movie Database can confirm your fear that you might have lifted the plot of *Terminator 2: Judgment Day* in your *American Dreamers* essay. Technology doesn't have a fix for this that I've found, so thanks for nothing Neil deGrasse Tyson.

**TRAVIS:** If by technology, you mean the breakfast machine at the beginning of *Pee-Wee's Big Adventure*, then it's a force for good and breakfast. If you mean the app on Justin's iPhone that emits a high-pitched squeal like a dog whistle, then it's a force for evil. That said, I could not live without my phone, or my dialysis machine. Unless there an iPhone app to remove waste from my blood. If, while cleaning my body of impurities, my phone could automatically update my Twitter feed that'd be cool.

Honesty time: I don't use a dialysis machine. I'm not even one hundred percent sure what it looks like, but I assume it looks like Pee-Wee's breakfast machine.

## *If you could change one thing, making the world a better place, what would it be?*

**TRAVIS:** I think that we are living in a "blame culture," where everything someone does can be blamed on some factor outside of their control making it not their fault. If people don't take responsibility for themselves, how can they improve their own situations? I would change that. If that's too unrealistic, it'd be pretty cool if we could make Endless Shrimp at Red Lobster a year round thing instead of seasonal. I mean, it's supposed to be ENDLESS, right?!

**GRIFFIN:** Teleportation. Then, we'd all just be citizens of the world, instead of citizens of countries and warring states, because there's really nothing you can do to stop anyone from going wherever they want. Yes, this would cause issues vis-a-vis banking, and preschool security, or any and all security in general, forever, and the more I think about it, the worse an idea it becomes. Maybe just I could have teleportation? I promise not to misuse it. Have you guys seen that film, *Jumper*? It's my favorite Hayden Christensen movie.

> MAYBE JUST I COULD HAVE TELEPORTATION? I PROMISE NOT TO MISUSE IT.

**JUSTIN:** I was going to say that I would change Travis' insatiable desire for buttered shrimp that will almost certainly lead to his untimely death, but I decided that's a little small-scale. If you're reading this, Travis (or, let's be realistic, Travis' grief-stricken widow), I just want to say that I'm really sorry that I didn't use my one wish to cure your shrimp addiction. I hope the shrimp is always endless in heaven, and I hope they have more varieties up there, as the choices always seemed a little limited, to me. I mean, just scampi, coconut, and traditional? How am I supposed to—wait, that's it! That's my answer! More Endless Shrimp varieties. That's going to make a difference. Moreover, it's what sweet, dead Travis would have wanted.

**TRAVIS:** If it is my fate to die by overwhelming flavor, then so be it! I take responsibilities for my own snack-tions! Also, I am very sad that I will be dead in the future.

## Who are three people who are changing things for the better?

**JUSTIN:** I mean, you're asking for three people changing things for the better and there are three of us, this one seems to be pretty cut and dry. I suspect you guys probably wanted us to choose ourselves, right? Wait, was this a test? Because if this is a test, I'm going with Gandhi, Mother Teresa, and that guy in the question mark suit that tells you how to get free money from the government. Again, though, if it's not a test, it's totally us.

**TRAVIS:** Guy in the question mark suit? Do you mean Lesko or Jim Carrey as the Riddler? I hope you mean Carrey Riddler. What's the name of the guy that made *Fruit Ninja* for the iPhone? Can I put him on my list? If not, then I agree with Justin. Mostly me though. When it comes to "world changing", I feel like Justin and Griffin are just riding my coattails.

**GRIFFIN:** President Robama is an obvious first pick. Robama, the android version of Barack Obama that really runs the country, as controlled by the Illuminati. That's what I said. I guess whoever operates his servos and speech centers and hope synthesizers should be on the list, too. For my third pick, anyone whose actual first name is "Bear," including (but not limited to) *Battlestar Galactica* composer Bear McCreary and renowned survival expert Bear Grylls, who won the goddamn cool name lottery twice.

# TIM WISE

*Tim Wise is one of America's leading speakers and writers on the topic of anti-racism. He has written multiple books on the subject including,* White Like Me: Reflections on Race from a Privileged Son.

timwise.org

## ALLYSHIP FOR TOMORROW

### *What is the future of America and how do we get there?*

First, if we are going to figure out what to do as a culture to pull out of our trajectory toward a dystopia, that so many are talking about and worried about (and understandably so), we first have to have a really clear assessment of why we are in the condition we are in, in terms of pessimism and defeatism. It is actually very understandable, in this culture and the United States in particular, for those who are relatively comfortable, those who are white, those who are men, those who are straight, those who are Christian, and those who are members of dominant social groups, have really been sold a bill of goods for years that poor folk knew was a bill of goods. Black and brown folk knew it was a bill of goods. Women mostly knew it was a bill of goods. LGBT folks knew. People of the marginalized groups knew the promise was only half real and that they were going to have to fight and scrape with everything they had. The dominant group members were able to think, "If we just play by the rules, everything is going to be okay. If we work hard, go to school, keep our nose down, and do what we are supposed to, everything will work out."

We are coming up against the limits of an economic growth model that is rooted in this industrial capitalist mode of production, this idea that we can just keep growing our way to prosperity, that we can just keep spending our way to prosperity and that is not going to impact the ecology, not affect our families, or not affect our communities. We are starting to realize, both because of environmental pressures and the economic collapse the country is currently facing, that maybe the system isn't all it's cracked up to be. If you always believed that the system was basically fair and just, needing a little tweaking but essentially okay, and you come to discover that maybe the poor folks were always right, that maybe the people of color understood the system better than you did, that can be incredibly disconcerting.

The people who are most knocked off stride by the economic collapse are not the ones hit the hardest by it. The ones hit the hardest are still people of color, low-income people, women, and still the folks at the bottom of the power structure, but they are more prepared for it. In the Great Depression, who threw themselves off of buildings when the market crashed? It wasn't poor people. They didn't care about the stock market. They were on the soup line the day before the crash and they were going to be there the day after. The rich folks reacted with, "Oh my God! I don't know how to cope with being poor!"

This fear and pessimism about the future is rooted in the realization, maybe for the first time in a lot of American's

> WE ARE STARTING TO REALIZE, BOTH BECAUSE OF ENVIRONMENTAL PRESSURES AND THE ECONOMIC COLLAPSE THE COUNTRY IS CURRENTLY FACING, THAT MAYBE THE SYSTEM ISN'T ALL IT'S CRACKED UP TO BE.

lives, that the system we have been sold and thought was going to be the most wonderful-perfect-last-forever kind of thing maybe isn't going to work anymore. We will have to think different and that is scary. In the meantime, while we figure it out, people start thinking about the future as a very scary place. "My God! It is not secure! We are not sure that our kids are going to be better off than we were." Well, people of color never assumed that their kids were going to be automatically better off. Poor folks never assumed that. I think that this is the 'come-to-Jesus' moment some folks are starting to have, realizing the system isn't all it was cracked up to be.

Once you get over the shock of that, once you get to the point where you say, "Okay, maybe I have been lied to," what do you do with that? If you are in your fifties or sixties when you come to that realization, you are probably really frightened because you think, "What can I do in the time I have left?" If you are in your teens, twenties, thirties, or forties and maybe realizing it earlier, we have some possibilities.

**THE PROBLEM FACING US IS NOT A LACK OF CAPACITY BUT A LACK OF WILL.**

The problem facing us is not a lack of capacity but a lack of will. Are we really prepared as a culture to reach across lines of race and ethnicity and culture and class and sexuality and religion to create real change? We are not going to survive as a country in thirty or forty years if we get to that place that demographers say we are going to reach, a place where 50 percent of the population will be folks of color and 50 percent white. We will not be able to survive as a productive society if half the population is still twice as likely as the other half to be unemployed, three times as likely to be poor, one-twentieth the net worth, double the rate of infant mortality, and nine years less life expectancy. If we stay on the current trajectory, it is a recipe for utter disaster for all of our children and grandchildren.

If, on the other hand, we harken back to the tradition of

allyship and solidarity which has been a part of our history (but is a part of our history that we have not been taught. White folks haven't been taught about the history of white allyship with people of color, men have not been taught about the history of male allyship standing against sexism, middle and upper-middle class folks have not been taught there is such a thing as solidarity with the poor, and straight folks have not been taught about the history of solidarity with LGBT folks), we rediscover this untold history and recognize there is a path. It is not a new path, it is an old path that has been trod by folks of past generations. Since it has been hidden from us, we don't know it is there, like a road you come to in the woods, covered by weeds and brambles. You don't know it's there until someone clears it for you and says, "Look there is another option."

## What are the success stories of the past, of that allyship? Where can we see examples of culture shifting itself in the right ways?

I do primarily anti-racism work and so my greatest familiarity is with the history of white allyship with peoples of color. It is not a history that I learned in school. I had to rediscover it myself, meeting heroes and sheroes of the Civil Rights Movement. They were not just leaders of color, though they were certainly the key to it, but also white folks who took great risk, more than we take today, to bring about the end of formal white supremacy and apartheid in this country. We still have informal white supremacy and informal apartheid but things are better because those folks stood shoulder-to-shoulder. I think about the folks in the Student Nonviolent Coordinating Committee which grew out of the sit-in movements. These white folks who were also white Southerners, they joined the struggle and turned against the dominant tradition in their own communities or their own families. They said, "We are willing to risk everything, our lives, our families, our friends, and our community in order to stand up for the real American ideal." The real American ideal, not the phony one being sold to us.

If you look back in history to the abolition struggle you find white folks deeply embedded in that struggle. Look at the entire history of the struggle against Jim Crow, even in the years before it finally collapsed, you find a history of white folks working to bring better labor conditions to places like Birmingham. These are places where we associate whiteness with repression, Bull Connor, and Governor George Wallace. Those are certainly part of the white tradition, but so too are the Bob Zellners of the South. Look at Anne and Carl Braden in Louisville, Kentucky, who were instrumental in the fight against white supremacy there. Looking all the way back to the Antebellum period, we see Lydia Child and the Grimké Sisters, names that are completely left out of history. Every time I pay for something with a twenty dollar bill, I am confronted with the visage of Andrew Jackson. I think about a man named Jeremiah Evarts whose name is lost to our history books. This was a white man who was steadfast in his opposition to Indian removal and the treatment of the Cherokee in particular under Jackson's administration. Evarts' name and the struggle he took part in against indigenous genocide is left out.

When I talk to young white kids in grade school, middle school, and high school, about this history of white allyship, they are amazed by it and amazed that they don't know anything about it. They are invigorated by it because they realize that they don't have to sit on the sidelines passively applauding for the Rosa Parkses and the Doctor Kings and the Fannie Lou Hamers (whose name they probably have not been taught). When they discover that for the first time it lights a fire under them. They begin to see that there is a different path.

## Following that from the past, what are the new struggles? Is there a movement?

I would say there is no new civil rights movement, it is the same as it always has been. It has different permutations, offshoots, and different struggles. They are not the same as fifty years ago, obviously. The lunch counters are integrated, the shopping centers are integrated, the hotels, the cemeteries, and the movie theaters, but in many ways we have gone backward. Our schools are more segregated today in many places than they were in the mid-1970s. We have gone backward in that regard. We have gone backward in wealth disparity, the wealth gap between white folks and black folks, between white folks and Latinos, is greater now than it was twenty and thirty years ago. The health disparities between whites and people of color have continued to grow, so that clearly has got to be part of a "new civil rights struggle." We can't figure out how to resolve health disparity with just a health care reform and ability to access. That is one piece but we know the research tells us that affluent, upper middle class, college-educated black and brown folk have worse health outcomes than low-income, non-college educated white folks. It is not just economics. There is something going on racially in this country in terms of health care. We need to look at it. I would say this is the opportunity that we have.

In Oakland, Detroit, and even places like Rochester, New York, you see mostly white activists defending homes that are being foreclosed on by banks, lived in by black and brown folks. That is evidence of real solidarity. I think that if we are prepared to examine Occupy, a naive and nascent movement early on, and help to develop it we can critique and we should critique. We need to work within it, to really say,

> PEOPLE ARE BEGINNING TO WAKE UP TO WHAT INEQUALITY PORTENDS FOR THE FUTURE OF THE COUNTRY AND IT IS NOT PRETTY.

"These issues of economic and racial injustice are one and the same. If it had not been for that racial injustice we ignored for thirty, fifty, and one hundred years, all the stuff working class white people are experiencing (foreclosure, inadequate health care, losing their jobs, not enough income for college), has been experienced by people of color for generations. If we had taken it seriously twenty years ago we might not be in this situation. If we can have that mentality, we can make issues of income and race inequality front and center in the American political narrative in the same way they were one hundred years ago. One hundred years ago these discussions about massive wealth disparity were front and center and the majority of working class people agreed with what we would now call a progressive or leftist position of, "This inequality is not acceptable."

There are signs on the horizon! People are beginning to wake up to what it means and portends for the future of the country and it is not pretty. When it comes to issues of justice, I have to be honest and as much as I try to maintain optimism, I have to remain agnostic about justice. I have never seen it and none of us have. We can say we believe in it and fight for it, after all, what else are we going to do with our lives? We have a very short period of time to earn our right to be here or to become "fully human", as James Baldwin said. We may or may not succeed.

I have to remain agnostic, but I think we are capable of it. I believe that we are capable of better. I could be wrong but I am willing to take the gamble and see what happens. I will say this, people ask me how I would know or look for a signpost for change, and I try to make is as simple as I can. I know things will have changed, particularly in regard to racial inequity, when I can drive into a community (maybe from out of town) and not know automatically who lives there and what color they probably are. Right now, I can go to any

> WE HAVE A VERY SHORT PERIOD OF TIME TO EARN OUR RIGHT TO BE HERE OR TO BECOME FULLY HUMAN.

part of this country and drive through its community and if no one was out walking, on their porches, and no people visible but I just looked at the quality of the infrastructure, roads, and signage on the buildings, I would be able to tell you with virtually 100 percent certainty whether it's a white, black, latino, wealthy, or poor neighborhood. So long as it is possible to drive through neighborhoods you have never been to and, without seeing a single person, know who lives there, we have a problem. When we have generated something like equity, that won't be possible anymore. We will be able to drive into a community and not know, just by seeing it is run down, that it is probably people of color. We won't know that just because it's nice and the lawns are neat that it is probably white people. We will understand that equity will be so much more prevalent that it won't be such an easy call. That to me, at the risk of seeming simplistic and naive, is the indicator. We will have made progress when I can't do that anymore.

## So what is the first step to getting there?

The first step is to figure out where we sit in this larger struggle. What is our role? What is our motivation? Why do we care? What is it that we are seeing and understanding now, when there was a time we didn't understand those things? The biggest danger for people trying to create justice is self-righteousness. It is that feeling of, "Oh, my God! I have discovered a horrible injustice. The polar ice caps are melting! I must stop it!" Or there is racism, "I must stop it!" Or there is heterosexism, "I must stop it!" The reality is that the folks who have been suffering could have told you a long time ago that those things were real. The fact that you now have discovered it can make you dangerous if you are not patient enough to step back and ask, "How do I join with those people who have always been fighting to save the environment, against sexism, homophobia, or racism rather than try to be the savior?" That is the fine line that we walk when we get involved, particularly as white folks fighting racism, men fighting sexism, or those who have a little money fighting the class system. It is hard because it is easy to have that savior complex. It is easy to think you will solve the problem. It has been hundreds of years of white supremacy in this country and for me to think, at forty-four, that I figured out how to solve it after hundreds of years of people of color trying, would be pretty arrogant. It would be pretty racist. It requires patience, self reflection, introspection, and to really know yourself. You need to understand that even when you are on the side of the angels there is a lot of conditioning to which you have been exposed that will allow you to screw up. We still screw up. Men who try to fight sexism still screw up and do sexist things. The reality is we have to be very forgiving of ourselves.

***How is the American Dream changing? Are the new dreams better for all of us?***

> ONE OF THE GREAT ARROGANT ASPECTS OF AMERICAN HISTORY IS THAT WE HAVE ACTED AS IF THERE WAS ONE AMERICAN DREAM AND IT HAD TO LOOK A CERTAIN WAY.

That has to be defined by each American. One of the great arrogant aspects of American history is that we have acted as if there was one American Dream and it had to look a certain way. It had to be this kind of house and this kind of family, but what that did was marginalize people of color who were never part of that picture, it marginalized working class folk, LGBT folk, and most women. Even heterosexual women who were in those types of families still had their voice marginalized. It marginalized non-Christian families and urban families. If you lived in the city the idea of the house with the picket fence and the yard didn't really work. That dream was always stifling and a very limiting dream and was dangerous. What it said to people was, "If you don't have this, you are not fully an American."

The American Dream has to be as expansive as the American population. We might have three hundred million different American dreams but if America means anything, it is the ability of each individual within the United States to have that dream, their own dream. It is their choice and right to not be told what that dream has to be. If we are going to actually define it, let's define it as the dream of the philosophy of the country, which we have never lived up to.

It is right there on paper. It is this notion that everyone is entitled to life, liberty, and the pursuit of happiness, the idea that we are going to maximize opportunity and equity and freedom and all of these things that we have talked about for hundreds of years but we never really delivered. If we have to define the American Dream, let us make it that, the doctrine of America, not this absurd materialistic notion of particular kinds of houses, a particular kind of car, a particular kind of family in image only. Substance and reality are often times very different than image and symbolism. We need to get to the substantive and realistic, not just the image. We have got to have a more expansive and inclusive definition of the American Dream than that. We have to be able to dream bigger and to dream better.

We don't always have to reinvent the wheel. We don't always have to find the next Doctor King or the next Malcolm X. Let's not ask who the next Doctor King is, let us ask who among us is ready to join the struggle and among the nameless faces and mass of people who really did the hardest work in the Civil Rights struggle. It wasn't just Doctor King. There were thousands of people whose names we don't know in the history books, whose names we don't get taught. They really did the hardest work. Each of us has a role to play. Most of us are not going to have our names

> THE AMERICAN DREAM HAS TO BE AS EXPANSIVE AS THE AMERICAN POPULATION. WE MIGHT HAVE THREE HUNDRED MILLION DIFFERENT AMERICAN DREAMS, BUT IF AMERICA MEANS ANYTHING IT IS THE ABILITY OF EACH INDIVIDUAL WITHIN THE UNITED STATES TO HAVE THEIR OWN DREAM.

in history books. Most of us will not be remembered by the masses one hundred years from now, but if we create a legacy for our children and our grandchildren than they will sing our praises irrespective of whether the history books do. That is the more important thing.

175

# MELISSA HANNA

---

Melissa Hanna is the founder of LoveThatBody.tv, an interactive comedy experience and workshop series about people's triumphs and struggles with body image issues.

lovethatbody.tv

## ARMS FLUNG OPEN

What our tomorrow holds:

The possibility of being happy and comfortable in our own skin.

The end of the battle with our bodies.

Abundant love for self and others.

A cognitive firewall that shuts out the media's negative messaging.

The dismantling of insecurities.

Guards let down and arms flung open.

A bright light shining from within.

Memories without shame.

Self-expression without taboo.

Choices made from a place of pride, not pressure.

Genuine communication.

Freedom from self-doubt.

Laughter at our inner critics.

Unabashed beauty.

Self-generated energy.

A vision that amplifies when we align ourselves with others.

Empowerment.

Connection.

Joy.

Feeling beautiful every day is a function of how willing you are to create yourself anew each morning.

Be courageous and willing to let go of what you think you know about yourself.

Let go of what the media says about you.

Let go of what others say about you.

Let go of what you say about you.

You designed your insecurities and you have the power to dismantle them.

Discover yourself in the mirror each day.

You are who you create yourself to be.

178 AMERICAN DREAMERS

# RICHARD NASH

*Richard Nash is VP of Community and Content of Small Demons. He ran the iconic indie Soft Skull Press for which work he was awarded the Association of American Publishers' Award for Creativity in Independent Publishing in 2005. He left in 2009 to found Cursor, an open-source community publishing project. The* Utne Reader *named him one of Fifty Visionaries Changing Your World and* mashable.com *picked him as the number one Twitter User Changing the Shape of Publishing.*

## POETRY WILL BE THE MOST POPULAR ART FORM OF THE TWENTY-FIRST CENTURY

The single most popular form of communication in the world right now, and for the foreseeable future, is speech. The next most popular is email (ten trillion non-spam messages in 2011), and the third is the SMS text message (one trillion non-spam messages).

What more fertile circumstances for the propagation of poetry?

Yet there is a pervasive assumption, in most of the

West at least, that poetry is dying. Poetry books don't sell, poets don't make money; it's the punchline in joke after joke about penury. Establishment literary culture bemoans the philistinism of American culture, and the Poetry Foundation, who after getting a massive one hundred million dollar donation from the pharmaceutical heiress Ruth Lilly, spent a wee chunk of it bribing public television to do some spots on how poetry isn't really that unpopular (always a sign of a truly unpopular thing when people spend money persuading you it's otherwise). Poetry is going the way of opera, it's assumed.

It is hard to pinpoint the basis of this perception, especially because it is completely wrong. Poetry is in rude health, even if every sign of ill-health I offered above is true. Poetry books don't sell very well, but they never did. Poets mostly do not make much money, but neither do knitters and no one thinks knitting is dying off. Establishment literary culture wouldn't function if it had to operate in a state of sunny optimism; it is Cassandra-like in its very being. Without barbarians at the gate, who would let them run the city? And it is the sad truth with any given nonprofit that while the worst thing for it is to have no money, the next worst thing is to have too much money; it goes in search of a purpose. So yes, poetry doesn't sell, and poetry denizens castigate a culture they believe has turned its back on them. So what then is "killing" poetry, if we are to believe it is dying? Ebooks are hurting independent bookstores, long seen as guardian of poetry. Google is making us stupid and shallow and unwilling to read anything more than a LOLcat caption; Facebook and Twitter compel us to read and write about cats. It's the Internet, isn't it, that's destroying poetry?

No. The greatest impediment to poetry is not technology; the printing press begat more poetry, not less; the Industrial Revolution produced more poetry, not less; the twentieth century book supply chain replete with wholesalers and tens

> POETS MOSTLY DO NOT MAKE MUCH MONEY, BUT NEITHER DO KNITTERS AND NO ONE THINKS KNITTING IS DYING OFF.

of thousands of bookstores worldwide engendered more poetry, not less; the web allowed more poetry to be hosted, not less; Web 2.0 sparked more conversation around poetry, not less; hell, even the great scourge of our times, spam, has produced more poetry by offering poets found texts in the same way the Surrealists and the Beats used the detritus of popular communication of the time as raw material for their work (I find myself continually remarking upon the astonishing power of human imagination—in this case our capacity to undo and remake language so as to express some intensity of experience—combined with our equally astonishing inability to comprehend the implications of the imagination. Given my own powers of imagination, one must surely assume these powers are universal, that children, adolescents, bankers, homeless persons, Grandad can all create poetry).

If not technology, then what? It is, I believe, education that is the greatest obstacle to poetry. For every *Dead Poets Society*, there are tens of thousands of teaching environments deadening poetry, extinguishing the spark. It escapes being squashed sometimes, here and there, typically through music, where singer-songwriters, indie rockers, but above all hip-hop artists, dodge the poetry-obliterating force of most formal education. The reality we all actually know, if we stop to consider it for a minute, is that most young adolescents are writing poetry when they enter high school, and they'll never read a poem, in love or anger, after they leave high school.

Education, after health, is probably the area in which we are most in need of compelling visions to make the world a better place. We need people in the fullest possible control of their physical capabilities first, then we need them to fully realize their minds. I know far too little of all the innovation going on in education to be able to articulate precisely how this will happen, but I can see how it is slowly

> GIVEN MY OWN POWERS OF IMAGINATION, ONE MUST SURELY ASSUME THESE POWERS ARE UNIVERSAL, THAT CHILDREN, ADOLESCENTS, BANKERS, HOMELESS PERSONS, GRANDAD CAN ALL CREATE POETRY

shifting from a top-down model to a bottom-up model, away from rote learning towards creative learning. As education becomes ever so incrementally less an imposition and more a discovery, the poetic impulse will endure less squishing, more cuddling, and we will have yet more poetry.

Now, I recognize I've not yet spoken of quality. I can imagine there are relatively few naysayers wanting to read about optimistic visions of the future, but I also believe that regardless of native or acquired optimism one must always be striving, always be questioning. So, how exactly can we have any confidence there will be more good poetry? Perhaps all of what I speak of here will simply produce bad poetry. I'm going to try to let the part speak for the whole here, a synecdoche as a poet might term it. When alluding to the perceived shallowness of the Web, I mentioned cat pictures. Pre-Internet, what's the best example one can think of the cat in cheap, bland, and sentimental commercial culture? To my mind, *Cats*. On what is *Cats* based? T.S. Eliot's *Old Possum's Book of Practical Cats*. LOLcats and T.S. Eliot do not exist in opposition to one another—pictures of cats co-exist with poems about cats; poems about cats co-exist with poems about paintings and food and love and death and shame and joy.

Here is one thing I demand not be misunderstood about this short essay. I am not advocating for poetry. I am not encouraging the writing of more poetry. I do not say we need more poetry. I am saying that more poetry is happening. I am saying more poets are being born every day, more poems will enter the world, more poems about cats, bad and good, more poets will slip the grasp of the poetry killers, more poems will enter the world, more poems will enter the world, there will be more poems than YouTube clips, more poems will enter the world, more poems will enter the world, more poems will enter the world than ever before.

> MORE POETS ARE BEING BORN EVERY DAY, MORE POEMS WILL ENTER THE WORLD.

Richard Nash 183

# MATTHEW DICKMAN

*Matthew Dickman is a poet. His first book,* All-American Poem, *was winner of the 2008 American Poetry Review/ Honickman First Book Prize in Poetry. His second full collection of poetry,* Mayakovsky's Revolver, *was published in 2012. Matthew, along with his twin brother Michael, appears in the film* Minority Report.

## ALL-AMERICAN POEM

I want to peel off a hundred dollar bill
and slap it down on the counter.
You can pick out a dress. I'll pick out a tie: polka dots
spinning like disco balls. Darling lets go
two-stepping in the sawdust at the Broken Spoke.
Let's live downtown and go clubbing.
God save hip-hop and famous mixed drinks.
Let's live in a cardboard box. Let's live
in a loft above Chelsea, barely human, talking about
the newest collection of Elizabeth Peyton,
her brilliant strokes, the wine and cheese.
You can go from one State to another and never
paint the same thing twice. In New Mexico

we could live by a creek and hang our laundry

on the line. Let's get naked in the cold waters of Michigan.

Let's get hitched in Nevada. Just you, me, and Elvis.

We could sell cheese curd in Wisconsin.

I could pay off my bills. You could strip

in some dive on the outskirts of Pittsburgh.

Let's bite each other on the neck.

Oh my sexy Transylvania!

We could be relationship counselors

for trannies in South Dakota.

It must be hard to have a woman living

inside you

when you're watching cows chew

the frozen grass of December.

You are everywhere, sweet Carolinas.

You're my boss, Tennessee, you honeysuckle.

Give us a kiss Hawaii. Who says were not an Empire? Fuck'em,

they need Jesus. They need the Holy Ghost.

Right Kansas? Kansas! My yellow brick road of intelligent design. We are not

monkeys. They're all in prison, right Texas? Texas,

I was with you on the Fourth of July watching the sky undress

with my friends

and we were Americans on America Day,

which is every day,

coming home from work, drinking a beer

and waiting for the dark,

for the night, the rocket's red glare, lying around

on a blanket in the backyard, a girl from your hometown

leaning against you, slipping her slender foot in and out of a saltwater sandal. She's wearing

cherry lip balm and taking ecstasy.

Later you can taste it.

The smooth wax along her mouth, her arms

stretched out in the grass and each narrow leaf of grass

like a separate lover, the horizon

of a summer tan rising above her low-cut jeans.

She looks different here than she did in her uniform, standing behind

the counter of the Coffee-Go, steaming milk,

rows of flavored syrup above her head: almond, blackberry, mint, vanilla.

This is the Fourth of July

and she looks like the end of summer. She's a wind

moving through the trees. She's the best thing

about high school assemblies. We are a country at war

and she's passing a note to you in class, your book open

to the chapter on dissecting frogs. How to keep the brain intact

when removing it from the small skull. The note says

Why were you holding Clare's hand after lunch?

We are a country at war but it's not really happening

here. It is not Clare or her brother or all the bourbon

in Kentucky. On the Fourth of July

I walk out among the fallen

watermelon rinds, the corn cobs, paper plates with chicken grease

being pushed by a little breeze

so they look like moons spun out of orbit.

I go inside. I turn the television on.

It's playing the Civil War again. The Battle of Gettysburg

remembering itself on the football field

at Lincoln Memorial High. A rush of gray uniforms

poised on the scrimmage line. The poor sons of Alabama

wearing the uniforms of dead soldiers.

The North marching down

toward cotton revenue and Big Tobacco. The South starving,

fighting, often without shoes, the narrator explaining

how the muskets were loaded, fired, and then re-loaded.

That's a lot of time

to think about the person you're killing.
That's a lot of time to wish you were home.
Unless, of course, you were home
and your house was burning down. Out of the smoke
there's always more smoke. There's always the hacking apart and crying.
You can go from one Civil War to another
and still not be free. The man in charge of the antique cannon
has lit his shirt on fire. The man in charge
of the horse runs Ray's Hardware on 10th and Main.
He's having a liquidation sale this weekend.
The show is over
in an hour. That includes commercials
and the slow, I won't kill you, pace
of the re-enactment. This is how it happened,
the narrator is saying,
while his producer plays a Negro spiritual. It makes you weep.
The vocalist calling out to God. Oh Lord! Oh Lord my God, she's singing,
have pity on our souls. You can go from one state
to another and pity will meet you at the Greyhound Station.
In the stands of the Lincoln Memorial football field
a little boy is eating cotton-candy while the dead men rise up
from the twenty-yard line and walk toward their families. I love
the History Channel. It's so foreign. The old reels of Germany
having the fascism bombed out of it. Kennedy waving
from the black sedan. It's almost real. Boston grieving. Pulling its hair out.
You can take the Chinatown bus from Boston
to the Chinatown in New York City. You can go
from one shop window
with peeled ducks hanging by their ankles
to another shop window
with peeled ducks hanging by their ankles.
In Oregon you can go from one hundred-year-old evergreen

to another hundred-year-old evergreen and never turn around.
They're everywhere, cut down
and loaded up, like paperbacks in bookstores.
My favorite bookstore is in Evanston, Illinois.
The owner is Polish and his daughter wore a wool skirt
that kept sliding up her legs
as she sat on the edge of his desk. God bless her
for it was cold outside and I was almost alone
but for my copy of The Idiot I carried with me everywhere.
You can go from one Russian novel
to another Russian novel and never have
borscht. You can go from one daughter to another
and eventually end up with your own. You can go from one
Founding Father to another and still have the same
America. The same Alaska. The same Baked Alaska
served on a silver plate in the same hotel
where the wait staff are all South American.
The same cows sleeping
in the same Wyoming with the same kids
getting drunk, shooting cans, peeing on the electric fence.
The same Main Street with the same True Value. The same
flags staggered between the streetlights
like marathon runners. I walked down that street in Tacoma, Washington
with Jennifer when Jennifer had red hair and listened
to Broadway musicals. We smoked
cigarettes in the town square
below a statue of one soldier carrying another. The plaque
read "Brothers in Arms". One soldier carrying another
in his arms. We were young and mean
and thought it was funny. You can go from one town square
to another and never fall in love.
Even in New Hampshire where people 'Live Free or Die'.

What kind of life is that

when you're on the road and the woman

next to you is hardly there, hardly speaking, her feet

on the dashboard like two very different promises.

How are you supposed to drive

under these conditions? Forget about the rain. Forget

about Vermont and the Green Mountain's majesty.

Forget Ted Nugent.

Forget Tom Petty and the Heartbreakers.

Forget the swimming pools in California

because if she doesn't love you

what chance have you got with L.A.?

In L.A. you don't get to be lonely.

You get skin peels and mud masks.

You can go from one spa to another

and watch the same lemon slices of cucumber

pressed against the eyes of 13-year-old girls and 70-year-old

women. You won't see that in Minnesota.

Minnesota! Cover me up in a wool blanket

and put me to bed. Let me sleep.

Let me have the dream again

where Kenneth Koch walks through my mother's house

looking for a leash. He's taking my dog for a walk. The dog

is scratching at the front door and Kenneth is saying yes, yes, I'm coming.

You can hear him telling the dog that one broken heart

deserves a heart that has been differently broken.

I had that dream in New York City. Times Square

looks like America throwing up on itself.

I want to hold its hair back. I want to sit in the park

where my brother and I drank coffee and ate donuts from Dean & Deluca.

We watched a man fly a little wooden airplane over the green benches.

We ate lunch at the Cedar Tavern.

The french fries I ordered were covered in pepper

like the poem Frank O'Hara wrote to Mayakovsky, saying

I love you. I love you,

but I'm turning to my verses

and my heart is closing

like a fist. The burger was bloody in the middle as if it wasn't through living.

My first girlfriend refused to eat meat.

She said she wouldn't be a tomb for another living creature.

But she privately cut herself on the arms

which confused both her parents.

Senior year she moved to Idaho. I miss her, my sweet potato.

You can go from one state to another

and still hate yourself. Hide in your room listening to The Cure, carving

little commas in your skin. You can go

to Arizona State and never leave your past behind. Arizona waiting

with open arms for the new blood. The great white hope

of tailgate parties and college football. Put me in coach, I'm ready to play!

I'm ready for the lobster rolls of Maine

and the co-eds of Maryland. In Maryland

I played miniature-golf with a waitress from Denny's.

I spent the winter sitting in her section, drinking Pepsi,

watching her hips hydroplane inside a green polyester skirt.

It was the year my Uncle Joe died. He was a G.I.

He was a G.I. Joe. A man who hid under the table

if a car backfired. He refused to eat rice.

He came back from Normandy

wanting ice cream. He had a friend from Arkansas

who ended up all over his uniform. An ear burned

into the helmet. He had a friend from Colorado

who got his hands cut off, slow, and forever. His pal

from New Jersey was thrown into the sky

like a human constellation of broken teeth. You can go

from one state to another and still feel pretty good about enlisting.

Joe lived in a trance. Love saved him.

He would scratch his wife's name over and over into the tough leather

of his boots. Hidden below the view-line

of a fox-hole, his knife drawn, the word Alice, written like a child

writes on the chalkboard. Alice, Alice,

like an antidote for death. Joe died in a hospital.

You can go from one pool of blood

to another and never see your own reflection.

Oh Mississippi, I worry about your boys.

Oklahoma City, Oklahoma, are you half empty?

Washington, D.C., the sons of senators

are sleeping between flannel sheets.

Darling lets go to Florida and sit

in the shade of an orange grove shack.

Let's meet some Cubans and Jews. The world is so big.

Why stay up all night and only have ourselves to keep warm?

I've never been to West Virginia. What the hell

are West Virginians doing this weekend? Or Iowa? In Iowa

there's a new Walmart opening and I'm gonna shed some dimes.

We'll take a bus there. A bus is a diplomat.

It throws us all together, our books,

hats, and umbrellas. I am never more human

than when I'm riding next to someone

who makes me shudder. If my body

touches his body who knows what will happen? Race issues

and cooties. The great unknown

coming home from work. You can go from one state to another

and still not know how to act. We are losing ourselves. We are somewhere

in Delaware. You are my Georgia peach. Your love

is like a field of buffalo when we still had buffalo and they looked like dark

rolling hills deep in North Dakota. America

I'm in love with your imports and exports,

your embargoes and summits!

Let's walk down to the river. Let's bless the paper

boats and turn the whole thing into wine. We can sit quietly on a blanket,

watching the transcendentalists come and go, talking

of Henry David Thoreau. Take me to the river,

Ohio, put me in the water.

Missouri goes down to the river and drinks Vanilla Cokes.

Rhode Island goes down and prays for money.

Connecticut goes down and washes its clothes on the sandy bank.

We go down to the river and the moon

pulls up in its silver Cadillac.

America, let's put our feet in the water! Let's tie a rock

around our waist and jump in.

The moon is revving up. The river

is rolling by. Tom Petty is singing about a girl from Indiana

and I am buying you another drink. I am trying to take you home.

193

# RAE BRYANT

---

*Rae Bryant's short story collection,* The Indefinite State of Imaginary Morals, *was released in June 2011. Her work has appeared in* StoryQuarterly, McSweeney's Internet Tendency, BLIP Magazine, Gargoyle Magazine, Redivider, *and has been nominated for the Pen/Hemingway, Pen Emerging Writers, and Pushcart awards. She is editor in chief of the literary and arts journal,* The Doctor T. J. Eckleburg Review.

## IS IT FUN? NOT SO MUCH. IS IT NECESSARY? ABSOLUTELY.

I see layers of gender on social biases, images of women, bones and flesh, over layed words, desire, oppression, and humor. I see vintage nudes and images of what women are and what women are "supposed to be." Socially, politically, artistically, gender biases cycle as they always have, waiting for the presidential ceiling to break. Being a woman, I can't help but desire a better future for gender understanding in general, but I don't necessarily see it through a feminist lens.

You see, I am a very bad feminist. I am a bad woman for

men and a bad woman for women. I sometimes do not make meals for my man and I do not want to be equal to my man in all ways. I like being a woman and wouldn't want to be everything male. I do not want all that testosterone. I do not want to give up birthing children.

I dream of a future when gender differences aren't differences to which we must blind ourselves and polarize our efforts, but rather, recognize and celebrate the diversities as well as the equalities. I dream of a future when we can collectively see both the commonalities and differences as necessary to the textures of life, art, literature. I see art and literature, new media, multimedia, intermedia, and virtual media, especially, as an exciting step toward this celebration of gender diversity.

I observe a "typical" man walking down the street, and I think, his gait is different than mine. His hair is shorter. He has stubble on his cheeks. His voice is lower. It does not make me want to be these things. It does not make me feel less capable because I am not these things. And I concede that he may be stronger and would likely beat me in a log-throwing contest. Not that I've ever entered a log-throwing contest. I just think it would be fun. But I would certainly get my ass kicked by a big burly man if I did enter a log-throwing contest. And I'm okay with that. I dream of a future when women can feel okay about men winning log-throwing contests, and men being okay with women winning log-throwing contests.

> I DREAM OF A FUTURE WHEN WOMEN CAN FEEL OKAY ABOUT MEN WINNING LOG-THROWING CONTESTS, AND MEN BEING OKAY WITH WOMEN WINNING LOG-THROWING CONTESTS.

This is what virtual media can do for us. It can let us walk into a gallery and stand in front of a video recorder and see our faces transposed onto burly men, extraordinarily muscular women in a presidential suit. Then we can see our transformed image throw a log, wining a body-building contest, or addressing the nation. Virtual media is the next step toward visualizing a different and sometime better future. It is a venue toward engaging our children in this visualization. It is also a venue for realizing, "Hmm, I really don't need to win a log-throwing contest to be a better woman, but I could see myself speaking to the nation." Virtual media can do this and far more.

We like to think we don't like to be told what to think, though, our traditional media often does this for us. When presented with two-dimensional explanations or propositions, we are hard-wired to absorb, regurgitate, and assimilate. We've been doing it since primary school. We try to be more critical, but essentially, we often fall into one of two camps. We either follow the obvious or subtle voice like sheep with an allusion of independence, denying our complicit ideologies and conventions, or we question the voice, with the allusion that we aren't already aligned with another ideology. Essentially, we approach each and every discourse, question, topic with preconceived structures, notions, conventions if you will, on top of the defined media with which we engage. We want to believe we are thinking for ourselves but essentially we seek someone to tell us what it all means in a format that is familiar to us, because it's faster and the "experts" know better and the "experts" have more education, more experience.

Once we've heard the experts, we need space to think for ourselves, but instead of educating ourselves and seeking new pathways toward learning and understanding, we return to the same standards and same formats our fathers and mothers sought knowledge—i.e. political entertainers, newspapers, strategists, big media, celebrity idols, and reality television shows (don't get me started on that one). We are "informed." It is all the essence of dumbing ourselves and following the herd. We are complicit in our quest for easy knowledge, and we go back to the same stalwart venues by which to understand laws, wars, social programming, socio-political trends, and financial trends ad nauseam. If we are to shake this, we really need to shake this not only voice alone but also format. How do we shock ourselves out of the norm? We engage more critically and creatively with the topic and we visualize ourselves in relationship to the topic as vested interests.

Don't just read about a war, put yourself there in its virtual space. Leave enough room for abstractions. I believe in abstractions as pathways toward building critical muscle. Be it on canvas, in words, video, or a mixture. Engaging with abstract forms is akin to a physicist nosing around open, incomplete formulas and theories. It is staring at a Rorschach test and seeing butterflies when someone else sees a vagina and someone else sees a Wall Street broker hiding money. The psychologist isn't telling the viewer what the abstraction represents. The viewer must find meaning and structure for him or herself. It's all in the ink and negative spaces. This is a necessary consideration, too, of negative spaces. Recognizing the absence of ink and paint and words, the negative spaces is as important as seeing the positive spaces and the lines drawn around them.

> **HOW DO WE SHOCK OURSELVES OUT OF THE NORM?**

According to Jacques Lacan, we give these negative spaces within art and literature our own language in order to form reality. This formed reality often symbolizes what we desire or sometimes fear. This reality is still a fantasy, it is a personal reality, which may be very different from another's "reality"—butterflies, vaginas, Wall Street brokers—but consider how training your mind to find its own language, forming its own reality, critically thinking in not only content but also structure, might benefit the act of reading an article on Bishop Blair and his Vatican initiative to bring nuns into compliance on women's issues. Or an article on Todd Akin's "legitimate rape" and "magical spermicide." Or an article on the Bush campaign's mission to fight terrorism. Or better yet, a contract with a mortgage broker on your new house with a flex interest rate.

Consider: you are given three words: Vatican, rape, mortgage. Then you are given a virtual space by which to create a scene, characters, storyline to reflect your understanding of these words and how they impact you today, how they impact your family. Then you step into this virtual creation. You engage with not only three hot topics, you give them nuance and meaning. You are bringing out the negative spaces of these topics and experiencing them, seeking to understand how they impact you on a more personal level than how the *New York Times* tells you these current hot topics are impacting you and the country at large. The act of creation gleans critical thinking and deeper reflection too often left out of the discussion, a far more in-depth and individualistic critical thinking experience, one that offers more connectivity, something D. F. Wallace described, in a 1995 BBC interview with Geoff Ward, as "leap[ing] over the wall of self."

I've recently completed a creative nonfiction multimedia and intermedia series, if there is such a thing, titled *Disembodied*. My dream exhibition for this would be a virtual media display in a gallery room—a box, white canvas walls—where readers and viewers can literally walk through the images and words as well as view them on a wall, ceiling, floor. The words tell the story of a rape I survived in college. Though it represents in this version as two-dimensional, within the context of the pieces, I see a virtual engagement of words and bodies, I can see myself within it. The series functions on two layers of negative space.

1) The lack of words that form and reform as the viewer progresses through the panels and the bodies of the women disappearing.
2) The absence of hope as symbolic of cyclical occurrence and need for change.

I try to employ elements of humor and satire, but overall, my work presents socially negative spaces, both qualitatively and quantitatively. I didn't fully understand this part of myself as a writer and artist before Frederick Barthelme made it clear for me. He'd published one of my stories, "Stage Play in Five Acts of Her: Matinee," in his journal, *Blip Magazine*. I asked if he'd take a look at my collection, *The Indefinite State of Imaginary Morals*. In short time, Rick came back with a blurb;

> *"Rae Bryant's stories yank at you over and over, desperate to give you the clue you never had and to point you, by what's left out, to a spot on this good earth where the heart might flourish. Getting there is your business, she seems to say, and she doesn't hold out much hope of your arrival, or of hers. Is it fun? Not so much. Is it necessary? Absolutely."*

After I read this, I thought, "The master has spoken, and somehow he knows my writing better than I know it, and he's shown me what I am." I'm pointing to what is not there, and though I may be realistic about the likelihood of collectively finding it, I do hope for our arrival individually and collectively.

I don't know if my work shapes a better future. I hope it does a small part to encourage reshaping. I hope my work opens readers' and viewers' minds to their own personal views of what our current state of gender understanding is and how it might be better, where the negative spaces are and how we might, each of us individually, fill them. Because, all in all, I do not believe one person or political party or country can make the world a better place. I do not believe what is good for one woman is good for all women. My dream future depends on one person at a time, thinking

**I DO NOT BELIEVE ONE PERSON OR POLITICAL PARTY OR COUNTRY CAN MAKE THE WORLD A BETTER PLACE.**

> MY DREAM FUTURE DEPENDS ON INDIVIDUALS ADDING CRITICAL THOUGHT AND CREATIVITY TO THE CRITICAL THOUGHT AND CREATIVITY OF MANY. IT IS A MESSY ENDEAVOR.

critically and creatively, willing to step out of the norm and conventions that have brought us to where we are. My dream future depends on individuals adding critical thought and creativity to the critical thought and creativity of many. It is a messy endeavor. All this individualism and critical thinking, yes. It leads to discourse and disagreements and sometimes fighting. In the words of Barthelme, is it fun? Not so much. Is it necessary? Absolutely.

201

# CRESTON DAVIS

*Creston Davis is a philosophy and religion professor at Rollins College. He grew up in the working class town of Hanover, Pennsylvania (famous for UTZ Chips and Synder's Pretzels), and served four years in an Airborne Ranger Recon outfit. Creston earned his PhD under mentors John Milbank and Slavoj Zizek at the University of Virginia. He has published several books including,* Theology and the Political: The New Debate, The Monstrosity of Christ *(both with Zizek and Milbank), and* Hegel and the Infinite *(with Zizek and Crockett).*

## EMBRACING THE FUTURE

When we think about creating a better and more optimistic future the standard strategy is either to overly romanticize the world ("Isn't the world beautiful and sublime—look at the precious flowers, the little children playing nicely, or the rainbow"), or else you graphically identify all the problems of the world (the world is shit and more and more going to hell—nuclear meltdown, pornography, Wall Street greed, and war). I claim that the best strategy is to accelerate both sides of this equation at the same time—to show the absolute absurdity that inheres within the logic of extremism (fundamentalism, politically correct, ideology, pessimism, romanticism, and so forth).

By revealing the impossible logic of extremism, what will emerge is the inversion of what the extremes themselves desire. So you will not get what the fundamentalists (rapture Christians) or the liberal fanatics (who peddle false multiculturalism in a very wealthy and elite context) want. What they want is certitude. By revealing the impossible logic of extremists, what you get is not certitude but contingency; you don't get mastery but humility. The fantasy of security gives way to radical risk and guns and violence turn into dialogue and forgiveness.

For example, Trish Dalton and Jesse Epstein's film *34x25x36* literally enters into the space of dangerous fantasy. This film takes place in a factory where old men are manufacturing their ideal mannequin of the female figure. Of course, their ideal figure does not really exist in concrete reality, as one man says in the film, "There are no perfect bodies out there; we make them." And that's the point. An ideal person cannot necessarily exist and this is because we are made of flesh and blood and not plastic. This further means that everyone must thus possess a "lack" of the ideal residing in you. We as fragile human beings cannot measure up to idealized types precisely because we are fragile and not necessary.

A strange thing happens in the very appearance of an "ideal" version of being human. There is a gap that opens up between this perceived and desired ideal version and the actual and concrete version of our everyday reality. This gap between the ideal and the real materializes in a void or lack that resides in us. Consequently, this lack creates a desire to temporarily overcome it by buying something (clothes) that look perfect on our mannequin, the "idealized woman" (and thus may look perfect on us). In other words, the perfect mannequin "ideal" creates a fantasy in the consumer we need to fulfill.

This structure of "lack-desire-fulfillment" is like religion; it extols an ideal image that doesn't really exist, but you believe in it anyway. The perverted old men in the film are materializing the fantasy of what a woman is supposed to be (but which can never be obtained). This is a male fantasy of a woman that can never exist, and one that a woman may actually want to be should she accept the male fantasy. In this sense, the gap enacts a certain symptom of death-drive in a woman because she wants to be non-existent, to exist in a state that is impossible to exist in! Or, said differently, a woman here only wants to exist in the space of man's desire. This is the kernel-core of misogyny—the hatred of women— which ironically is reproduced by women.

Notice that the logic of hatred is premised on a religious ideal. Like the mannequin in the film, religion gives you an ideal reality that you desire but can never fulfill. If Dalton and Epstein's film gives you the coordinates of misogyny, idealized religions thus give you the matrix of masochism and self-hatred. So, you can see where extremism leads directly to self-destruction. It gives us an ideal that we cannot fulfill—the perfect body, the perfect soul, or the perfect resume.

Next, we realize the necessary failure in trying to achieve this end-goal, and this leads to self hatred. The lesson we must take from this is that we must not buy into these fantasies; that, as Jacques Lacan said, "the big Other" (i.e., God, Nationalism, Capitalism, etc.) does not exist. Once we are freed from these idealized fantasies or extremisms, we can live with our own truth, and thus be able to accept the truth of others in all their fragility.

Thus I propose that the way forward into a brighter

> ONCE WE ARE FREED FROM THESE IDEALIZED FANTASIES OR EXTREMISMS, WE CAN LIVE WITH OUR OWN TRUTH, AND THUS BE ABLE TO ACCEPT THE TRUTH OF OTHERS IN ALL THEIR FRAGILITY.

future is to stop playing the sadistic "existential-set-up" game in which we set ourselves up just so we can fail (and enjoy doing so in the process!) Perhaps what we need for a better, more just, and peaceful future is not ideals (visions of a better world: rapture, the Apocalypse, liberating the Middle East into Western styled democracies, or a pure multiculturalism), but the hard sober work of reaching out your hand, your flesh and blood, to someone else risking a relationship with all your fragility. It may be, that in the lack, we as human beings (our shortcomings, letting each other down) may just be enough to save us from our own self-destruction. That is what we need to risk today—we need to risk forgiveness, acceptance, and togetherness. It is our fantasies that are killing us. It is time to embrace our lack and accept it as we are. This is a real politics of flesh and blood.

> IT IS OUR FANTASIES THAT ARE KILLING US. IT IS TIME TO EMBRACE OUR LACK AND ACCEPT IT AS WE ARE.

206  AMERICAN DREAMERS

# KURT ANDERSEN

---

*Kurt Andersen is a Renaissance man. As a writer, he has published several books, including* Reset *and his most recent, the novel* True Believers. *Kurt is also the host of the Peabody Award-winning* Studio 360, *a national public radio show about culture. Kurt regularly contributes to* Vanity Fair *and* The New York Times, *and has founded magazines and web sites, and written for film and the stage.*

kurtandersen.com

## RESET

In this new era, Americans will surely have to adjust the ways we think of ourselves. Still an exceptional country, absolutely, but not a magical one exempt from the laws of economic and geopolitical gravity. A nation with plenty of mojo, sure, but in our third century informed by the traditional wisdom of middle age a little more than the pedal-to-the-metal madness of youth.

Now that our long era of self-enchantment has ended, however, each of us, gobsmacked and reality-checked by the harrowing new circumstances, is recalibrating expectations for the timing and scale of our particular version of the good life. However, even though most of our hypothetical individual futures don't look quite so deluxe, as a nation we have three special strengths that, managed correctly and given a little luck, could allow America to remain at the top of the heap for a long time to come.

**IMMIGRATION**

No other nation on earth assimilates immigrants as successfully as the United States. There are those who argue that we can no longer afford to open our doors so wide, but in fact precisely the opposite is true. Beyond giving sentimental, self-flattering lip service to our history as "a nation of immigrants," the sooner we can agree on a coherent and correctly self-serving national immigration policy—that is, to encourage and enable as many possible of the world's smartest and most hardworking and open-minded people to become Americans—the better our chances of forestalling national decline.

---

### *How does American benefit from others?*

I think that immigration and people those who don't grow up with the complacency that growing up in America during the twentieth and twenty-first century can breed will be the good we are talking about. As people are going through the enormous struggles and dislocations and risks that immigrants do experience to get here, whether or not they have a conscious patriotic idea of America, they do have an idea about America and themselves as Americans. That is not only good to have by the millions, but is also a model for the rest of us. It says, "This place is worth something. There is a reason people want to come here and build new lives here." We should be inspired accordingly.

## TECHNOLOGY

For most of the last two hundred years, a great driver of our national prosperity and power was the extraordinary physical scale of our land, our natural resources, and our population, the more the better—a mostly empty continent ripe for exploitation and settlement, vast deposits of essential industrial material, many millions of laborers to build new cities from scratch and operate Brobdingnagian assembly lines turning out steel and automobiles and aircraft.

Muscular industrialism gets you only so far. In the twenty-first century, further increases in productivity and prosperity require ingenuity and enterprise applied at the micro scale—digital devices and systems, fantastic new technical materials, biotechnology, subatomic nanotechnology. As China and other developing countries finally achieve the industrial plenty that we enjoyed fifty and one hundred years ago, the United States can once again pioneer the new, next-generation technologies that the increasingly industrialized world will need.

---

### *What innovations do you see happening now that will hugely shift society?*

Technology itself doesn't determine the systems by which it will evolve. There are lots of choices and I think we make a mistake if we assume, "Oh, technology is this neutral thing that will just develop." On a certain level that is true but as a matter of systems and ways we develop, those are matters of choice. We have to watch those.

I write things to figure out what I think. As I continue to think of these issues, I will end up somewhere in the middle,

> **TECHNOLOGY ITSELF DOESN'T DETERMINE THE SYSTEMS BY WHICH IT WILL EVOLVE.**

not as a radical dystopian saying, "Oh, My God. We will be in *The Matrix*," or as a hysterical optimist of the Ray Kurzweil kind saying, "It's all wondrous and as we evolve into posthuman machines our intelligence will spread to the ends of the Universe!" I am somewhere in the Goldilocks mode of hoping. I am slightly more optimistic than I am pessimistic about what technology will portend for us in fifty or one hundred years.

## THE AMATEUR SPIRIT

The American spirit really is the amateur spirit. The earliest settlers were amateur colonists. "I see democracy," the historian Daniel Boorstin wrote twenty years ago, as "government by amateurs, as a way of confessing the limits of knowledge." In the early nineteenth century, Alexis de Tocqueville approvingly noted the absence of "public careers" in America—that is, the rarity of professional politicians. Back then, "amateur" was an entirely positive, noble, virtuous description of someone. An amateur pursuit meant something that one pursued—a field of study, an artistic enterprise, a craft—not unseriously, but out of passion rather than merely to earn a living. The Latin root is amator, or "lover."

Amateurs are passionate. They do the things they want to do in the ways they want to do them. They don't worry too much about breaking rules and aren't paralyzed by a fear of imperfection or even failure. They embrace new challenges. And it's that attitude, infusing our occupations as much as possible with the joy and excitement of avocation, that will get us through this wrenching time of creative destruction, confusion and change.

## THINKING THE UNTHINKABLE

So this next couple of years is our window of opportunity for a carefully considered reset. The elements of the untenable status quo, most obviously and critically how we use energy and pay for health care and educate our citizens, but also the ways we define contentment, are not immutable givens. Rather, they are the results of choices we made and habits we acquired and systems we built back in the twentieth century. Different, twenty-first century choices are now available to us. Dysfunction and profligacy aren't inevitable, and the American tendency to magical thinking can be kept in check. The die-hard opposition of powerful institutions (oil companies, agribusiness, the health care industry, teachers' unions, and more) to fundamental change is implacable, for sure, but it isn't invincible. We can rediscover common sense and the better angels of our nature. We possess the ability to rejigger and renovate our lives and our country as necessary. But to get there, we have to keep thinking the unthinkable.

> WE ONLY NEED TO CAREFULLY AND CLEARLY DECIDE WHAT THE MOST IMPORTANT THINGS ARE, AND THAT ARE ACTUALLY FIXABLE, AND FIX THEM.

---

*There is no guarantee or surety about the future but what can we do today to be hopeful?*

The pendulum has swung too far in believing we cannot collectively solve problems, making our lives and the lives of our children better. There is evidence all around of what we can do. Look at aviation safety, crime going down, or rivers being cleaned. We can do things. We only need to carefully and clearly decide what the most important things are, and that are actually fixable, and fix them.

After World War II, we had won the war, freed people

> THAT KIND OF BLACK OR WHITE THINKING ABOUT ALL THINGS IS THE GREATEST DANGER WE FACE. IF I WERE GOD AND COULD ORDER EVERYONE TO BE AT LEAST 55 PERCENT POSITIVE, THAT'S WHAT I WOULD ORDER.

from tyranny, and didn't get invaded ourselves. No wonder it was such a happy time for another twenty years. However, it was another twenty years before the late 1960s happened. That initial sense of happiness, of "Yeah! We can do anything! We can make the poor not poor! We can get to the Moon!" It's not all narrative but that is a lot of it. Progress is happening and can happen. Despite whether the media accentuates only the negative, the national outlook can pick up and become self-fulfilling. That is what periods of prosperity are all about. Confidence in the future reaches critical mass in a Ponzi scheme where everyone is happy, investing, and working. That is the way it happens. The problem is our tendency towards being bipolar, either, "Everything is great! America is perfect!" or, "America is terrible! We have lost our mojo and there is no going back." That kind of black or white thinking about all things is the greatest danger we face. If I were God and could order everyone to be at least 55 percent positive, that's what I would order.

**NOTE:** *This excerpt from the book* Reset, *by Kurt Andersen, published by Random House in 2009.*

213

# DR. ROBERT ZUBRIN

---

*Dr. Zubrin is an aerospace engineer and advocate for Mars exploration. He founded Mars Society in 1998 and has since been leading simulations on Earth. Dr. Zubrin is the author of many books including,* How to Live on Mars.
marssociety.org

## TO MARS!

There are three reasons to go to Mars. One is for the science. The second is for the challenge. The third is for the future.

As far as the science is concerned, Mars is the Rosetta Stone for letting us know the truth about the potential prevalence and diversity of life in the Universe. Mars is a planet whose early history mirrors that of Earth. It was warm and wet. If the theory is correct that life originates wherever you have appropriate physical and chemical conditions, life should have appeared on Mars. We now know that most stars have planets and every star has a habitable zone depending upon the brightness of the star and where you have the right temperatures for liquid water. If life can originate wherever it has a decent planet, man's life is everywhere.

Since the entire history of life on Earth is one of

development from simpler forms to more complex forms manifesting greater capacities or activity and intelligence and evermore rapid evolution, we can guess that if life is everywhere it means intelligence is almost everywhere. This is worth finding out. We can find this out by going to Mars and looking for life, either fossil life on the surface or extant life underground. The scientific motive for going to Mars is tremendous. We will be able to resolve the question of whether or not we are alone in the Universe. This is something that thinking men and women have wondered for thousands of years.

The second reason is the challenge. This is the challenge that has been staring our space program in the face ever since the end of Apollo. It is the challenge of society if we continue to be a nation of pioneers. Are we capable of leading humanity to become a space-faring species, a multi-planet species with a wide-open frontier and a wide-open future? By embracing this challenge we won't just benefit the future, though I will get to that, we benefit the present. Society grows when we are challenged. We stagnate when we are not challenged. The "Humans to Mars" program would send out an invigorating challenge, particularly to the youth of every country that participates. "Learn your science and you could be an explorer of new worlds." Out of that challenge we would get millions of young scientists, engineers, inventors, doctors, medical researchers, and technological entrepreneurs.

> ARE WE CAPABLE OF LEADING HUMANITY TO BECOME A SPACE-FARING SPECIES, A MULTI-PLANET SPECIES WITH A WIDE-OPEN FRONTIER AND A WIDE-OPEN FUTURE?

These are the kinds of people that advance society. They advance technology, health, defense, and the economy. These are the people we need. This is the basis of our prosperity and our strength. A "Humans to Mars" program would bring them into being by the millions.

Finally, there is the future. Ask any American, "What happened in 1492?" They will say, "Well, Columbus sailed in 1492." That is true, of course, but a lot of other things happened in 1492: England and France signed a peace treaty in 1492, the Borgias took over the Papacy, Lorenzo de' Medici died in 1492. No one today cares about any of that stuff. Very few people even know about it. What matters is Columbus. He made our world possible. Five hundred years from now, nobody is going to care who came out on top in Iraq or Afghanistan. No one will care who won the election or whether there was a 4 percent tax cut or increase. What we did to make their life possible, those billions of people living on thousands of planets in this region of the galaxy, will matter. This is what matters for the future. If you can do something that matters, you should.

### *What are the goals beyond Mars? What are the longer-term goals for distant planets?*

Mars is not the final destination, it is the direction. Mars is the closest planet that has all the resources needed for settlement. Other places are more difficult. As the European colonists settled the East Coast of the United States they developed the skills that made tackling more difficult frontiers possible. If we become a space-faring species and we master the technologies that allow us to settle Mars and transport ourselves back and forth to Mars increasingly and effectively and we make use of resources that are found on Mars, than we become capable of settling the asteroids and the moons and the outer planets. Columbus sailed the Atlantic in ships that fifty years later, no one would have dreamed of sailing. In his day there was no trans-Atlantic traffic, no ships designed for that. By transforming European civilization to a trans-Atlantic civilization they brought into being the three-masted caravels and the clipper ships. Then came the steamship and the ocean

**MARS IS NOT THE FINAL DESTINATION, IT IS THE DIRECTION.**

liner and the Boeing 747. The first people to go to Mars will go with chemical propulsion. It will take six months to get there in tight and cramped quarters. They will have stories to tell their grandkids that will be difficult to believe because the grandkids won't be doing it that way. They will be in spacious accommodations with every luxury. They will do the trip in four weeks and fusion power. Those new technologies that make it routine to cross interplanetary space to Mars will make travel to the outer solar system practical and travel to the stars marginally possible for the truly daring.

> THOSE NEW TECHNOLOGIES THAT MAKE IT ROUTINE TO CROSS INTERPLANETARY SPACE TO MARS WILL MAKE TRAVEL TO THE OUTER SOLAR SYSTEM PRACTICAL AND TRAVEL TO THE STARS MARGINALLY POSSIBLE FOR THE TRULY DARING.

***Fifty years ago, having a man on the moon was a giant step. Having a rover on Mars was a giant step. What is the timeframe for humans on Mars and how do we make it a reality instead of a science fiction dream?***

First, we have to decide to do it! Fifty years ago Kennedy gave his famous speech, "We choose to go to the moon in this decade and do other things, not because they are easy, but because they are hard." We were there seven years later. They got to the moon because they were serious about getting to the moon. The technical obstacles of getting to Mars today are significantly less than they were getting to the Moon when Kennedy started the Moon program. If we had serious political leadership we could have humans on Mars by the end of the decade. Do we have serious political leadership on this? At the moment, no. They are cutting the Mars exploration budget. They are wrecking the program and this is not how we are going to get to Mars. We will get there by deciding we want to and then doing it.

***What technology do we have now that allows us to get there? What are the advancements we have made in the last, say ten years, that have made that possible?***

Well, in the last fifteen years we have had a series of probes to Mars that have been successful and told us a lot more about Mars. We have mapped the planet in high resolution and are now capable of picking out good landing sites. We have just demonstrated a system for soft landing large payloads on Mars. They put down Curiosity like it was a crate of eggs instead of bouncing around with airbags.

The human spaceflight program has largely been marking time. The current program is to keep it marking time into the future or until people get bored with sending people up and down to orbit and just cancel the whole show altogether. It really needs an objective.

The general level of technology in society has, of course, advanced. We got to the Moon before there were pocket calculators! We started going to the Moon before there were push-button telephones, certainly before there were camcorders let alone cell phones, smart phones, or home computers. The general level of technology in society is advancing and it becomes more and more possible to do these things quite easily. The computer that they had in the Apollo lander was less powerful than most people have in their phones.

***What is the ideal Mars journey astronaut? Are the astronauts of the future similar to those of the past—specialized Air Force pilots—or are they scientists, engineers and citizens?***

On the first mission to Mars, the two most important skills will be mechanics and field geology. One person may have both these skills or you might have two people on the crew that specialize in one or the other. These are really the two most important skill sets. Someone good at fixing things and a real field geologist who can pick up a rock and tell you that water was flowing from north to south three billion years ago. They need to sniff out where fossils are likely to be. Apollo astronauts were fighter pilots or test pilots and those are not primary skills on a Mars exploration. We don't need people good at shooting down MiGs, we need people good at fixing plumbing, circuits or this and that. That may include a really good hacker, a fix-it type or two. In *Star Trek* terminology, I would like two Scotties and two Spocks.

On our current Earth missions, we have had quite a variety of people. We have had over seven hundred people as crew members in our desert station. We have had one hundred and twenty crews of six people each. They vary in quality but some are quite first rate. We have had terrific geologists and terrific fix-it types. We have also had people who don't have the required skills or character set. That is one of the things we are finding out. You put people out there and find out what the skills are that really come in handy. What are the character types that really come in handy?

The best character type is somebody with a sense of humor because if you lose your sense of humor on the way to Mars you are finished. You need to have people who can take innumerable small difficulties and and just laugh at them. You don't want people who are too uptight.

**IF YOU LOSE YOUR SENSE OF HUMOR ON THE WAY TO MARS YOU ARE FINISHED.**

## *When humanity becomes truly interstellar, what will become of Earth? Will our problems follow us or will they seem small?*

One of the real problems we have had on Earth in the past one hundred years is not overpopulation but people who thought there were too many people and tried to do something about it. This idea of limited resources, that there is only so much to go around, encourages us to fight over them. It is ultimately the cause of war. Germany did not need living space in 1939. Germany is smaller today than it was in 1939 and has a much higher standard of living in spite of, and perhaps because of, a larger population. This idea, that there is only so much to go around, is what turns the world into war of all against all. If we can show that wealth does not come from ownership of resources but comes from creativity that can open up endless new frontiers, then we can have peace. Then you have a world where nations are not enemies but are friends. You have a world where it is not a problem for America that the sons and daughters of Chinese peasants are going to college, becoming engineers, buying cars, and using oil (which we want for ourselves). No, it is a great thing because they will start inventing in proportion to their numbers. We will massively increase the rate of global technological progress and prosperity. Similarly, it won't be a problem for China that America is here and using oil that they want for themselves because we will be making our share of inventions.

By showing that the future is open and resources are as infinite as human creativity we can defeat this ideology which sets people against each other.

**Will our future explorations, Mars and beyond, be projects of NASA and America or will they be international projects, made possible by collaboration?**

It is unclear. Mars will go to those who go there. WIll it be America acting alone? Will it be a group of nations including America? Will it be a group of nations not including America? That is for the future to decide. I would like to see many nations and cultures moving out into space. I do not prefer it to be collapsed into one cooperative international program because that is a formula for stagnation. I would rather have an Olympics style competition to see who can do the most to advance the human frontier.

*And will the successful mission be a project of governments and nations or will the first people to Mars be private enterprise?*

That is hard to say but now, given the mismanagement of NASA it is hard to see how NASA is going to go. That could be corrected. If it is not corrected perhaps it will be a private venture, whether that is SpaceX or someone else. We are going to go. We will find a way to go.

Humans have this drive to want to go where they have never gone before, to see what has never been seen before, and to do what has never been done before. Whether we do that through government formations or corporations or things people haven't thought of yet we are going to find a way to make it happen.

*What can we as everyday citizens do to engage and support exploration?*

The space program that we have a voice in is the government space program. We can insist that we want a space program that really goes somewhere and we have a right to it. They should not be cutting the Mars exploration budget, that is absurd. It is one of their most successful programs. To celebrate the Curiosity landing by ripping out the program funds is outrageous. People should contact their congressmen and say, "Turn that around." We need to say, "Look, we want a space program that goes somewhere! We don't want to do it to send astronauts up and down to make observations of how their bodies react to zero gravity! We don't want guinea pigs we want explorers. We are willing to accept risks. The

**WE DON'T WANT GUINEA PIGS WE WANT EXPLORERS.**

astronauts themselves are quite willing to accept risks. That is why they become astronauts. So let's get the show on the road!"

**How do we respond to detractors who complain that the money could be better spent on homelessness, hunger and issues here on Earth?**

Since 2008, U.S. government spending has increased but NASA spending has not increased at all. There may be a budget blowing out but it is not NASA that is responsible. If you want to impose budget discipline you should not hit the agency that has been fiscally responsible but those that have not! Otherwise, you are in fact accelerating the fiscal blowout. The government is here to do things that the private sector finds difficult or impossible to do. With the opening up of Mars to human settlement, at this point, it is not obvious how the business plan for that closes. That is the the kind of thing that government should be doing.

Before I became an engineer, I was a teacher. I taught in a variety of good schools, bad schools, and in-between schools. There is one thing I learned. Anybody can teach kids who want to learn and nobody can teach kids who don't want to learn, period. if you want to improve American education, don't spend money on LCD projectors for schools, more teachers, or this or that. What you want to do is something that says to the kids, "Science is the great adventure. Intellect is the great adventure."

If we had a "Humans to Mars" program we would get tens of millions of kids excited about science. They would be teachable and teach themselves. They would run off to the library, dig into every book they can, and build model rockets. They would build terrariums and watch plants make oxygen for the fish and animals. You don't improve education by drilling kids to pass standardized tests; that only creates a system that cares about passing that test. You improve education by showing that intellect is the great adventure. The "Humans to Mars" program would be an invitation to adventure that would revolutionize education in this country. We doubled the number of scientists in this country out of Apollo, doubled it! The number of science graduates doubled. We are still benefitting from that intellectual capital today. Who were the old technological entrepreneurs who built Silicon Valley in the 1990s? They were the twelve year old child scientists making rocket fuel in the basements during the 1960s.

This is how we grow. If you want to benefit society, don't spend your money keeping state police employed so they can harass motorists. Spend the money on something that will mobilize intellect passion, industry, and inventiveness of America. That is what a Mars program will do.

There is a lot and lot of potential for surprises out there. We have to know that all the answers are not in the back of our current textbooks. There is a lot that remains to be discovered. That is why we need to go and look in new places. We are trying to open the future, full of endless possibilities.

> IF YOU WANT TO BENEFIT SOCIETY, DON'T SPEND YOUR MONEY KEEPING STATE POLICE EMPLOYED SO THEY CAN HARASS MOTORISTS. SPEND THE MONEY ON SOMETHING THAT WILL MOBILIZE INTELLECT PASSION, INDUSTRY, AND INVENTIVENESS OF AMERICA.

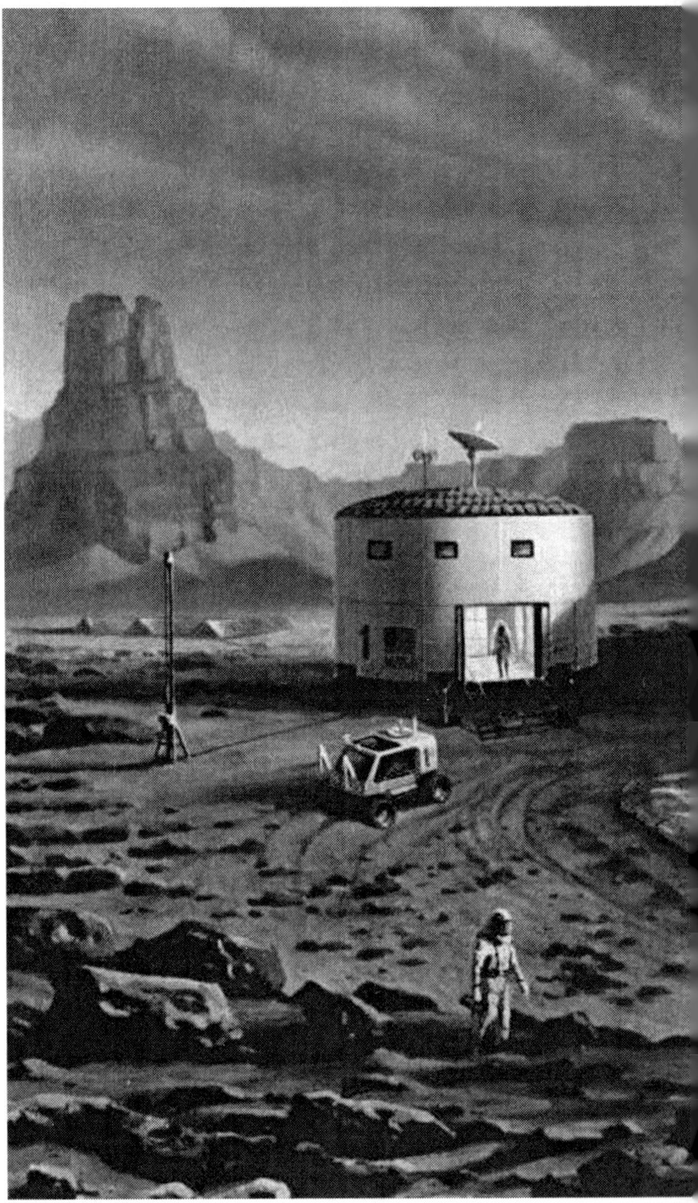

*Image by Robert Murray, Courtesy of Pioneer Astronautics*

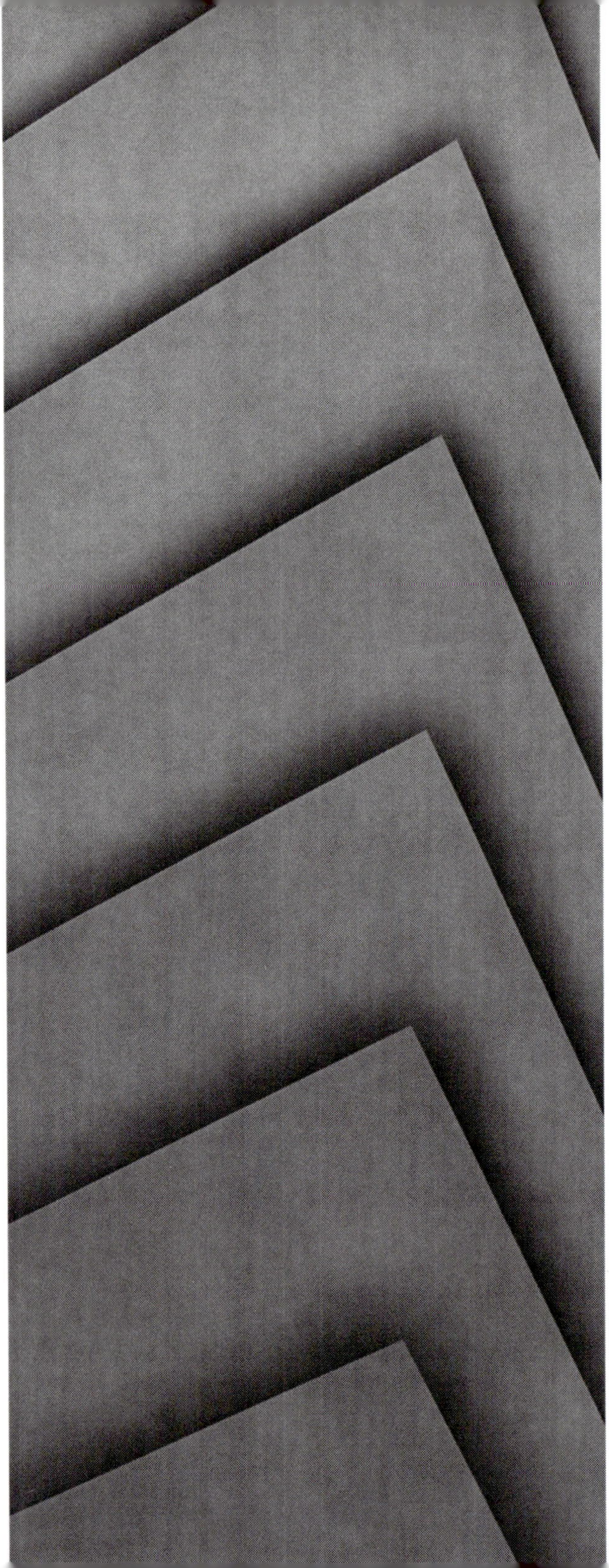

# AMBER CASE

---

*Amber Case is a researcher exploring the field of cyborg anthropology and the interaction between humans and technology. She is the founder of Geoloqi Inc., a company bringing the future of location to the world.*

caseorganic.com

## CYBORG ANTHROPOLOGY

I work in the field of Cyborg Anthropology, a way of understanding how humans and technology work together and how technology is affecting humans. It is hard to step back when you are in a space that is so new and continuously evolving.

---

Traditionally location technology has been used to surveil people and not to empower people. Now, in exchange for your location you get local weather patterns, Wikipedia articles, things texted to your phone. You can subscribe to layers of reality. All of this stuff has been stuck in the web; if you wanted the information you had to go to the website and look at the map. With something that knows where you are, you can have that data at the point in time that you are interested in it and when you are at that location. As people have phones the most important things in the future will be maps and data.

---

If you think about optimism, extreme optimism is embodied in that song "I.G.Y" which stands for International Geophysical Year. Donald Fagen sings, "What a beautiful world this will be/What a glorious time to be free." If you listen, the song refers to spandex jackets for everyone, it is hilarious. It was his attempt to talk about the amazing things that science and technology could do for the future.

But of course, we have to talk about the converse. A lot of technology has been used for government and private enterprise but now, when we get to play with it, it becomes interesting. People ask if technology is bad or good and my response is that technology is completely neutral until applied to a human. A human, depending on who they are, will decide what they want to do with it. Someone who would have watched six to eight hours of television in the past will use their phone, iPad, or Youtube for six to eight hours a day. They are the people who used to go to the tavern and drink for hours because that was the original television. You consume something and it pacifies you.

Creative people are going to use technology as a tool in creative ways. It is not a consumption device. It is a tool. At the beginning of the Internet you had to create more than you consumed because there wasn't anything on the web. It was all handmade. BBS systems in 1978 were something you created, the text was you and you became embodied in text. As time went on, people made lots and lots of websites and

**YOU CONSUME SOMETHING AND IT PACIFIES YOU.**

after a while you could browse the Internet without creating a thing. Now, everything is premade for you.

---

There is a big difference between creating and consuming. Your brain can conceive of anything but it takes so much energy to get something out of your head, to convince someone to believe in it, and then building it is almost impossible. Creative people end up getting severely depressed because they think something is wrong with them.

---

That is changing. We are all seeing it. Kids who are good with technology are considered amazing. They are like miniature gods. They can create an experience and distribute the experience using a computer at the back of a classroom. When I was in college a friend ran his online business from the seat next to me in communications class. Everything he learned in class he applied to the business. Real time business development. Kids can now build and make 3D objects and make their own toys.

> **KIDS WHO ARE GOOD WITH TECHNOLOGY ARE LIKE MINIATURE GODS.**

---

We have an overabundance of crappy technology. We also have an abundance of crappy bands, an abundance of crappy restaurants, an abundance of crappy people, and an abundance of junk. There will also always be things that are amazing. Who gets to experience those amazing interfaces? That is the issue. As it always has been, it is a privileged class that can experience these. We can say we will give every kid a laptop and therefore, they will teach themselves calculus. Most of them will watch Youtube, just like everyone else. One may actually do it though. Those few who really want to get out of their circumstance or make it will be able to connect with people and actually use the tool. Technology allows us to be empowered. There is a lot more justice going on. Anonymous is the new Robin Hood.

---

There is the idea that everyone in America is a temporarily disadvantaged millionaire. We all think that at some point we could have a million dollars, that at some point we can access the American Dream. In reality we have one of the most stringent social class structures out there, it is just very hidden. We don't like delayed gratification or having to wait for five years. The people who play *Farmville* don't have any delay. They click on stuff because everything is a reward.

---

> WE USED TO STORE MEMORIES IN PEOPLE BUT NOW WE STORE THEM IN MACHINES

There will be a class of people who become the historians for reality. We are already seeing this. I see Internet Archive as one of these historians. They are the equivalent of the old woman on the corner who tells all the stories for the village, passing them on from generation to generation. We used to store memories in people but now we store them in machines. The problem with machines is the required maintenance and stuff degrades.

---

Humans are a very stable code base that have been around for a long time. I would rather have a guide dog than a program on my phone telling me when to turn left. A guide dog can reproduce itself, be easily trained, and can figure out situations.

---

If people try to make machines that are like humans we will produce humans that are like machines. Technology will never take over humanity. We have always symbiotically produced it, hand in hand. We have become completely reliant on it and technology has become completely reliant on us to reproduce. We need more mundane science fiction where we take the information we have now and accentuate some of it, writing it out into the future. Then we can see how it will impact us.

> **IF PEOPLE TRY TO MAKE MACHINES THAT ARE LIKE HUMANS WE WILL PRODUCE HUMANS THAT ARE LIKE MACHINES.**

---

Technology is the new American Dream. "I will get wealthy from creating this software." I just sold Geoloqi. I am living it but now I need to do the next thing. It is not about money but making sure people are fulfilled and doing great work otherwise there is no point. We don't get that much life, maybe eighty years. People are fragmented and one thing that keeps us unfragmented is the Internet. Now we can go to conferences. Now we can meet people and do weird stuff. Americans are very creative and very good at design. They write beautifully elegant code and they push the boundaries. We will have severe limitations with money and careers but a few who will keep going on will be great, creating genius innovations. We have to make our own reality. I graduated in

2008, the beginning of the recession. A lot has to be rewritten and we have to find creative ways of surviving.

## WE DON'T HAVE RESOURCES BECAUSE THE OLDER GENERATIONS ATE THEM ALL.

The old dream is not achievable by our current generations. We don't have resources because the older generations ate them all. People are not connected anymore. The generations don't hang out and young people don't hang out with grandparents. But the people I meet in the tech community are all different ages. There is a camaraderie between ages and perspectives that makes for a valuable experience. You don't need a lot of money or these lost resources when you have people. People are resources.

233

# JOHN ZOGBY

*John Zogby works as a national pollster and veteran analyst. He is a well-known interpreter of the American and global scene. As author of* The New York Times *bestseller* The Way We'll Be: The Zogby Report on the Transformation of the American Dream, *Zogby continues to put his finger on the pulse of America, creating a portrait of the trends that drive our society today, and in the future.*

## WE DON'T NEED DATA, WE NEED PEOPLE

I am an optimist and maintain that. I didn't start out that way. I let my numbers do the talking. I think that America has increasingly come to grips with spending less in tougher times. There has been a redefinition of the American Dream, away from what I call "traditional materialism" towards "secular spiritualism." We do not want our lives to be defined by what we own, but want them to be defined by what kind of legacy we are leaving. It is in terms of leading a genuine life and making our world, community, and even our family, better than when we started. I think that, at least generationally, we will be doing less but being smarter consumers, using credit cards a lot less, and not living beyond our means as much.

## *What effects does that shift from traditional materialism to secular spiritualism have? Where else do we see the impact of that in our lives?*

It is a redefinition of work. Sociologists told us we would be working thirty-hour work weeks by the 1990s. That turned into thirty-hour work days. The future will bring a convergence of living and working, as working becomes an organic part of our genuine life. Whether we are entrepreneurs, and more and more of us will have to become so, work and play and networking and relationships are all going to converge. We will not define our lives as working a forty-hour or sixty-hour work week. We will not be living in cubicles during the day at work, with a living space at home. Many of us will be living, working, and recreating in one space. The look and feel of our homes will change.

**I AM EXCITED THAT YOUNG PEOPLE MAKE DECISIONS DIFFERENTLY THAN THE REST OF US DO.**

## *What excites you about the future? What is our best feature that will make things better?*

It is the diversity. It is the fact of our blurring racial and ethnic lines. The young people, whom I call America's First Globals, see themselves living, more and more, in a post-racial world. There is an appreciation for things that are planetary and multicultural among young people. I am excited that young people make decisions differently than the rest of us do. Decisions will be made horizontally, via networking, as opposed to vertically and through chains of command. I see a leveling, equalizing, and greater appreciation of peers. There is a greater opportunity to do real problem solving, as opposed to kicking the can down the road. Socially, there will still be diversity but less conflict about it. There will still be conflict but it won't be tribal or national. There will be new paradigms for global changes not based on organizations of nations but rather multicultural NGOs working with wealthy corporations to resolve problems. We will not wait for the slow wheels of governance.

There will also be a cognitive revolution. Africans will no longer be seen as those people who are far away. Asians will no longer be seen as people who are different from Europeans or Americans. The less "other" people become, the more difficult it is to go to war with them, or exploit them economically.

I am portraying a very optimistic picture here but others have too. I have read Steven Pinker's *The Better Angels of Our Nature*, and as an historian, not only a pollster, I subscribed to his notions. We are becoming less violent and the next less fifty years will make us less so.

We also need to take a broader view and look in terms of epochs. We are in one of those epochs that is similar to the fall of the Roman Empire, for that matter, similar to the decline and fall of feudalism. We are experiencing major global changes that require massive structural changes, cognitive changes, and cultural readjustments. We are in the middle of it now. It feels overwhelming and ugly. We are living this minute-by-minute through the communications that we have. This is a tremendous fundamental shift in everything. Things will be slow and uneven but we are in the position for it to happen even faster. There will be destabilizations. Just around the corner is a bigger, better, and global economy but we have to survive the next bit first. History offers the perspective.

We see movement globally, when Brazil and Turkey work together to come up with a plan dealing with Iran. They said

**THE LESS "OTHER" PEOPLE BECOME, THE MORE DIFFICULT IT IS TO GO TO WAR WITH THEM, OR EXPLOIT THEM ECONOMICALLY.**

to the United States, "Hey, we are major powers. You can't call all the shots all the time."

On a personal level, I coached my son's soccer teams when they were little. I remember a father coming up to me and saying, "I expect you to teach these kids, the five-year-olds, the fundamentals of soccer." I said to him, "Great! I don't know a fucking thing about soccer. I have never played in my life." Now we are into the world of soccer, joining the rest of the world. American kids have a common denominator of soccer that they never had before. There are common denominators being built.

We have been defined by splendid isolation. That is essential to our culture. But there is so much that mitigates against that. Like being able to fly to London in an hour and a half and having porous borders. We will not stop immigration. We will be begging people not to retire because we need their skills. It will be a completely different world than what we have and it is starting already.

You can't go to war with people carrying Louis Vuitton bags and wearing Benetton sweaters. There are universal experiences, across all cultures. The more we experience those cultures the more difficult it is to fight. In a war you have to kill the "other." Our communications and transportation revolutions are slowly and steadily destroying that concept.

There are, however, huge problems like hunger, malnutrition, disease, tribal hatreds, terrorism, and technologies that can destroy whole swaths and regions. Fighting this will take vigilance and infrastructure. There will be pain. People are losing jobs but they are losing jobs that are obsolete.

All of these tell us that we need to get beyond ourselves. We need to get beyond our borders and that is automatically happening.

Technology is pushing this along. We are in touch with

> YOU CAN'T GO TO WAR WITH PEOPLE CARRYING LOUIS VUITTON BAGS AND WEARING BENETTON SWEATERS.

the world via handheld devices. This is all happening and will continue to happen. Our culture demands it. You can talk to someone in Beirut and if the phone goes dead we say, "This goddamned technology doesn't work!" We don't step back to see that in the palm of our hand we were just talking to someone in Beirut! We couldn't do that before. Each new technology comes with a whole new set of expectations and with that set of expectations comes a whole new slew of entrepreneurism to help perfect it. Without that, we would still be operating with transatlantic cables and Morse code.

In terms of technology that is coming, the next fifty years belongs to high-speed rail, space travel, and satellite technology that will make our dependence on any energy drawn from the earth obsolete. Technology much like the Hubble which reflects light and beams images from light years away, can also reflect the sun and transmit energy in such abundance that energy could be free of charge. What that does is level the field. Now, a hut can be transformed into a place that provides livable space for tens of millions of people. It also allows people to mechanize. A handmade business can be sold to more people. You don't have to worry about an energy bill. Mobile technology is already doing similar things. Mobile phones throughout Africa are empowering farmers to check weather conditions and food prices.

### *How do we get involved in these changes?*

**WE DON'T NEED TESTS ANYMORE. WE DON'T NEED THE TREMENDOUS DATA DUMP INTO LITTLE KIDS' HEADS ANYMORE.**

We should support education. We need to allow for flexibility and to redefine education. We need to monitor our school boards. Elementary and secondary schools are so outmoded. Too many resources go to sustaining our institutions rather than to make fundamental changes that are required. We don't need tests anymore. We don't need the tremendous data dump into little kids' heads anymore. If you ask me a question and I don't know the answer, I can look it up in four seconds.

We need more access to information. More importantly, we need to be trained and experienced in what to do with the information. How do we work in teams? How do we crowdsource? How do we sift through responses from peers and make decisions? This creates direct democracy. I am not going to say that Congress is obsolete but I am going to say that corporations will have a hell of a time buying off a hundred million people. It is now a hundred million party system.

The two political parties are vying for their very existence. It is not even a question of wins and losses. It is a question of people saying, "Well, the Democrats suck and the Republicans suck!" People want problems to be solved. The parties are on the firing line. The same is true of corporations and businesses. Most of them are based on structures geared for an earlier time and they no longer make any sense. Now structures need to be mobile, nimble, flexible, and less bureaucratic.

> WE NEED TO BE OPTIMISTIC, OPTIMISTIC AND VIGILANT WITH PERSPECTIVE.

We need to be optimistic, optimistic and vigilant with perspective. Just because I am going through a rough patch right now does not mean it is permanent. We have a resilience. Humans beings have a resilience. We read about people who die unnecessarily but we don't read about people who live and survive hardships, or people who are able to put together their lives. The United States during this recession is only catching up with the rest of the world.

I live in upstate New York near a little city called Utica. When we read about the recession we say, "This has been our community for the last thirty years." But people start new businesses every day and people put food on the table. That is the story of survival and the triumph of of humans. Watch the changes that are taking place and have a perspective. We have gone through this before.

*240*   AMERICAN DREAMERS

# ANI ZONNEVELD

---

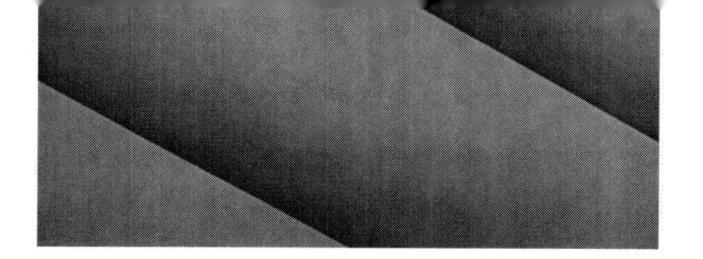

*Ani Zonneveld is Co-founder and President of Muslims for Progressive Values, a nonprofit founded in 2007. She has organized numerous interfaith arts and music festivals and is a strong supporter of women's and LGBTQ rights. Ani performs Islamic wedding services for mixed faith and gay couples and, in 2006, she was named a Muslim Leader of Tomorrow by the American Society for Muslim Advancement.*

mpvusa.org

## ISLAM AND AMERICA, BETTER THAN EVER

My dream for the future is a planet that extends equality to all. I believe the only way our world can become a better place is when our intention is expressed simply by the phrase "justice for all" and when our laws and lives live up to it. It is only when human beings exercise and live out the values of equality that we can have a peaceful and just world. In order for us to attain those values we must completely shun and ostracize those who are divisive, and hateful. And we must include both our political and religious leaders in this list. We must truly want for our brothers and sisters what we want for ourselves. Religion taught us that, but we have instead used religion as an exclusive club to build up our ego. I am hopeful though, because at the core, we all want a peaceful life. We want to love and be loved. It is that simple.

People become hopeful when they feel they matter. They want their voices heard, their identities and issues respected. Sometimes I get calls and emails from strangers who are distraught. They write from Bahrain or call me from Malaysia and Sweden. They are angry that their societies discriminate against them because of their faith, that their sexual identity is evil and they are therefore treated with contempt. Sometimes these strangers cry on the phone but with some assurance, they feel empowered. Sometimes, however, it is not that easy to help them overcome self-doubt. Optimism can only survive when everyone's voice becomes relevant, equality exercised, and when opportunities flourish.

America gave me the opportunity to be me. To truly be who and what I want to be, no holds barred. As an immigrant, I strongly reject the naysayers who speak of the American Dream being dead. Yes, America is not perfect, but it is a country that inspires. If societies and thus governments of the world can focus on inclusivity and equality, building societies that benefit all rather than divide and conquer, then there would be more optimism in this world.

> I STRONGLY REJECT THE NAYSAYERS WHO SPEAK OF THE AMERICAN DREAM BEING DEAD. YES, AMERICA IS NOT PERFECT, BUT IT IS A COUNTRY THAT INSPIRES.

### *How do you hope your work inspires people for the future?*

I'm a mother, a wife in an interfaith marriage, and a musician. Tying them all together is my activism. The meaning of the question, "What is your purpose in life" took a new turn post-9/11. As a songwriter it used to mean getting that next song published, or getting that next award. Although I've had some level of success in the music business, that treadmill didn't lead to a fulfillment of the soul.

9/11 was a turning point for many people. For me, a Muslim in America, it has been life-altering. In the aftermath of 9/11, America became an ugly place for Muslims, but there was beauty in it. It tested me. With the freedom to think and read, for the first time, I allowed myself to discover pure Islam. What I discovered was liberating. All the cultural baggage about a woman not being allowed to do the call for prayer or to lead prayer went out the window. The discrimination and many social ills such as female genital mutilation were cultural and branded as Islam. So the next step was for me to ask, "How do I practice an Islam that is truer to its teachings, if the mosque I attend isn't good enough?" The simple answer was to start my own community.

> IT IS ONLY IN AMERICA THAT ISLAM CAN BE REJUVENATED AND REINTERPRETED WITHOUT ANY CULTURAL CONSTRAINTS.

Fortunately I wasn't the only Muslim in America experiencing this soul-searching. Collectively, a progressive Muslim movement was born, namely Muslims for Progressive Values. I know taking a stand against a tradition that is unjust ruffles feathers. Changing peoples' habits and beliefs is difficult, but it is only in America that Islam can be rejuvenated and reinterpreted without any cultural constraints.

The best way to live a fulfilling life is to challenge yourself and to ask, "Is what you say or do good enough?" What actions can you take to make a positive impact on someone listening and watching? By challenging tradition, many Muslims here in America, and throughout the world, are starting to see a different way of practicing Islam. Simply put: if the Islam you practice discriminates, is unjust, abusive, is hierarchical, is patriarchal, and misogynistic, then how can you call it Islam?

As Muslims, the *al-Fatihah* is the all-important verse in the Quran that sets the tone, the direction on how we are to live our lives—"Guide us to the path that is right." I interpret this for my own life simply—to live an honest life, and to do so, especially, when it is the difficult choice to make.

Living an honest life means thinking honestly, sincerely, not maliciously, and not deviously. When you think honestly, the words you utter are sincere and lead to honorable actions.

Marriage is an individual, family, and communal event. At one interfaith marriage I officiated, the mother of the Muslim bride had requested I give a five-minute talk about interfaith marriages, in other words, to address the many family members at the reception who had an issue with the marriage. My message to the reluctant family members discussed the historical and cultural origins of their unwillingness to accept "outsiders". In the past, women lost their religious, cultural, and tribal identities to accept that of their husband, and so, Muslim women could not marry non-Muslim men, in fear that their Muslim identities would be shed. But this is not the culture we live in today in America. Obliging cultural norms by having the groom convert to Islam would have been a lie. Deep down in their hearts, everyone involved would have known it. Starting their lives together on the straight path of honesty is what the newlyweds had chosen to do. Their marriage was a true example of *al-Fatihah* at its best. Several of the elders, men and women, came up to me after my short speech and thanked me for reminding them about the meaning of *al-Fatihah* and for showing a new way to interpret Islam. Some even offered support for more female imams!

We Muslims need to be honest. We need to speak the truth about the shortcomings within our societies, and we need to have an honest discussion about solutions. Parroting the phrase, "Islam is a religion of peace," runs hollow when we are unjust toward each other. Peace cannot exist without justice. Justice can only be upheld with truth.

Through the centuries, as human beings, we have become better on issues of human rights, but we still have ways to go. The Internet and telecommunications technology

> PARROTING THE PHRASE, "ISLAM IS A RELIGION OF PEACE," RUNS HOLLOW WHEN WE ARE UNJUST TOWARD EACH OTHER.

have expanded our communication capacity. From villages beating drums as a form of communication to cell phones via satellites and video conferencing on the Internet, our new technologies have enabled freedom of speech and of thought. If it wasn't for the Internet, 1.3 million people from around the world would not have been able to witness how we conduct our prayer services, a woman leading prayer. Our sermons for human rights and equality are videotaped and viewed. This alternative message of Islam is now being heard by anyone with a cell phone, and there are hundreds of millions of them. Mind you, this Islam is not new but the difference is that it is being lived out. Just as technology enables for messages of intolerance and hate, it is now our responsibility to counter that with messages of justice and human dignity for all.

What we are seeing is that when messages of hate and murder are directed at a particular gender, sexual orientation, religion, or race there are many who now come forward in the spirit of collaboration and humanity countering the hate and violence. Thanks to technologies, our consciousness and awareness of injustices have become more acute and our actions point to a humanity that is well—more humane.

It is only through knowledge, reading, and communication that we can fathom that we truly are in this together. And only when we have understood this, can we understand the values of equality. Using these values as the tool of measurement, we see a direct correlation between our actions and how it affects others, whether they are our neighbors next door or our neighbors thousands of miles away. For example, voting against marriage equality affects the spirituality and the finances of same-sex couples; my consumption of gold can severely impact the environment and health of others in the African continent. The values of equality force us to respect each other. And we have already started to see this respect come to fruition.

Consciousness is the change that needs to happen in each individual. Once our collective consciousness is raised, then the issues we have today such as the right for girls to attend school, who you marry, sex slave, child prostitution, and many more, are issues we know we can overcome.

In its current form, American Islam does not reflect Islamic values and neither does it reflect the American values of "justice for all". For future generations of American Muslims it is imperative that Islam retains not just its values but its relevance and relatability to America and in the twenty-first century. Given the diversity of America's religious and non-religious citizens, the separation of church and state is probably one of the most important core principles to keeping the peace. Allowing any one religious group to dominate, or to allow religious laws as an alternative means to settling disputes, such as the Jewish halakhah or Islam's sharia law, is a mistake. Secular laws cut across race, religion and in most instances, class. It is these laws that enforce equality.

> THE QURAN OFFERS AN IDEAL, AND AMERICAN LAWS GIVE US THE SPACE TO LIVE OUT THOSE IDEALS. THIS IS HOME.

Only in America, and not even in most European countries, do we have the luxury of freedom of expression, even blasphemous ones. To support any form of laws against blasphemy is to support the thought police. Only in this free environment are we forced to hear different perspectives, and it is only from learning about each other can we be better human beings. This actually fits neatly for Muslims as we are mandated in the *Quran*:

> *"We have created you into nations and tribes for you to learn from each other and not to hate each other"* (Quran: 49:13).

The *Quran* offers an ideal, and the American laws give us the space to live out those ideals. This is home.

247

# ROSS BORDEN

*Ross Borden is the founder and CEO of Matador Network. He has traveled to over 60 countries and lived in Spain, Kenya, and Argentina. He currently splits time between New York City and his native San Francisco.*

matadornetwork.com

## GET OUT THERE

Americans don't travel much. Only 33 percent of us even own a passport, a figure that's been inflated since immigration began requiring more than a driver's license to visit Cancun. With this being the number one destination Americans make it to abroad, we can safely assume the percentage of us who visit countries in addition to Mexico is much lower.

I was lucky enough to travel when I was younger and caught the bug at an early age. After going on to study abroad in Spain, work in Kenya, and spend time "in between jobs" in Argentina, I can look back and point to travel as the most significant source of education in my life. Along the way, I've observed the numerous benefits that travel offers people who make it a priority. And I've witnessed firsthand how friendly, open-minded American travelers, simply by making the effort to travel to faraway places, can tear down stereotypes and spread a message of peace.

You could argue that the other 67 percent of Americans don't have enough money to travel. To which I could call, "Bullshit!" and highlight the fact that most countries are far less expensive than the U.S. Instead, I attribute the trend to fear. Fear of the unknown, fear of disease, fear of crime—or for some, fear of a violent death at the hands of terrorists.

Indeed, we're led to believe the world is a very dangerous place. If you asked most Americans what they thought of a trip to Colombia, they'd probably warn you of rampant kidnappings. If you said you were headed to hitchhike through Rwanda, most would recoil as they imagined getting caught up in political violence. If you announced you were leaving for Iran, they'd assume you'd be destined for a secret government prison.

The fact is, all three of these counties are perfectly safe for the average independent American traveler. Unfortunately, a combination of our media, Hollywood storytelling, and the ulterior motives of our government has the average American Jedi mind-tricked into thinking overseas travel is a risk not worth taking.

Here's why they're wrong, and why that's a problem for everyone. More travel = more peace.

Perhaps the most important reason Americans should travel abroad more is the collective benefit we realize from meeting people of different ethnic and religious backgrounds. In turn, they benefit from getting to know us. Due mostly to our decades of aggressive foreign policy, and the size and ubiquity of the U.S. military, there are millions of people in the world who don't like America. I've been challenged dozens of times while traveling abroad by people who think of America as a juggernaut that strides around the world doing whatever it pleases, leaving war and poverty in its wake. Regardless of how accurate you find these assertions, America's military

**MORE TRAVEL = MORE PEACE.**

presence abroad lends plenty of fodder to those trying to rally sentiment against the U.S.

Less than a year after the terrorist attacks of 9/11, I was hitchhiking through Kenya, stopping in places like Lamu, Kilifi, and Mombasa—towns with many predominantly Muslim neighborhoods. Since I was traveling alone, I spent a lot of time chatting up anyone who would talk to me, a practice that one afternoon landed me in a Mombasa restaurant full of working-class Muslim men. A TV in the corner blared an English newscast featuring a particularly hawkish speech being delivered by George W. Bush. Everyone there knew I was American. To say it was tense would be an understatement. As the speech went on, I started receiving verbal attacks from the others in the restaurant: "Your country has declared war on Islam! Why?" Instead of getting up and leaving, I held my ground and chose my words very carefully. I explained that the views of our President were not shared by every American. I explained that the Americans I knew had absolutely nothing against Muslims, and that we understood the fact that Muslim extremists and terrorists account for a miniscule percentage of the total Islamic faith. I also shared my opinion that there is absolutely no excuse for extremism rooted in violence that kills innocent people, Muslim or American.

The group of men, who moments ago had been passionately berating me, now sat and listened to what I had to say. A full hour of sensible political discussion later, I'd gained a new perspective on how East African Muslims see America, and the men at the restaurant had learned that not all Americans hate Islam. One of them invited me to dinner with his family that evening. I accepted and met him at his house nearby. We sat at a low table on the rug and ate a dinner of spiced fish and rice with his wife and three children. We spoke about travel and what had brought me to Kenya, and I answered dozens of questions about everything from my family to what it felt like to fly in an airplane. A chance encounter abroad had resulted in an unlikely friendship and changed the way an entire group of people thought about my countrymen.

In *The Clash of Civilizations*, Samuel Huntington argues that because our respective views of the world are so different, Islam and the West will always be at war with each other. Watching the news today, it would be easy to support the conclusion that we're destined for endless violent conflict.

I'm not in favor of giving up so easily.

Global understanding between Islam and the West will not come via a top-down process. It will be based in real experiences with ordinary people. On the other hand, the "clash of civilizations" will most certainly transpire if we leave it up to heads of state and purveyors of radical rhetoric on both sides. The fact is, most Americans are ignorant of the complex history and regional variations of Islam, and I'm sure most non-North American Muslims are ignorant of daily life in the U.S. The only way this will change on a large scale is if Muslims and Westerners meet face to face and find that they have more in common than they thought.

Mark Twain said it best:

> "Travel is fatal to prejudice, bigotry, and narrow-mindedness, and many of our people need it sorely on these accounts. Broad, wholesome, charitable views of men and things cannot be acquired by vegetating in one little corner of the Earth all one's lifetime."

We have a powerful and important opportunity as Americans to be our own ambassadors when we travel—proving to people in all the world's countries that we are respectful, hard-working, open-minded, and peaceful, regardless of what our government does or says. And stepping into the role of being one of these ambassadors should start when people are still young.

Travel is essential for America's young people. In 2010, only 1 percent of college students from the United States elected to study abroad. Although that number is increasing, progress is slower than it should be, and America as a whole would enjoy massive advantages if the figure were closer to 60 percent.

In the 1960s, the United Kingdom developed something they called "gap year." Still widely practiced there, and in other parts of Europe and the world, gap year encourages students to take up to a year off between their secondary and higher education and travel abroad to pursue internships, volunteer opportunities, or shoestring-budget backpacking. Many American teens graduating from high school and moving on to college (though they may have performed successfully on the SAT and taken the advisor-recommended number of AP courses) are far from intellectual maturity. Many lack a realistic understanding of the world, as well as the basic notion of just how lucky they are to have been born in the United States.

Widely adopting a gap year in the U.S. would better prepare our young people to participate in the globalized world we're already living in. Adapting to a new culture during a semester or year abroad and learning how other people live—through language, food, music, custom—becomes a transformative experience. It eliminates misguided preconceptions about the differences between "us" and "them." At the same time, young people (and Americans in general) can benefit simply from removing themselves from the United States for a significant period of time, regardless of where they travel. Mainstream American culture, and its obsession with material gain and celebrity worship, can make us lose sight of what's universally important: strong families, meaningful relationships, and overall happiness in our day-to-day lives. Equally worthwhile is an escape from mainstream American news media, whose content when it comes to foreign affairs is primarily rooted in fear-mongering and sensationalism, with the only things that seem to qualify as "news" being death, tragedy, war, and violence.

Freed from these insidious elements of "modern American life", young people are better able to figure out who they are and what inspires them. During an extended travel experience, they begin to emerge as open-minded adults. The students who return home are more worldly, knowledgeable, and compassionate—some in larger measures than others, of course—than when they left. Many will also be on a faster track to finding something they're genuinely passionate about—just in time to apply themselves in college.

As the founder of an independent travel community, I have read hundreds of stories and seen firsthand through interpersonal connections how travel acts as a force in uniting good people. A passion for travel is something millions of us have in common already, and people who are curious about the world also tend to share a sense of optimism about it.

When you travel, you often find yourself in need of assistance from strangers. You might be lost and needing directions; you may even be looking for a meal and place to stay the night. Throughout my travels, I've been continually shocked by the warmth and generosity of the complete strangers I've encountered.

It is so healthy for humanity as a whole to know that most people are good, and that in 99 percent of situations, we can count on and trust one another. The only things holding us back from unlocking this optimism and a better world are fear and excuses. Put them aside and we will all have a more enlightened America.

**PEOPLE WHO ARE CURIOUS ABOUT THE WORLD ALSO TEND TO SHARE A SENSE OF OPTIMISM ABOUT IT.**

254  AMERICAN DREAMERS

# NATALIE BAILEY

---

*As a foreign correspondent based in Bangkok, Natalie traveled to some of the most remote parts of South and Southeast Asia with her notebook and camera as her only companions. Her creative non-fiction and journalism have appeared in* GOOD Magazine, Reader's Digest Asia, Forbes Travel Guide, The Boston Globe Sunday Magazine, Real Simple, Military Times, *and* IRIN News.

## MCDONALD'S 2.0

I am not proud that I called McDonald's at four o'clock in the morning. And much to everyone's befuddlement, it wasn't for my usual hot fudge sundae.

Please, first understand that though I have an acute aversion to television, country music, and fast food when in the United States, I am drawn to these beacons of American familiarity when I find myself far from home. Though I love sticky rice and bamboo salad with an undeniable passion, during my time in Bangkok, I occasionally delighted in forking over three dollars for a Happy Meal to appear at my doorstep. My pleasure derided from more than the soggy fries and plastic toy, it was the promise of avoiding the madness of the hot streets clogged with motorcycles and strange goods. For once I could "press 1 for English" and have limited miscommunication. To boot, it was like America improved—McDonalds 2.0—I had never experienced the distinct luxury of fast food delivery. Quite simply: I was lovin' it.

Though the McDonald's twenty-four-hour hotline did have an English option, giving directions to my residence —a condo slightly off a street with an impossibly difficult fifteen-letter-long name (Krungtepkreetha) and with no true landmarks in sight aside from a herd of goats (one was purple, so that could have helped in a pinch) and a train station that was about a mile away—was not an easy task... for me at least.

But one lazy Sunday, I hedged my bets and spent a good thirty minutes trying to communicate my location. Within minutes of hanging up I was rewarded with the aforementioned hot fudge sundae (ice cream seemed risky in case they got lost, but I was feeling lucky).

A few weeks later, a domestic disturbance startled me from sleep and continued to confuse and terrify me into the wee hours of the night—Did I hear someone in my house? What were these people yelling in Thai? Why was that man banging on the gate and honking? It was at this unlikely hour that my time invested with McDonald's delivery paid off again. As my heart pounded and my groggy mind tried to make sense of the continuous shouting, I peeped out my window to the confounding scene below and considered my options:

- Do nothing and hope whatever is happening stops (that hadn't worked so far).

- On second thought, rolling over and playing dead in my nightgown if someone really did break into the house did not sit well with my intuition.

I decided to call the police. I dialed the Thai emergency number...no answer. I tried and tried and when I finally heard a "Krahp?" I discovered, in stringing together the longest Thai sentence I could muster, "Poot Angrit dai mai?" (Do you speak English?), that they only spoke Thai.

After exhausting my other options (friends who all turn off their phones at night and the United Nations emergency number, which was outright unhelpful in all of the bureaucratic glory I had come to expect), I did the aforementioned laughable act: I called McDonald's for help.

When I explained my predicament in the simplest terms possible in a quivering whisper: "There is danger, you have my address, can you call the police for me and tell them how to get here?" they laughed in that nervous Thai way often elicited by a foreigner asking something ridiculous and they put me on hold.

About an hour later, three police arrived outside. Turns out it was a neighbor's belligerent ex-boyfriend causing the ruckus. Nonetheless, as the sun rose, I felt the weight of having been through a harrowing, life-threatening ordeal as I caught my work flight to Hong Kong.

Though ultimately, I am not certain exactly how the police were delivered to me; did Ronald McDonald step in? All I know is that they were neither fast nor food. In all of this, I learned a few lessons. Firstly, I devised a better contingency plan. If there is a next time, I'm ordering a Filet-O-Fish whether I want it or not. But mostly my encounter with the presumed Hamburglar forced me to reassess what I was doing in this far-flung country, with my support system precariously resting on a food delivery service. Why was I so extremely removed from my comfort zone in a place where I did not speak the language or have absolutely any ties?

The short answer was that I craved the exotic. Moving away from my Midwestern roots to the East Coast after graduating college satiated my wanderlust for a few years, but eventually the brunch and beggars I found in New York were no longer enough. I wanted to live somewhere hot and sticky and rugged, with a ceiling fan and that vague threat of monkeys and lizards. I wanted a place where I would confront life's real challenges; a place that would give me a bird's eye view of the United States.

The choice I made to move to Bangkok straight out of graduate school, following the great recession of 2008, was unthinkable to many, especially for those in my parents' generation. But I represented a new American Dream that traded the stability of a house, car, and even couch, for one thing: adventure. Ironically, it was outside of the land of liberty that I felt free. From Bangkok I traveled far and wide; I built my savings; I became part of the global community.

Of course, living abroad is no longer what it was when the American Dream consisted of picket fences and 2.3 children. I had a cell phone that worked in the middle of nowhere, email at my constant disposal, Facebook, and video chat—the list goes on, and yet, acute culture shock and homesickness sideswiped me upon my arrival. I realized how brave travelers before me had been—going off into the great unknown, with no comforts to speak of, not even hamburgers. Nevertheless, being tens of thousands of miles away, I came to identify with my appreciation for the special, and simultaneously for the usual.

I knew I didn't want to be an expatriate forever. I wanted to return to the U.S. an improved version of myself, enriching the fabric of the culture through my own reversed immigrant experience. My dream was to come back somebody new. After swinging between countries with rich histories, untrustworthy governments, and a relatively low regard for safety in the midst of several natural disasters, the sweetest words were those of a border control official at JFK who

> I REPRESENTED A NEW AMERICAN DREAM THAT TRADED THE STABILITY OF A HOUSE, CAR, AND EVEN COUCH, FOR ONE THING: ADVENTURE.

said, after flipping through the eighty pages of visas in my passport, "Welcome home." But what I overheard in passing, a few days later, was similarly comforting thanks to that harrowing night on the other side of the world: "Would you like fries with that?"

Why yes I would.

260 AMERICAN DREAMERS

# PANTHEA LEE & ZACK BRISSON

---

*Panthea Lee and Zack Brisson are the founders of Reboot, a service design firm tackling global governance and development challenges.*

thereboot.org

## A FIGHTING CHANCE

We dream of a future where everyone has a fighting chance. Luck plays an enormous role in all of our lives. Where and when we're born largely dictates the opportunities we're afforded. Unluckily, much of the world is born into difficult, debilitating circumstances, without the chance to realize their ambitions and dreams. Some of these circumstances, such as geography, are a result of forces outside of man's control. Others, including global development policy, are within our control. We hope for a future where we proactively manage what factors we can, to ensure that everyone has at least the opportunity to care for themselves and their families.

Good work today means carefully considering the consequences of our actions, now and into the future. It means understanding the connections between social, political, and economic forces worldwide, and it means making informed and responsible choices that, at the very least, mitigate crises instead of exacerbating them.

Most disasters are not random acts of fate—they are man-made. Terrible events, such as earthquakes and floods, are unavoidable, but they only devolve into true disasters through bad decisions and ineffective systems. A powerful example of how the bad decisions of a few lead to disastrous consequences for millions happened in Somalia. The country's 2011 drought could be called an act of fate but it was only a disaster because faulty foreign interventions resulted in an extremely fragile country that didn't stand a chance in the face of crisis.

**WE CAN'T AVOID DROUGHTS, EARTHQUAKES, OR FLOODS. BUT WE CAN AVOID THE WORST DISASTERS IF WE ARE THOUGHTFUL ABOUT HOW WE ENGAGE WITH EACH OTHER.**

We can't avoid droughts, earthquakes, or floods. But we can avoid the worst disasters if we are thoughtful about how we engage with each other. People often talk about wanting to "do good work" that "helps the world". A great place to start is by minimizing the harm we and our governments inflict on the world.

We've observed a general lack of public interest in global development and, specifically, the role of government and multilateral organizations therein. Many people think these institutions are irrelevant, at least in their daily lives. There's also a halo effect over them; the nature of their work—"saving the world"—gives them an air of unimpeachability.

But these institutions have enormous impact worldwide, and the decisions they make affect billions of lives. Further, the global structures they've set up and maintain will continue to have outsized impacts for generations to come. And there just isn't enough critical examination of their activities.

There is a growing societal consciousness about how corporate policies affect lives and livelihoods worldwide. We should take that same critical perspective toward our governments and global development actors. The good news:

it is becoming easier to understand and contribute to the processes of governance and development. Empowered, often by new technologies, citizens have been able to pressure powerful institutions to be more transparent in their decision-making. Technology has made it easier for us to realize our collective ideals by democratizing access to information, by sparking the imaginations and firing the ambitions of those previously marginalized when they compare their situations to others, and by enabling dreamers and doers around the world to collaborate in realizing an improved, shared future.

To bring change to the world, we need to first understand how the world works. We need to become informed global citizens.

Most mainstream media doesn't encourage people to engage in global issues, and actually prevents them from understanding other populations. U.S. media often portrays poor or troubled regions of the world as having intractable challenges, and the implication is that it's always been that way. That's just not true. If you look at the history behind certain troubled places of the world, the dark secret is that often the great Western nations of today had a hand in their downfall. It's less true of the U.S. than the European powers, but American policies and interventions have done their part in causing turmoil worldwide.

If more people understood the United State's role in today's trouble-spots, more may be compelled to act. That's not to say a sense of guilt (which can become a modern-day "white man's burden") is the only or best way to understand the suffering of the world. We believe basic empathy is more important. If people saw a clearer picture of the unmet needs and egregious violations of human rights faced by billions worldwide, we think they would act.

We've met women who have seen five of their own babies die from diarrhea for lack of clean water. We've met people

> TO BRING CHANGE TO THE WORLD, WE NEED TO FIRST UNDERSTAND HOW THE WORLD WORKS. WE NEED TO BECOME INFORMED GLOBAL CITIZENS.

who have gone crazy because of the constant hum of the drones flying above their heads, killing "militants" as well as innocents and devastating their communities. And time and again, we meet people who only want a better living for their families, just like the rest of us. It's only due to the circumstances of birth (luck and happenstance), that they go through extreme hardship and/or exploitation as they seek to fulfill this basic, human desire.

We're trying to make these stories palpable for more of the world. A lot of Reboot's work involves ethnographic research—we listen to the stories of people who often don't get to tell their stories. Ethnography literally means "a portrait of people." Having talked to thousands of people whose lived experiences are so different than our own, we've learned to recognize our own flawed assumptions, and we try to paint more honest, accurate portraits of people's situations and needs. We then take these portraits to policymakers, to push them to act, and we work with institutions with the ability to improve these situations to design programs that do so.

Reboot strives to improve lives around the world, and we work on global governance and development challenges. While we've never described ourselves as a "think/do-tank", it's a good approximation of our daily work.

We engage in a fair amount of advocacy work (the "think" bit), as we evangelize for new and more inclusive ways to tackle human development challenges. We believe that public-sector and development solutions should be designed with a greater emphasis on the actual people who are on the receiving end of those policies and plans. And we spread these practices in the field, working with a host of world-changing organizations—the "do" part.

Unlike traditional think tanks that research and propose solutions to policymakers, we also do the hard work of implementation. It's great to have an innovative policy idea or

> UNLIKE TRADITIONAL THINK TANKS THAT RESEARCH AND PROPOSE SOLUTIONS TO POLICYMAKERS, WE ALSO DO THE HARD WORK OF IMPLEMENTATION.

talk about how you might want to change things, but it's very different when you get down to the hard work of actually changing things. When the rubber hits the road, does your idea work or not?

No matter how sound a theoretical framework, if a plan can't sustain real-world factors, there's no point. Not only does Reboot study the human, contextual, and institutional factors that will make or break a solution, we also test interventions in the real world and adjust them based on how people really react to them. That takes a long time, but it also ensures that solutions are useable, and thus will be used.

We help organizations understand where their resources can be most effectively applied, and we work with them and the communities they serve to design solutions that are truly fit for purpose. We mostly work with institutions that we believe have the ability to affect positive social change at significant scale—this often means multilateral organizations, international NGOs, and large corporations.

Some pretty thorny questions come across our desk. After a country has toppled its autocratic ruler, how can the international community support its democratic, post-revolution ambitions? In the wake of a devastating natural disaster, how do you organize resources and design systems to help people rebuild their lives as quickly as possible? In countries with tight state controls on media and information, how do you inform citizens of their basic rights so they can demand more accountable governments?

We use systems thinking and design principles to break such questions down into their component parts; to identify, assess, and prioritize potential points of intervention, then to design effective policies and programs to address them. Design provides a robust set of tools to navigating and improving complex systems. It's very helpful for answering questions like: What are the motivations, constraints, and

> NO MATTER HOW SOUND A THEORETICAL FRAMEWORK, IF A PLAN CAN'T SUSTAIN REAL-WORLD FACTORS, THERE'S NO POINT.

capacities of different actors? Where do diverse interests intersect and diverge? How can we align opportunities and challenges to maximize the odds of successful interventions? That said, practitioners must remember that design only provides a set of guiding principles and analytical tools—the biggest mistake we see people making is to treat them as dogma.

In our work, time and again, we see practitioners forced to make assumptions about people they serve or places they work in. They often do so based on existing literature or "expert" opinions, but in international development work, literature can be scant or non-existent and even experts are often far away from ground realities. Even here in the U.S., policymakers in D.C.—most of whom have never been poor—sit in boardrooms poring over presentations filled with impressive graphs and tables, working to "solve poverty" in America.

**RIGID RULES AND TECHNOCRATIC BLUEPRINTS ARE USED TO ADDRESS CHALLENGES THAT ARE FLUID, COMPLEX, AND IN UNFAMILIAR CULTURES AND PLACES.**

Too often, policies and programs are designed based on theoretical constructions of reality or "best practices" taken from wholly different contexts. Thus, it should be no surprise when such solutions don't work. But governments and development organizations—for a variety of reasons—are largely set up to solve problems this way. Rigid rules and technocratic blueprints are used to address challenges that are fluid, complex, and in unfamiliar cultures and places.

Thankfully, there is a growing recognition that program design needs to be more grounded in field realities and driven by the communities they serve. In the age of Big Data, we think there is something to be said for engaging face-to-face with the communities you serve. For us, we know it drives us in a different way; it makes us less willing to settle for poorly thought-out or poorly executed solutions because we know the people it's going to impact. They are people with names and faces, people we've shared tea with, people we've laughed with, not just random points in a dataset.

The world's challenges are interrelated. There are people who champion health, education, clean water, or any number of important factors as key to solving the world's problems. But we see each of these issues as symptoms of deeply rooted and structural challenges. Thus, we don't choose to focus on particular sectors or regions; rather, we increasingly work on cross-cutting issues in government and institutional accountability.

What we do maintain is a very keen focus on services, which are the transactions between institutions and people. These are the most concrete means of improving livelihoods, and thus of realizing human rights.

We believe that the sum total of the basic services people receive is an accurate measure of a society's real-world embrace of human rights. This is an inherently practical approach to human rights, and an evolution in the theory of how societies can be improved.

It's important for everyone to have a theory of change—a well thought-out and workable strategy for how your own actions and work can make a difference. And passions can originate from the most unlikely of places. We have a friend who traveled to Latin America, fell in love there, and thus has continued to focus on the region. Another decided to devote his life to improving education in America after having watched a moving documentary on the topic. And all that is great—more people should run with what their heart tells them, regardless of whether that issue is trendy of whether there's a strong body of evidence to back up their choice. There are enough challenges plaguing our world, this work isn't easy, and so you need to really care about whatever topic you care about to be able to stick with it, and to be able to make the sacrifices you're going to need to make.

> WE BELIEVE THAT THE SUM TOTAL OF THE BASIC SERVICES PEOPLE RECEIVE IS AN ACCURATE MEASURE OF A SOCIETY'S REAL-WORLD EMBRACE OF HUMAN RIGHTS.

208 AMERICAN DREAMERS

Panthea Lee 269
& Zack Brisson

*Courtesy of Panthea Lee*

270 AMERICAN DREAMERS

# JON FRIEDMAN

---

*Jon Friedman is a designer who has been shaping the next generation of sustainable consumer products for top consumer brands. His professional experience with product development has put Freight Farms on the map for its innovation and sustainable design.*

freightfarms.com

## FREIGHT FARMS

Freight Farms introduces a scalable farming platform that can be operated anywhere. By up-cycling shipping containers into a source for high yield crop production, Freight Farms makes food accessible in environments where farming has never been possible.

Freight Farms eliminates the inefficiencies associated with commercial farming and streamlines every element of the growing process, from seed to harvest. Each unit is outfitted with advanced climate technology that creates the optimal growing conditions needed to maximize any harvest. The configuration of the system delivers high quality production at a low cost of operation and uses a fraction of the energy compared to traditional and greenhouse production. Unlike these other methods of commercial farming that grow food by the square foot, Freight Farms grows food by the cubic foot. This allows up to three thousand plants to be harvested at one time in a single unit.

A world full of Freight Farms would mean that EVERYONE would have access to fresh, quality, and affordable food. Our food system would no longer be harmful to our environment (the current food supply system accounts for one-third of humans' carbon footprint). Freight Farms are built for universal access, commercial growers, and community farmers alike. The system provides a turnkey solution to farming in places that lack the infrastructure or climate to grow food.

Freight Farms also puts the profitability back in the hands of the farmers.

My dream for the future is that our global society will progress in more conscious and sustainable directions. There is a lot of room for American innovation. Technology is progressing at a rate that leaves room for different applications of older technology. An app can help make a product better, but is not always the best answer. As a country, we still have a long way to go in making sustainable practices the most profitable method of doing business.

We have a lot planned with Freight Farms. We have only scratched the surface of what we can do with our system. We are expanding our product line to offer more crop varieties and soon, even expand beyond plants. Our goal is to make food accessible everywhere, so we plan to bring Freight Farms to everyone who needs them.

> A WORLD FULL OF FREIGHT FARMS WOULD MEAN THAT EVERYONE WOULD HAVE ACCESS TO FRESH, QUALITY, AND AFFORDABLE FOOD, AND OUR FOOD SYSTEM WOULD NO LONGER BE HARMFUL TO OUR ENVIRONMENT.

273

# NADER TEHRANI

*Nader is the principal of NADAAA, a design, architecture, urban design, and industrial design firm in Boston, Massachusetts. He is the founding principal of Office dA, which he headed for twenty-five years. Nader also heads of the School of Architecture at MIT and for the last twenty years has taught at MIT, Harvard, and RISD.*

nadaaa.com

## CHANGING THE FOUNDATION OF OUR KNOWLEDGE

### What is the current state of design?

One of the most radical things that has happened is the Internet. It has taken a discipline that had a rarified and highly tuned knowledge base and made it accessible to a much vaster population. The education that may have once only been accessible to people at Princeton, Harvard, and MIT is now something that is affordable and accessible to people in all corners of the world, from Chile to Iran to China. Design is more accessible. Design becomes more democratic. Design can be afforded, implemented, and intuited by much larger populations.

We have also seen a shift in production. If modernism was defined by mass production, digital fabrication affords mass customization. The kinds of forms, construction protocols and configurations that are possible geometrically and affordably are the result of what computing has been able to render. These two things, together, are changing the landscape altogether. Both the intellectual landscape as well as the physical landscape.

### How do we build for the future?

There are some things that have already changed and I don't think the discipline has caught up with them. In the old days we used to think of cities as organisms that evolved over decades or centuries. Now, if you look at places like Shenzhen, among other Chinese cities that have evolved, they sprouted up out of a village and gained millions in population over twenty years. This is unprecedented and there are few techniques and urban design protocols that have prepared neither the academy or profession for that. This is a work in progress.

At another level, the kind of research being done at MIT is formidable. For instance, in our course, How to Make (Almost) Anything, in which digital fabrication and interactive technologies are being taught, we create a more responsive environment. You do not just exist in space. Architecture is another protagonist. There is a call and response in relation to your environment. At the most mundane level, heating is not just something you turn on and off, it knows when to turn on and off in relation to your body's presence.

In material sciences we are investigating materials that at the molecular level—the nano level—are changing in their behavior. Things that have no insulation quality will now gain a much larger insulation potential just because of their makeup. The ways in which concrete or metal behave will be

> YOU DO NOT JUST EXIST IN SPACE. ARCHITECTURE IS ANOTHER PROTAGONIST. THERE IS A CALL AND RESPONSE IN RELATION TO YOUR ENVIRONMENT.

different to how they behave today. The way we can control the density of materials is also important because if you look at the composition of a beam it may have different properties at the top versus the middle. The gradient by which you can begin to manipulate structural systems will optimize them, make them more efficient, save money, and be more sustainable. These are just a few examples in which you get to control the parameters of the elements that go into design. Think about how many materials and resources are wasted per building. If you look at the major wastage of resources in the world, the construction industry eats up a good portion of that. The kind of research that we do at the molecular level of materials can contribute a great deal to that change.

## *What does the city of the future look like? Will we use buildings differently?*

The question of how things look versus how they perform is an age-old architectural predicament. If it has proven anything it is that there is a complete divorce between how things look and how things work. Digital fabrication affords, with the same economy, the ability to build almost anything, any variable of geometry. You should see the way they have optimized the way they make Doric columns and Ionic columns. They do it through CNC fabrication. We know that the means by which certain freedoms have been created through digital fabrication do not produce future looking forms. They deal with the very substance of history as much as they do with forms of innovation invoked today or maybe ten years from now.

When you get into the question of performance however, we have a lot to look forward to. When you look at both how we are operating within the academy as well as in practice, the lines between design, architecture, engineering, industrial design, product design, and urban design have all

> **THERE IS A COMPLETE DIVORCE BETWEEN HOW THINGS LOOK AND HOW THINGS WORK.**

been completely blurred. Much of this is due to the way in which each of these disciplines has begun to impact each other. A lot also has to do with the environment we live in right now. Not only is the economy strained but the natural resources of the world are cornering us so that we need to ask the questions, "How do we get things to work? How do we establish reciprocity between design and what it gives back?" To that end, my sense is that we will be able to have a much clearer understanding of the repercussions and performance of piece or artifact that we design in the future. That will be done on a simulation basis. If the computer of the last twenty years has been dedicated to constructing form and imaging in different ways, the computer of today is dedicated to managing fabrication protocols, and the computer of tomorrow will anticipate by simulation all of the repercussions: structural, environmental, resources, and so forth. Effectively, every platform and software is heading in this direction. Not because they are a consultancy to design but they will become the very substance of design itself.

**THE COMPUTER OF TOMORROW WILL ANTICIPATE BY SIMULATION ALL OF THE REPERCUSSIONS: STRUCTURAL, ENVIRONMENTAL, RESOURCES, AND SO FORTH.**

*What are the issues facing America today regarding our cities and design? How will these be solved?*

The American city of the last half century or more, since World War II, has been centered around the expansion of the city through the suburban condition. Even the exam you take to become a registered architect is founded on examples that deal with the suburban condition way before they do the city. Suburban sprawl has demonstrated all of the ways it requires and is dependent on fuel, transportation, infrastructure, and a great waste of resources. One of the issues that needs to be dealt with, not purely at a design level, but at a political and administrative level, is how we can get Washington, D.C. and the states to work around agendas of city making. We need

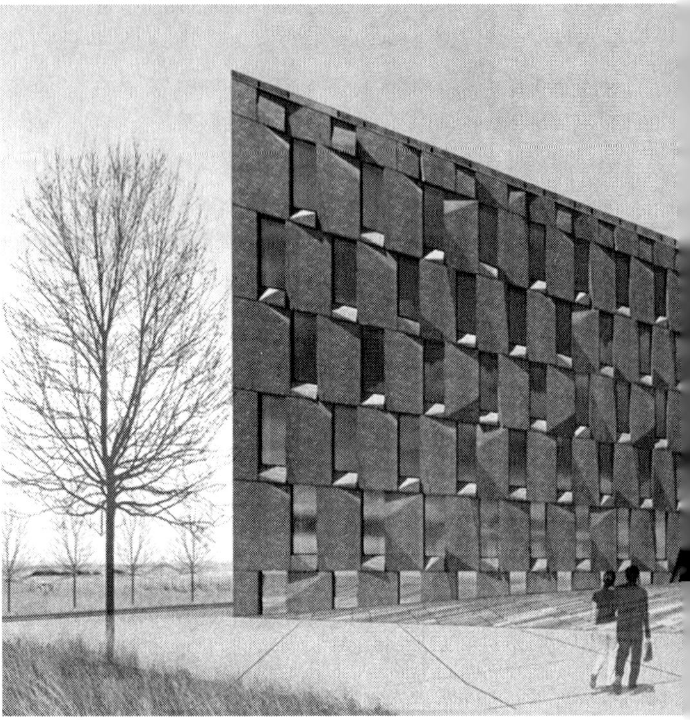

*Courtesy of NADAAA*

to create zonings and codes that offer alternatives to sprawl by densifying the existing suburbs, creating new centers (that do not require transportation to a central hub), and that innovate with existing conditions.

The second issue is that we need to begin imagining how federal funds, now going into highways and transportation networks, which are of no public value outside of transport, may be imbued with a public function outside of just transportation. Right now there are no monies put into the design of the public space, and no resources put into infrastructure as a public mandate. The city of the future may tap into this potential to transform at a public level—this after decades of privatization in the United States.

My sense is that beyond the grassroots level of what we do in our studios and academies, this is one big political obstacle that awaits us. The only other way I can imagine it changing is to alter the structure of patronage. That is not a question of educating architects further but is a matter of educating the clients. The only way to do that is by introducing design, the arts, and the city as curricular agendas at the beginning of our education. The city is the foundation of our knowledge and our societal platforms. How is that left out of the curriculum?

> **THE CITY IS THE FOUNDATION OF OUR KNOWLEDGE AND OUR SOCIETAL PLATFORMS, HOW IS THAT LEFT OUT OF CURRICULUM.**

***If you had one area to focus on, and in so doing change the world, what would it be? What is your progressive soapbox?***

That is a big question. I will speak to it from the perspective of what I do on a daily basis. There is no limit to design and there is no limit to innovation. The scales of design have an impact on society at every level whether you are designing silverware, a chair, a room, a house, an institution, or a piece of infrastructure that gets you from here to there. The way in which design culture can impact and alter the world is boundless. It seems that, beyond myself, who operates in all of these areas, we are really invested in design as a way of producing new forms of knowledge and a transformation of culture. This is how we can impact the way communities work. Design is everywhere.

And so, we need to construct patronage in ways that can take advantage of what design thinking brings to society. Design thinking is not built on linear knowledge. It is rooted in lateral thinking—making unexpected connections you would never expect—and built on the risk to fail. Design thinking is based on making the unexpected. Bringing design thinking back into the core of education is an important factor.

The integration of design into education and patronage as a central pivoting point of politics is important. Look at how public funding has been chipped away over the years. This is where design thinking can do the most for culture. Design has ways of integrating diverse ways of thinking. Architecture, for instance, is not a precise discipline. When you are an architect you have to know about engineering, environmental engineering, space planning, urbanism, material properties, and you have to know a little bit about a great range of disciplines. It is also one of the unique forms of production that has the potential of producing new forms of knowledge based on speculation, experimentation, and risk.

## *Does design have the power to change the world or is it just a by-product?*

Neither is right or wrong. We are programmed and led by a certain form of patronage, we learn from culture. But there are also key moments in design that produce new forms of knowledge and transform culture. No, I don't think that design or architecture can end world hunger but the ways in which we plan cities, create transportation, and change

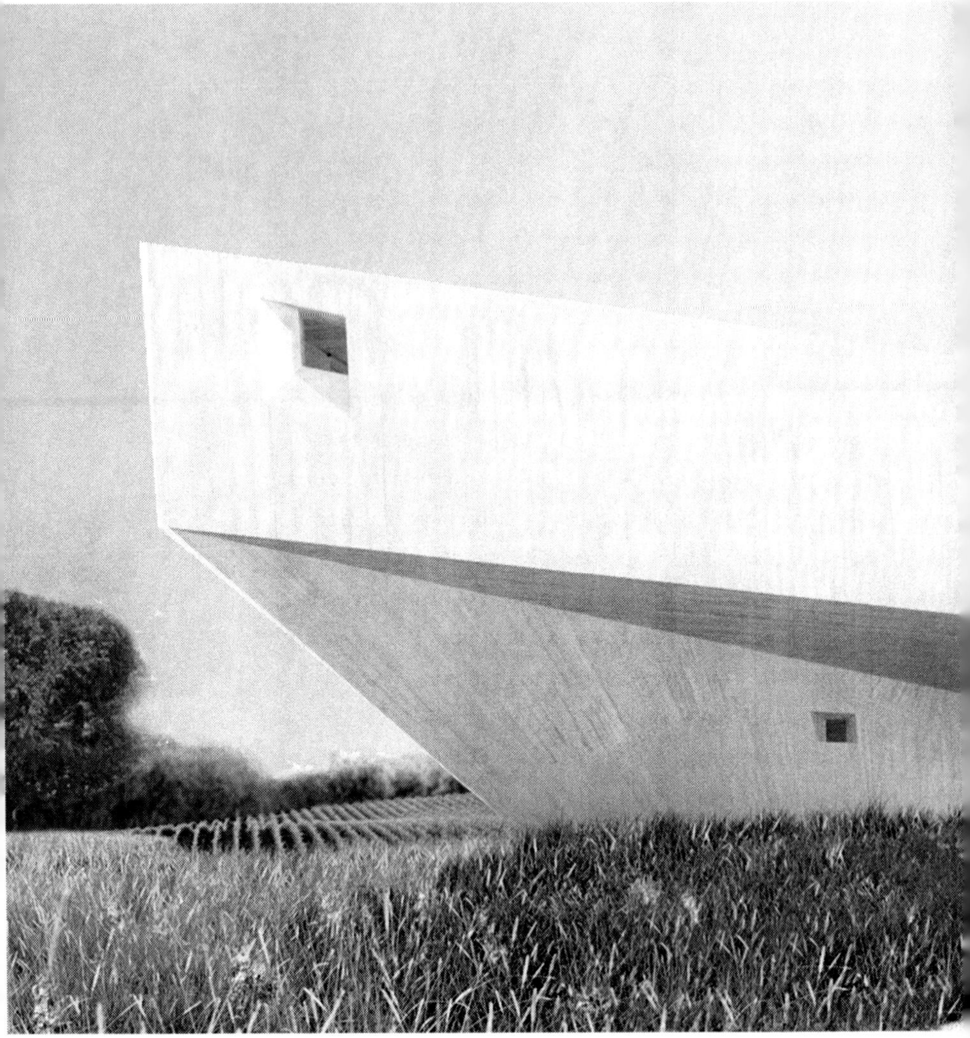

*Courtesy of NADAAA*

> THE WAYS IN WHICH WE PLAN CITIES, CREATE TRANSPORTATION, AND CHANGE OUR ENVIRONMENT ALL HAVE MASSIVE IMPACTS ON THE WAY WE USE RESOURCES.

our environment all have massive impacts on the way we use resources. They impact how we produce better environments for people to live in.

As much as everything has changed, it is amazing how much does not change. A lot of sustainable strategies that people adopt today are not only high tech but are absolutely low tech. With all of the most sophisticated solutions of how to "green up" a building, there is nothing like opening a window to circulate the air. Daylighting is the same thing. We have some of the most sophisticated lighting devices, some of which are very expensive and are very green, but that does not compete with daylighting.

There are cultural questions that need to be brought to the table and be able to operate within many paradigms. They need to operate between the traditional city, the modern city, the suburb, and the city of the future in ways that leverage smart thinking as a basis for flexibility. There are many ways to be flexible, but part of it is to not take on a monocular vision towards this or that technology.

285

# ELLEN DUNHAM-JONES

---

*Ellen Dunham-Jones is an architect and professor of architecture at Georgia Tech where she coordinates the Master of Science Degree in Urban Design. Her research focuses on redevelopment in suburbia and she co-wrote* Retrofitting Suburbia *with June Williamson. She is also the chair of the board for the Congress for New Urbanism, an organization that removes the obstacles to designing and building great urbanism.*

## RETROFITTING SUBURBIA

***Does retrofitting suburbia mean reworking the existing structures or tearing them down and starting over?***

It depends! We have approximately one billion square feet of vacant retail space in the U.S. right now, in addition to loads of aging office parks, garden apartment complexes and zombie subdivisions. Different strategies apply in different conditions. In some cases, the availability of such "cheap space" is a boon to entrepreneurs, new immigrants, and community-serving uses. Hundreds of "ghostboxes" (dead big box stores) and strip malls have been reinhabited as schools, libraries, theaters, medical clinics, gymnasia, churches and spaces for artists and restaurants. In other cases, where there's access to mass transit or a strong market it often makes sense to clear the site, connect a walkable grid of tree-lined streets and parks, and build up with a mix of retail at the ground floor and several floors of housing and offices above. Over forty dead malls have been redeveloped to provide their communities with downtowns, Main Streets, and urban lifestyles they never had before. But, densification won't work everywhere and sometimes the best strategy is to re-green the site whether by reconstructing the wetlands that may have been displaced when the project was first built or by constructing parks or community gardens. In addition to the ecological benefits, the provision of such green amenities tends to increase property values and attract new investment, providing a double win for the community.

## How does retrofitting suburbia change how we live and how we interact with and in our spaces?

It minimizes the distinctions between what a city is and what a suburb is. The model most of us carry in our heads of a metropolitan area is of a dense urban downtown core and rings of "bedroom suburbs" extending outward at lower and lower densities. This American model was identified in the 1920s but is really out of date today. We now have more office space, more industry, and more retail outside the downtowns than inside – but they're separated by zoning such that the amount of time suburbanites spend in their cars vastly outweighs that of city dwellers.

It isn't only the uses in suburbs that are changing. The demographic shifts are dramatic too. We tend to think of suburbs as family-focused and yet since the year 2000, two-thirds of suburban households have not had kids in them. The baby boomers have become empty nesters (for the most part) while growing chunks of those suburban office jobs are held by childless Gen Y folks. Counter to the Gen X suburbanites raising kids, both of these groups are looking for opportunities to live a more urban lifestyle within suburbia. They are looking for walkable Main Streets, buzzing with activities and opportunities for engagement, nightlife, restaurants that are not just fast food, and a social life that doesn't just center around a school. Retrofitting is both helping revive the old suburban downtowns and creating new centers. Instead of the old model, the city of the future is a metropolis that has multiple, diverse, mixed-use centers and re-greened and reinhabited corridors.

**THE CITY OF THE FUTURE IS A METROPOLIS THAT HAS MULTIPLE, DIVERSE, MIXED-USE CENTERS AND RE-GREENED AND REINHABITED CORRIDORS.**

## *What practical effects does that have?*

It does a number of things—mostly by reducing the number and length of car trips. The average suburban household generates about ten trips per day. Even if you get one of those to be on foot or bicycle that is a 10 percent reduction in dependence on oil and a reduction in pollution. It is significant. By combining live-work-shop-play in compact, walkable neighborhoods, suburban redevelopments enable residents to substitute up to 45 percent of those trips by foot – even more if transit is available. This has tremendous benefits to the environment, the wallet, public health, and the community's social capital.

Plus, once you start getting a series of nodes of denser development transit in suburbia becomes much more feasible. Whether extensions of heavy rail, new light rail systems, streetcars, Bus Rapid Transit, regular bus, or shuttle services, there has been a tremendous surge in recent years of access to transit in the suburbs. This has triggered a great deal of retrofitting around station stops while improving ridership. This is especially helpful for the suburban poor and elderly—both of whose numbers are growing more rapidly than the nation's as a whole.

## What cities are doing this right? Who has planned right or is currently changing for the better?

The Washington, D.C. area has undergone an amazing transformation. The successful transit-oriented redevelopment of five suburbs on the Roslyn-Ballston MetroRail corridor in the early nineties resulted in the highest per capita ridership levels in the country and a high-density mix of uses. Continued extensions of MetroRail further into the suburbs coupled with revised zoning codes that encourage urban development patterns have led to impressive redevelopments and increasingly exciting places. The new planning codes encourage new buildings to be built close to the widened, tree-lined sidewalks with pedestrian friendly frontages. Well-used new town squares and public greens provide civic anchors and green infrastructure to the new density and more sustainable lifestyles. .

Denver is also an exciting place to watch. There, the trigger for redevelopment has been reuse of dead mall sites. Eight out of thirteen of their regional malls either have or have announced plans to be retrofitted into something more resembling an actual Main Street and a two to four storied urban neighborhood.

Other cities with less strong markets are doing innovative reinhabitations and re-greenings. Cleveland has been encouraging interesting, green reuses of vacant lots. Neighbors can get together and reuse vacant lots for community gardens, put in geothermal heating, or put in bioswales or rain gardens. This can reduce the need for expensive repairs to aging stormwater infrastructure while improving the neighborhood.

There are many, many more examples. We have almost five hundred case studies in our database of various kinds of retrofits all over the country. I get a kick out of documenting all of the creative ideas people come up with.

***I can see these kind of things working well in cities like Detroit and Cleveland. They are full of empty lots, struggling to maintain vast sections of town and it is easy to rezone and push new development. How does this work, however, in cities like New York, San Francisco, or Los Angeles, where space is at a premium and it is hard to rebuild an entire area?***

There are definitely different strategies. In places that are losing population, like Cleveland and Detroit, the strategy is primarily one of re-greening, whether it's farming or reconstructing the wetlands. What market there is for redevelopment is better steered downtown. In Flint, Michigan, city leaders recognize that water is just as finite a resource as oil and may well be the main asset they can leave their grandchildren. The county established a model land bank program for tearing down abandoned homes, cleaning up former industrial sites, and promoting green uses of the land that will contribute to clean water for future generations.

In growing cities like New York, San Francisco, and Los Angeles we find much more redevelopment. Often, this is as simple as building on top of the parking lots and infilling between existing buildings.

There is a great example of this in Hyattsville, Maryland called University Town Center. It was a 1960s office park with fully leased ten-story office buildings and surface parking lots until DC MetroRail opened a station kitty-corner to the property a few years ago. At this point the owner thought, "Hey, those surface parking lots don't make sense anymore." He built a parking deck, inserted a new Main Street between the office buildings and built housing, a cinemaplex and plans for a new grocery store on top of the old parking lots.

***How do we balance between the mixed-use benefiting the community and simply cramming potential customers close to a mall? It seems developers could be densifying purely for-profit and not for sustainability.***

It is up to every community to incentivize the kind of development they seek. They do this mostly by controlling the zoning and, in many retrofits, by covering some of the infrastructure costs. This gives planning officials leverage to demand a certain minimum number of affordable housing units, X percentage of public space, or, simply better design. This is key to integrating density so that it contributes rather than burdens the existing community. Design is also often able to resolve the differences between what a community wants and what a developer can afford to provide.

**IT IS UP TO EVERY COMMUNITY TO INCENTIVIZE THE KIND OF DEVELOPMENT THEY SEEK.**

The real estate profession has picked up on the idea that urbanism is both more fashionable and more profitable than the old mall. When developers hear from communities, "We'd like a Main Street but we also want some affordable housing and some offices," it is not really twisting their arms because they recognize that this is where the market is going. The best developers are well aware that density for densities sake won't hold value. Rather, it is about making great places that people want to walk in and be a part of.

Outside of Denver there was a very large regional mall in the town of Lakewood, Colorado. Lakewood was a collection of subdivisions. It never had a downtown. So when the mall died their first reaction was to find a developer to fix it. But, we really aren't building big malls anymore. One-third of our 1,100 enclosed malls are dead or dying. So instead, Continuum Partners said to Lakewood, "We will give you the downtown you never had." Instead of a one hundred-acre super block sea of parking, Belmar is now twenty-two blocks of very walkable, publicly owned streets. Two of them are lined with retail but have housing, offices and condos above them. The other blocks have a broad mix of townhouses and apartment buildings, all of it green construction and at a range of price points. There is a green park and a hardscape public space, both of which are reached by eight public bus routes. It's well-designed and well-built and provided a more urban lifestyle option for a segment of the population without taking away other choices. It's been a boon to the community's tax base and despite tripling density on the site, no new traffic lights were needed because so many of the trips are made by walking. Although Lakewood did not initially want a new downtown, they worked closely with Continuum all the way along and got a great place that they have embraced heartily.

### *As the environment, economy and need for housing changes, how do we change our development?*

I'm convinced that generational change is a big driver, but it will be evolutionary as attitudes catch up to reality. For instance, many of the people who serve on local planning boards or volunteer with their city councils are retirees. I admire them tremendously for taking the time to do civic service. However, having seen decades of suburbanization lead to traffic congestion, declining property values in aging subdivisions, and bypassed shopping centers, their primary motivation is often to protect their neighborhood from any change. They want to preserve it for future generations that they assume will look just like they did when they moved in forty years ago. As a result, they tend to resist densification, multi-family housing, mixed-use, or transit. And yet, the reality is that 90 percent of new households through 2030 are expected to look a lot more like the retirees. The percentage of Americans over age sixty-five will just about double and the percentage over age eighty-five will triple by 2030. Will it take the loss of one's driver's license for older, suburban Americans to begin to value the more urban neighborhood characteristics they resisted?

While elderly Americans fear the isolation induced by losing their drivers license, we see quite the opposite amongst younger folks. Sixteen to thirty-four year olds are driving almost 24 percent less today than that same cohort ten years ago. Getting a driver's license the minute you can, on your sixteenth birthday, is down 20 percent. The love of the car and the freedom it implied is ingrained in the older generation. They can't imagine that this younger generation is not as enthusiastic about cars. The younger group grew up chained to the car, shuttled everywhere by mom and dad. 75 percent of Gen Y grew up in the suburbs and yet 77 percent say they want to live in an urban core.

The challenge is in figuring out how to negotiate between those two generations.

## *How do we build cities now, meeting current needs, while also being flexible with future needs? We can't just rebuild every generation.*

I think we would lose more than we would gain even if we could rebuild every generation. There's a lot to be said for cities that incorporate the patterns and patina of multiple generations and lessons learned over time. They tend to be much more appealing places than "instant cities".

This is actually one of the biggest criticisms of suburban redevelopments and other examples of new urbanism. Yet, as charming as the incremental city is, we can't improve the economic, social, or environmental sustainability of suburbia incrementally, one building at a time. We need to retrofit suburbia in big chunks in order to integrate a walkable street network, affordable housing, public space, green infrastructure and transit. Yes, we have to learn how to do a better job of designing "instant cities."

**LET'S TAKE ADVANTAGE OF THIS LULL TO CHANGE OUR REGULATIONS AND POSITION OURSELVES SO WE CAN ATTRACT THE KINDS OF DEVELOPMENT WE WANT.**

One of the new tools in this regard are Form-Based Codes. They establish the framework of building mass and frontage in relation to an approved master plan of streets, blocks and lots. This balances predictability of the urban form (which is necessary to protect property values and encourage investment) with flexibility on use. This is very different from conventional suburban zoning codes which are inflexible about uses and segregate them with very little attention to overall interconnectivity. When done well, code-writing engages the community in democratically deciding on the shared framework of streets, public spaces and infrastructure while allowing private uses to evolve over time

***How do we create incentives and engagement in the poorer and needy areas? How do we push development where its most needed instead of new shops for those who already have them?***

That's in fact much of what retrofitting suburbia is about. Since 2005, more Americans in poverty have been living in suburbs than in cities and that's before the recession and foreclosure crisis hit! Before the recession, most suburban poverty was concentrated in inner-ring suburbs built in the 1950s and 1960s. New development was out at the sprawling and ever-expanding periphery. Retrofitting those underperforming properties along dying commercial strip corridors in the poor but closer in communities was a way to take advantage of existing infrastructure in a relatively central location while giving those communities a boost. During the boom years as urban lifestyles were increasing in popularity, most such suburban retrofitting was market led and planning departments were simply in a reactive posture

Since the foreclosure crisis, there have been two particular changes. Poverty has expanded into the outer suburbs and planning departments have been able to catch their breath and become much more proactive. They're updating their zoning codes, their capacity to engage in public-private partnerships and they're learning how to better leverage their public land. Many are realizing that they can no longer afford to deliver services at low densities and are incentivizing higher density, mixed-use development as a means to both respond to the emerging market and be more fiscally responsible.

One example of a place where local planners are being very innovative at responding to multiple needs is Covington, Georgia, about twenty-four miles east of Atlanta. In this small town a subdivision built about eighty homes out of a planned two hundred forty before it went bankrupt, becoming what is now often referred to as a "zombie subdivision." The city recognized that it would pull down the entire city's property values if they didn't do something. Even though politically they did not want to be interventionists in the market, they were uncomfortable letting these empty houses sit and attract crime. So they set up a redevelopment authority and essentially empowered it to become the master developer. Nine different banks were holding the various parcels and it was a nightmare to acquire ownership of a critical mass of the partners.

It required trolling the foreclosure auction websites. Then, they engaged in a suite of strategic partnerships. They partnered with Habitat for Humanity to clean up townhouses that had been built but never occupied and got families in them. They partnered with a low-income tax credit developer who replatted some of the larger lots into small lots with fifteen-year leases to purchase homes. They partnered with their housing department and several nonprofits to build housing for seniors and the disabled and to bring in a few offices, an incubator kitchen, and a café. The result, still under construction, is that what had been designed to be a regular owner-occupied subdivision will now be a diverse place where low income households should be able to thrive. It took an incredibly visionary planning director and a supportive city council to be willing to take some amazing risks.

The Covington example also gets at the crux of the difference between urban and suburban. Under the suburban model any new development or any new additional house is just another car on the road adding to congestion. It means more kids into the school system and raising taxes. It is perceived as a negative. Suburbia has a tendency, because of development patterns, to see additions as negative. In urban conditions, the more you add the more there is to support the community. It is seen as positive instead of growth being seen as negative. That is the goal.

### What is your dream for our future?

It's clear to me that the auto-dependent pattern of suburbia is simply not sustainable. Sprawl increases per capita energy use, ecological footprint, chronic disease, and social segregation. It's also no longer affordable. The cheapest land and consequently, the cheapest housing, tends to be the furthest out. For generations, our country's default model of affordable housing has been "drive 'til you qualify." That worked fine and provided access to the American Dream for the past sixty years. Now, however, the cost of gas has risen to the point where the savings associated with that cheaper house are eaten up by the additional costs of transportation. We do not have an alternative model of affordable, healthy housing and that really worries me. Publicly provided affordable housing is a drop in the bucket compared to the needs of ordinary working households. My dream is to provide affordable housing with affordable transit while retrofitting the abundant underused and underperforming properties lining our aging commercial strip corridors.

Every community has its commercial strip with miles and miles of fast food joints, strip malls, tire shops, motels, some tired office parks, and garden apartment complexes. Some of the properties have been reinhabited with entrepreneurial new businesses and community-serving uses. But, for the most part, there are more underused, out of date, inefficient buildings, and empty parking lots than can be used in their current form. These are the opportunity sites, but of course, in their current condition no one who has a choice would want to live along one of those streets. They are depressing, unsafe, and ugly. If we retrofit commercial strip corridors into walkable, transit-served boulevards lined with trees and compact, great housing, we get the triple affordability of transit, energy-efficiency, and affordable housing while meeting goals of health, sustainability, and affordability. It could also be an enormous jobs program, rebuilding our infrastructure that we desperately need.

> MY DREAM IS TO PROVIDE AFFORDABLE HOUSING WITH AFFORDABLE TRANSIT WHILE RETROFITTING THE ABUNDANT UNDERUSED AND UNDERPERFORMING PROPERTIES LINING OUR AGING COMMERCIAL STRIP CORRIDORS.

### What is the tourist pamphlet pitch for the city of the future?

Design matters! Especially the design of the public realm. Great cities attract tourists and residents less because of their specific indoor amenities as for their vibrant street life, beautiful squares, parks, and waterfronts. Design in suburbia has tended to focus solely on the attractions of private space, allowing the experience of public space to degrade into soulless suburban commercial strips, vast parking lots, and commercialized shopping centers. A renewed focus on employing the techniques of urban design to retrofit the suburbs is bringing great design to suburbia. The Congress for the New Urbanism, whose board I chair, continues to be a leader in redesigning suburbia to increase our happiness, our health, and our sense of community. The MSUD program I coordinate at Georgia Tech is preparing the next generation of urban designers to retrofit the habitat most of them grew up in to craft the kind of forward-looking, stimulating, and beautiful public realm they want to live in. I'm optimistic!

299

# ALEXANDER ROSE

---

*Alexander Rose is the director of The Long Now Foundation, a group dedicated to providing a "counterpoint to today's accelerating culture and helping to make long-term thinking more common." Alexander is also one of the leads on the 10,000 Year Clock, a project that will build a giant clock inside a mountain, left to tick away for ten thousand years.*

longnow.org

## BUILDING FOR THE FUTURE

### What is The Long Now Foundation and how did it come together?

The Long Now Foundation began as an email discussion by a group that eventually became the founding board. One of the early inspirations was a story of the beams at New College, Oxford. In the 1200s, when they built the college, there were large oak beams over the main hall. About five hundred years later the beams had become rotten and infested with beetles, they needed to be replaced. The school didn't know what to do because you couldn't buy trees and beams like that in Europe anymore, they had been deforested. It wasn't until they spoke to the school forester who said, "Well, we have the trees that you planted." It turns out that when the school had been built they had also planted a grove of oaks to replace beams like this. This kind of future thinking, something as simple as spreading out acorns on the ground and leveraged over five hundred years, solved a totally intractable problem. It is this type of thinking that inspired the eventual founding board of The Long Now Foundation. People like Stewart Brand, Kevin Kelly, Brian Eno, and Danny Hillis, who had all been in the tech industries.

There are certain issues, like the environment, climate change, hunger and education, that can't be solved on a very near-term horizon. They have to be solved on a long-term horizon and if you only prize the fast solutions, it makes all those problems totally intractable. The notion was to provide a kind of example and inspiration to doing much longer-term projects so that we can build stories, myths, and concrete examples of long-term projects.

Some examples of this have come out of the recent tsunamis. In the Indonesian tsunami there was a tribe in the Andaman Islands that everyone assumed would have been wiped out because they are a coastal tribe. Pretty much all of the coastal tribes had been wiped out by the tsunami in the direction of Indonesia. When they got there however, they found all of this tribe still alive. The rescuers asked what happened and it turned out the tribe had a legend that traced back several thousand years, "When the ocean retreats it will always come back even higher." This was a tsunami legend. What was interesting was that this tribe of people, considered basically a Stone Age subsistence fishing tribe, were vastly better prepared for a tsunami than the modern people of Sri Lanka, who, when they saw the water retreating, walked out on to the mudflats with their cellphones recording it. They were killed. There are times

> WE CAN HOPEFULLY BUILD STORIES, MYTHS, AND CONCRETE EXAMPLES OF VERY LONG-TERM PROJECTS THAT WILL GIVE PEOPLE THE EXCUSE TO ACTUALLY WORK ON SOME OF THESE MULTI-GENERATIONAL PROBLEMS

302  AMERICAN DREAMERS

*Image by Rolfe Horn, courtesy of The Long Now Foundation*

when, if you pay attention to that ancient knowledge, and if you have the ability to pass it down from generation to generation, you can leverage it.

**With this in mind, how do we start projects that increase options? How do we begin something today that has impact later on down the road?**

The first thing you should always be sure of is: "Is the project worth making a long-term project?" Sometimes it is worth making a whole institution around it and sometimes it should only be short-term. We have found cases where people have thought too long-term, take nuclear waste for example. The United States wrote a law that said we have to protect the future for ten thousand years, literally. That has actually hindered them from being able to come up with nearer-term solutions that would make waste safer. Because all of the solutions are required to last that long they can't do an iterative solution which is probably a better idea in their case. So first, get your time scale correct.

In terms of our projects, like the *10,000 Year Clock*, we are very rigorously trying to build a device that can plausibly last on that longer time scale. Figuring out that right time frame for issues like climate change or reducing carbon in the atmosphere, you probably need to look at them as multi-hundred year projects. If you tried to solve them in the next election cycle, you clearly can't do that. But if you were going to do it over three hundred years, what would be the way you would go about it?

*Image by Rolfe Horn, courtesy of The Long Now Foundation*

***To plan for the future, we have to start now, but we can't anticipate every event. What contingencies do we plan for? How do we build something that lasts and how much does hope and optimism play into it?***

There are some examples of other things in the past that have survived on the millennial time scale. For instance, the Pyramids at Giza are about 4,500 years old. They were robbed of all the treasures inside the tombs not long after they were built. They were robbed of their outside casing stones much later, after an earthquake loosened a lot of them and they were used to build mosques. We still have the pyramids fundamentally, and they are still a great tourist attraction and a UNESCO World Heritage site. They have succeeded in lasting for a very long time by having some easy to steal trinkets. Another place that used this technique (and both of these were obviously accidental) is the Taj Mahal, which was covered in expensive jewels. It was taken over by the British and instead of destroying the building (which did happen to many), they spent time prying the jewels out of the walls. By the time they finished, they felt they had extracted the value and didn't need to destroy the building. That is one technique; having some kind of highly valuable thing that can get taken away. People felt they had taken all the value away even though they had left a certain amount of it.

Another technique is to have an institution that can survive alongside it. You change your project from designing a clock for example, to designing an institution to last a very long time. There are examples of this in Japanese temples. One of the oldest standing wooden structures in the world is about 1,400 years old and is a Shinto temple. For a very long time it was the largest wooden structure ever built. It has been maintained by generation after generation of people.

There is another set of temples in Japan at Ise, which

are rebuilt every twenty years in an exact replica in adjacent sites. They disassemble one and reassemble another. This has been well documented for well over one thousand years, and with sketchy documentation, closer to two thousand years. This is an interesting example because the act of rebuilding the next temple is a very physical act that requires a master to teach an apprentice. The Shinto religion has survived the waves of other religions coming through Japan. I suspect that some of these temples, generational behaviors, and rituals have helped that.

**GET LOST AND FOUND AGAIN.**

Another technique for lasting a long time is to get lost and found again. The Dead Sea Scrolls or the paintings in the caves at Lascaux were lost for thousands of years and re-found at a time when people were ready to decide they were antique valuables and preserve them. Other things have been found at really inopportune times, like in the middle of a war, and have been destroyed.

The other thing that happens, one of the biggest dangers around things lasting, seems to be ideology. We often associate religion with very long-term survival, Shinto and Catholicism as examples. The problem with religion and ideologies is that they can lose out and there is a time when they become unfashionable or even threatening. Then people actively destroy all those artifacts. In very recent times, the giant Buddhas of Bamiyan in Afghanistan were all destroyed by the Taliban. Even as innocuous a symbol as the Buddha is, the Taliban felt it was upsetting and insulting to their religion. They spent many, many man-hours blasting these giant Buddhas out of the cliff face.

***So the best way to plan for the best is to plan for the worst and hope it doesn't happen?***

Planning for the best generally means you do nothing, right? Sometimes predicting an awful future is the best way to stop it from happening. I wouldn't take all of the negative views of the future as something bad. There were large predictions of overpopulation in the 1960s causing us to run out of food but people saw those and engineered our systems to solve them. We didn't run out of food by 1982 like they had thought we would. By making dire predictions, we often come up with ways of making those very predictions untrue. They can be very motivating.

> BY MAKING DIRE PREDICTIONS, WE OFTEN COME UP WITH WAYS OF MAKING THOSE VERY PREDICTIONS UNTRUE

### *What positive changes do you see?*

The Middle East, two thousand years ago, was one of the greatest places for mathematics. Then there was France. Then it was Germany. We in America had a peak in science around the time of the atomic bomb development and the Moon landings but this has been declining ever since.

Some people, who are actually changing the way we learn, might have a longer term influence. They are people like Sebastian Thrun at Udacity. Sebastian left Stanford to start teaching only over the Internet. Projects like this could fundamentally change the game. It turns out there is a lot of interest once you open the gates wide enough. There is not an interest problem. When Sebastian Thrun taught his Artificial Intelligence class at Stanford there were two or three hundred people who signed up. Up to 160,000 students signed up worldwide for the online course. That is a fundamental change and a very positive one for the future. If a poor kid in India can find Internet access, and have an aptitude for math and computer science, they can now take a class from one of the best A.I. designers in the world. That is a very positive thing. Projects like that are changing things in a fundamental way and doing great things for the future.

308  AMERICAN DREAMERS

# HIDESHI HAMAGUCHI

---

*Hideshi Hamaguchi is considered a leading mind in creative concept development, strategy building and decision management on both sides of the Pacific. In 1994, he developed Japan's first corporate Intranet. Hamaguchi also led the core concept development for the first USB flash drive that was introduced in 2000. Hideshi has spoken internationally on topics of innovation and strategy, received numerous design distinctions, including IDEA Gold awards, and served as a juror for the Red Dot Design Awards.*

## BREAKING BIAS

*How do we change the world? Where do we start?*

One of my theories is that the first thing you have to do is identify the bias. We are living in a bias and the new ideas and steps should be built by breaking biases. We have the bias of "robots help people." Can we switch that to humans help the robot? Do you remember the robot dog named Aibo? This was a beautiful idea. We know the robot is not perfect. Aibo is not perfect. Sometimes it would malfunction, hit its head on the walls and not understand commands, but it was cute. Because of imperfections we can give love and that switches the paradigm; and this is a very important moment. We feel that the imperfections are okay.

So this is an important step. We need to make unique things and break biases. We fail if we don't plan or don't make steps to the future. If we have a distant future goal, we need to have a step now. If we miss step one, we can't get to step two.

> **WE NEED TO MAKE UNIQUE THINGS AND BREAK BIASES. WE FAIL IF WE DON'T PLAN OR DON'T MAKE STEPS TO THE FUTURE.**

It is okay to dream the future, it is okay to dream. It is very important but the first step should be to go against the bias. The first step has to be unique. It is human psychology that if you see something already known, it is hard to be excited. We need excitement to move and progress is always asking humans to do something different. You can drive there with money, pushing an idea towards the future and some people do that.

When I was a kid I always had a pad of paper and drew the future. The future had tubes and cars but that never happened. It might happen in another five hundred or one thousand years because we are moving towards it, but the timeline is much longer that we thought. In one of my pictures, I was talking to a friend through my wristwatch. This has happened with my iPhone, and even more. I can talk with anybody on Earth. The future is coming, not broadly, but focused, like a tiny crack. So if you see the future you should carefully look at where to start making cracks.

The first era of the Internet provided people with the power to read and access information. After that, the Internet created the power of writing through the blog. Everyone can write a blog. Sharing information is the next era. We are entering this era and it is more complex. We have to make it happen in a unique way. It is not just reading or writing, it is more sharing and more communicating. To make it unique, we have to identify if it is a handshaking model or a broadcasting model.

We are in a very interesting era. There is a model and it can go back and forth and there is also a wrong way. We are seeing a lot of wrong ways and that means we cannot go back. With the environment, for instance, we are already past the threshold where we can go back. That is the reason we are freaking out. But we have information and that is good. We have more and more information and we will share it.

There are a lot of new things coming. Do you remember the arrival of Google? We freaked out and thought, "Google is a god!" It is not God. Now we have Facebook and Twitter. Once a corporation is established, they have DNA. The reason they grow is because they follow the DNA. If they don't follow the DNA, they fail. It is a dilemma. Google has a DNA. They are a search engine and then they put some advertisements on that, but that is them. If they go a little different way, they fail. Successful companies have to focus on their DNA.

**THE FUTURE IS COMING, NOT BROADLY, BUT FOCUSED, LIKE A TINY CRACK.**

*When our DNA causes problems, makes us consume too many resources or expand unethically, as examples, is it possible to change DNA? Both as a corporation and as a culture?*

That is a good question. I have never seen a company drastically change their DNA, even Microsoft. At first Bill Gates was against the Internet but suddenly shifted. If he had not shifted they would have failed, but he did. I have still never seen a company drastically shift their DNA though, that is why it is called DNA. In the future someone might. We are getting into that interesting era that I mentioned. One to two hundred years ago we were in commercial capitalism. If I took an apple to Japan, it had a big value. So if you have a ship and can reach the location in time, you can get the money. Now we are into industrial capitalism. That is a different paradigm. You have to have a technological innovation of some kind and that innovation can live in the machine or factory.

It is about the ideas. This is maybe called the Information Era or the Idea Era. It is easy to get money. There is a lot of floating money. The paradigms used to be high-risk/high-return or low-risk/low-return. But now, we have low-risk/no gain or low-risk/high return. If you come up with a new concept, you can make it online. You don't need a server, just rent or buy some part of the cloud from Amazon and market it by yourself. If you fail you just lose a small amount, but if you succeed, you have a chance for a high return. The system is changing. Younger people know that.

In this new era, you have to focus on technology. There are huge opportunities. I am pretty much optimistic about the future because it is about breaking the bias. If we break the bias we can make an innovative future. Our only fear should be, "Do we have bias?"

## *What are the biggest biases that need to be changed?*

I have discussions with consulting groups, principals and partners, and they ask me about the future and about trends. "How do you see that world?" They ask a bunch of questions and I answer, "I don't know." If you know the future, what are you going to do? Trends are trends. I don't want to spend my time on this planet thinking about that. We don't know the future or which way we will go. One way to attack a trend of the future is to just follow it. That is a wrong way to approach things. A second way is to just pick an option, A or B, or A and B.

The third way is to just break it. Create something totally

new. Create a totally new uncertainty which just absorbs the others. Innovation is this third way. If you are talking about innovation, not just survival, knowing the trend is not important. You don't have to spend millions of dollars analyzing the future or having a report.

Start thinking different. Start from a small amount of information. Think from nothing. People are afraid to build something from nothing but that is very important.

Even with climate change, the system is so complicated. People are freaking out but they don't see on their own or think by themselves. They don't feel by themselves. They follow someone's eyes, thoughts, and feelings, like Al Gore. But I am not Al Gore and it is dangerous to follow someone else, even someone with some authority.

Another important part is knowing what you can do. You have to do something you like. You have to do to something you can do and do something where you can contribute. This cross section is very important. For instance, if it is something you like and can do but people hate, you shouldn't do it. If it is something people like but you cannot do it, then you shouldn't do it.

There is a boundary that I can impact and a line where I cannot. I cannot help stop global warming. I cannot help a poor community in Uganda. There a lot of people talking about these big things, things they cannot solve. A lot of people also talk about things too close to them. We go to extremes, either out of the boundary or too close to our capabilities. The important thing is figuring out the edge and working on the edge. If everyone knew their boundaries and tried to solve some problem at the edge of their boundaries, that would be the best for human beings. Push outside what you can do and your boundaries will be much bigger than you think.

> THE THIRD WAY IS TO JUST BREAK IT. CREATE SOMETHING TOTALLY NEW. CREATE A TOTALLY NEW UNCERTAINTY WHICH JUST ABSORBS THE OTHERS.

314 AMERICAN DREAMERS

# JOHN MAEDA

---

*John Maeda is a graphic designer, computer scientist, academic, and author. His work in design, technology, and leadership explores the area where the fields merge. He is the current President of the Rhode Island School of Design.*

maedastudio.com

## STEM TO STEAM

### *What is the future role of art and design in the greater context of the world?*

The role of art and design has always been in flux, and the one thing we can be certain of is that it will continue to be so. The world will be an older world than the one we occupy —warmer, and more resource depleted than it is now. With greater despair will come greater hope—and greater art. With fewer resources will come greater ingenuity—and greater design. I truly believe that artists and designers will be the next great leaders. We know the world will be volatile and uncertain—and we know there are no better people to handle that kind of world than artists and designers.

## What is the future of art and design education?

> FOR THE PAST SEVERAL YEARS, I HAVE BEEN ARGUING THAT WE NEED TO ADD THE "A" FOR ART TO TURN STEM TO STEAM.

It depends on what it's like right now where you are. At a place like RISD, where we have been teaching art and design for 135 years with a deep, immersive foundations-based curriculum, I expect the timeless central tenets to stay the same. But a RISD education will also be in step with advancements in materials technology, fabrication tools, and knowledge platforms because of the people—who are constantly integrating new thoughts and practices. There are all kinds of questions about the value of higher education these days. There is also an increased acknowledgement that creativity and innovation are what will keep us competitive in the future. Science, Technology, Engineering and Math—the STEM subjects—alone will not lead to the kind of breathtaking innovation the twenty-first century demands. For the past several years, I have been arguing that we need to add the "A", for art, to turn STEM to STEAM. My experience as the President of Rhode Island School of Design has reawakened me to the world of physical creation. RISD is the ultimate culture of makers. There is no greater integrity, no greater goal achieved, than an idea articulately expressed through something made with your hands.

## Where is the world heading in regards to art and technology?

There's a definite disconnect that is gradually dissipating. Twenty years ago when I was talking about software as art to museum people, they literally ran me out of their houses. Today, when the Guggenheim holds a symposium on software as art, we think nothing of it. Change is happening, and change is gradual.

## What is the future of the "hybrid space" between art and design?

Any hybrid space is the best space to be in, but expect to be lonely. I heard Yo-Yo Ma talk about how when you have two ecosystems right next to each other, there is an incredible bio-diversity that emerges where the two intersect. It is deep, he said, yet it is sparse. To me, this says that people who cross boundaries bring a rich diversity of thinking, but are rare and lack the reassuring comfort of a community of like-minded others. RISD is an especially fortunate environment for hybrid artists and designers because we are half fine arts majors, and half design majors, and our campus is so small that the intersections are often frequent, unplanned, and joyous.

**PEOPLE WHO CROSS BOUNDARIES BRING A RICH DIVERSITY OF THINKING.**

318  AMERICAN DREAMERS

# LESLIE BRADSHAW

---

*Leslie Bradshaw is the President, COO, and Co-founder of JESS3, a creative interactive agency specializing in data visualization and visual storytelling. A native of Northern California and Oregon, Leslie is a sixth generation Oregon Trail pioneer who farms wine grapes with her family in her downtime. Leslie also is a regular contributor at* Forbes *on the topic of female entrepreneurship.*

jess3.com

## DATA DREAMING

The twenty-first century is a fantastic setting for playing oracle, not because it's any easier to make accurate projections, but because in so many areas of technology and media it feels like we're already getting a head start on tomorrow. We're now in the era of Big Data and we're moving into a future of Even Bigger Data. My dream, though, is a future of More Meaningful Data. And for that, we need two things: literacy and design.

When I talk about data, I really mean two things: data, lowercase and plural, are all of the quantitative and qualitative measurements we take of our world and ourselves;

*Courtesy of JESS3*

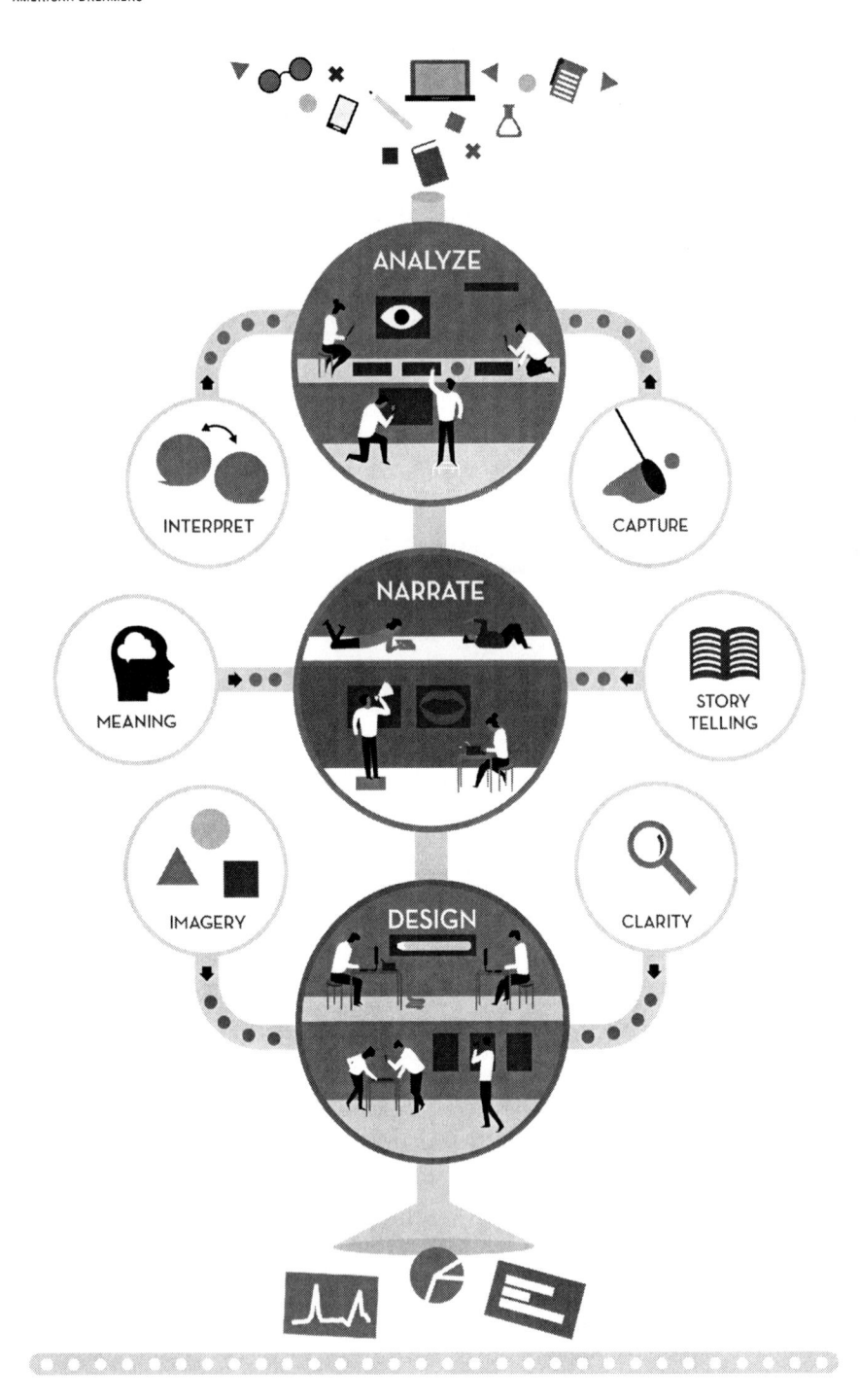

Data, capitalized and singular, is a whole that's greater than the sum of its parts, a bundle of actions and outcomes that, ideally, speaks to the relationships between those actions and outcomes. Visualization and storytelling are tools that help us understand and describe those relationships.

Data literacy isn't as simple as an ability to read numbers. On the production side, it's a process that involves different competencies at each step; on the consumption side, it's an acumen in judging the credibility of a final product. On both sides it's an understanding of the fundamental problems that can crop up along the way, from strategy to data collection to filtration to analysis to presentation:

*The things we want to measure, but don't know what data to collect.*

*The data we want to collect, but don't know how to capture.*

*The data we've captured, but can't use because they're not accurate.*

*The data we've captured, but don't know how to interpret.*

*The data that we misinterpret, because there's too much noise and not enough signal.*

*The data that we misattribute, because we mistake correlation and causality.*

*The data that we misuse, because we want them to support an agenda based on falsehoods.*

Without data literacy, we end up in one of the following scenarios with regard to Data: we don't collect it; we ignore it; we look at it, but don't apply it; we apply it incorrectly; we extract the wrong meaning from it; or twist it to support our (wrong) ideas. Data literacy can help us solve those problems, but it's only one part of the puzzle. Anyone can throw a few numbers together to make a quick statistic, or compile tons of them into massive spreadsheets, but without any real meaning to be extracted we're left with numerical gibberish, or "data salad," if you will. This is where design comes in.

Design is a process of making complex things understandable. It's a wonderful tool for communication, because it doesn't require a minimum level of functional literacy to understand it—it teaches to the student and, if done well over time, can help the illiterate become literate. Design is storytelling. Design is clarity. Design is empathy. Design is representational. Design is intentional. Design is meaning-making, and design is meaningful. And it's been that way since early humans first converted abstract thoughts and memories into concrete messages by painting them on cave walls. Design is a major facet of humanity; it's how we make the inhuman world more human. As Victor Papanek wrote in his seminal 1971 book *Design for the Real World: Human Ecology and Social Change*, "The only important thing about design is how it relates to people." On that note, I believe the only important thing about Data is how it empowers people.

> IT'S NOT THE SIZE OF YOUR NUMBERS, IT'S HOW YOU USE THEM.

It's not the size of your numbers, it's how you use them.

Data isn't particularly fun or interesting right now, but it can be, especially with the help of design and visualization. When we combine Data with meaning (story) and intention, we get better, smarter, faster, and more reliably predictive decision making. When we do so with clarity, conscientiousness, and empathy for our audience, we get more attention, more engagement, and less frustration.

If we collect the right data, filter and analyze them intelligently, and visualize them properly based on the right set of logic (establishing an elegant concordance between data as stimuli and graphics as responses), then Data can be transformative in so many aspects of society, from public policy to business to sports to finance to economics, and so many aspects of our individual lives, from health to work to time management to the "quantified self."

324  AMERICAN DREAMERS

# AARON KOBLIN

---

*Aaron Koblin is an artist and designer specializing in data and digital technologies. Aaron's work takes real-world and community generated data and uses it to reflect on cultural trends and the changing relationship between humans and the systems they create. His work is part of the permanent collection of the Museum of Modern Art in New York, the Victoria & Albert Museum in London, and the Centre Pompidou in Paris. He received the National Science Foundation's first place award for science visualization and two of his music video collaborations have been Grammy nominated.*

aaronkoblin.com

## ART AND DATA

### What kind of future do you dream of?

To me, the ideal future is a lot like the present, but, to paraphrase Carl Sagan, with human beings who have more of our strengths and fewer of our weaknesses. I'm a techno-optimist and I hope that technology will continue to make us more efficient, more intelligent, and more human.

*How can good work today make tomorrow better?*

Good storytelling passes down ideas to the next generation, so that hopefully they have an advantage that we didn't have. And they don't repeat our mistakes. Good work should have that effect.

Tell stories in the most thought provoking way possible. To me, this means making them interactive and explorable rather than passive. I'm excited about creating new possibilities by combining existing technologies. The future should involve things we're not even thinking about right now, so the first step is to keep thinking differently and continue trying new things.

Right now, I'm thinking about how to tell new kinds of stories with technology, especially mobile technologies. I don't know what will come of it, but it's something that'll happen eventually. It's just a matter of technology improving to a high enough standard and the right idea coming along.

Hopefully, it'll make storytelling more egalitarian and more suffused into our lives. I think of my phone now as a device for social networking and casual gaming. What else can it become?

*You've talked about the Internet giving us the ability to work together to create things that would otherwise be impossible. What is the next 'impossible' we are overcoming?*

> THE POWER OF COMBINED HUMAN INTELLIGENCE IS THE STRONGEST FORCE THIS PLANET HAS EVER KNOWN.

The ability to make stuff; check out Raspberry Pi... cheap, configurable computers are going to change the world. Also, personal fabrication. Amazing things are happening with 3D printers and computer- controlled milling machines. DIY culture is more powerful than ever.

## What will change in the way we use machines?

I hope we'll get back to building machines instead of just using them. I'm afraid of closed source. As the Maker's Bill of Rights states "If you can't open it, you don't own it." I'm also really excited about the potential of new interfaces. Not that I want a mobile phone built into everything I own, but smart sensors and common protocols may enable us to understand ourselves and our lives in more granular ways, and to interact with our surroundings in some new novel ways. I've seen the surface scratched with home automation—things like the Nest Thermostat, Nike+/FuelBand, Wii, etc. I'm eager to see interfaces with greater levels of detail so we can have simple high-level interactions, but quickly and easily dig down to the more granular preferences, options, and details.

## What can the small simple actions of many add up to?

Data, and data with the right angle can tell you amazing things about the world. No time in history have small actions been more powerful, as they can now be quantified so readily. I honestly believe the power of combined human intelligence is the strongest force this planet has ever known.

## Does more accessible and malleable data lead to more knowledge? Does it help us know each other better? Can it bring us closer together?

All of the above—but not without effort. Data alone doesn't create knowledge, it requires intelligence and research. Tools that bring us together can also push us apart. First and foremost we need drive, compassion, and a heavy dose of curiosity.

FIRST AND FOREMOST WE NEED DRIVE, COMPASSION, AND A HEAVY DOSE OF CURIOSITY.

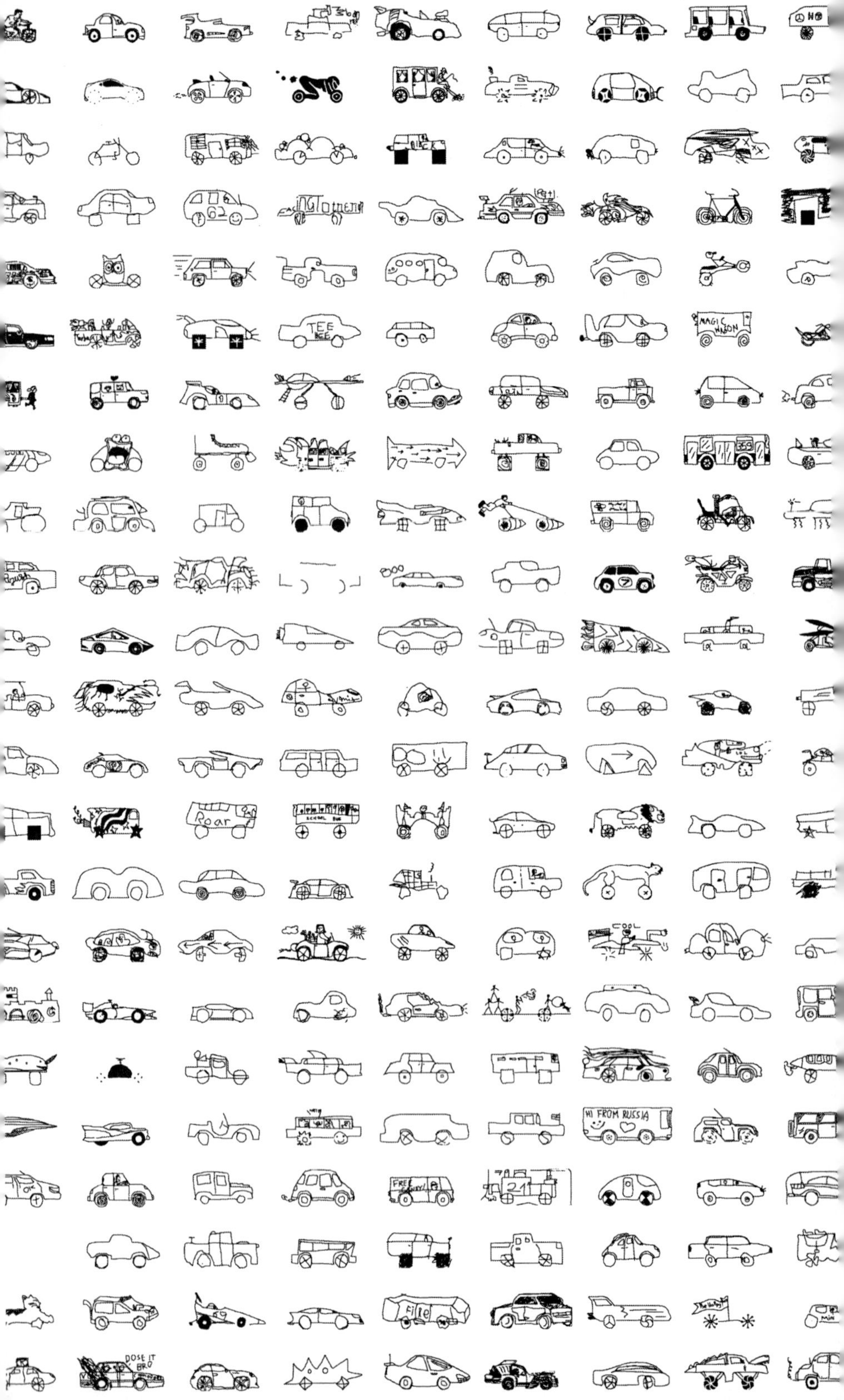
TEE HEE
MAGIC WAGON
Roar
COOL
HI FROM RUSSIA
DOSE IT BRO

*Courtesy of Aaron Koblin*

### *What is data unable to tell us?*

Honestly, data doesn't tell us very much at all. Data is usually the result of a very precise question, specifically a quantitative response to some kind of sensor. It's not our eyes that see, it's our brains. In this sense the term "tell" is problematic; data can provide a picture that we can use to tell thousands of stories. The real answers in life come from deep reflection, analysis, and play, which all start from data... but virtually none of the pursuits end there.

### *In a world where there are no technological limits, what other limits would you impose?*

Moral limits are the bedrock of our society. I think we limit ourselves too much in some areas, while at the same time giving too much leeway in others. What these limits are is one of the fundamental debates of civilization, if not THE fundamental debate. In a world without technological limits, morality becomes even more important than it is today.

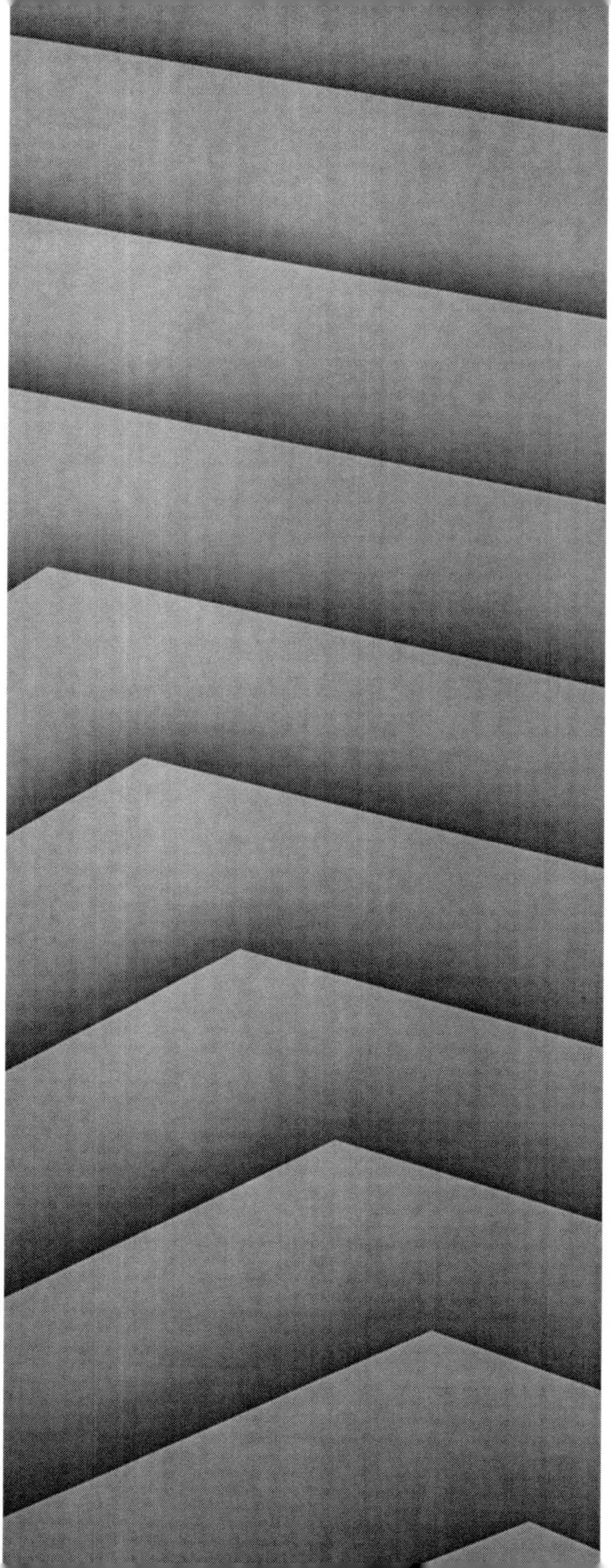

# RICHARD SAUL WURMAN

*Described by* Fortune *magazine as an "intellectual hedonist" with a "hummingbird mind", Richard has written, designed, and published eighty-three books on topics ranging from healthcare to atlases and the Olympics. He received degrees in architecture from the University of Pennsylvania and created the TED and TEDMED, conferences. He is currently developing the WWW conferences and continues to work on his global cartographic initiative, 19.20.21. Wurman is the 2012 Lifetime Achievement recipient of the Smithsonian, Cooper-Hewitt National Design Awards.*

wurman.com

## PATTERNS AND MORE PATTERNS

I am seventy-seven years old, born in 1935. Recently, I've thought the sociological model of life is a silo in which you start off as a private and you end up as a general; a tall silo of improving one's skills in a particular subject and getting better and better at it. For some inexplicable reason, early in my life, probably in my early twenties, my silo fell over. I didn't get better at anything. I just kept on doing different things. The different things were spurred on by this terrifying epiphany of ignorance; that I was a wellspring of curiosity, but not very intelligent.

It took a long time to get over this terror, but I embraced it. I accepted the fact that I could be interested in lots of things and find a cobweb of patterns between things. Maybe I would never be very smart or do anything very well, but I would maintain my curiosity. I would see a world that was all connected in this lattice of things. For most of my life, I was unsuccessful in terms of the world. I wrote a lot of books. People asked me to talk. I taught a lot. It seemed like I was okay. Financially, I was desperate. My abrasive, but charming, personality didn't always work. At forty-five, I found that I was basically destitute. I didn't have a job. I was fired from jobs. I didn't do anything different from forty-five to seventy-seven. Somehow there was a switch. Slowly all the work I had done before reached a critical mass. It became okay to be not so smart, but to be curious.

> **MAYBE I WOULD NEVER BE VERY SMART OR DO ANYTHING VERY WELL, BUT I WOULD MAINTAIN MY CURIOSITY.**

The work I've done has just been in the work that interests me. I started out in architecture. I did very well in the beginning. I graduated first in my class at the University of Pennsylvania. I got the gold medal in design. I took more courses than anybody. I had the highest average. They skipped me a semester. Then I got both a Bachelor's and a Master's in Architecture in 1959, one in February, one in June. I had never worked so hard in my life. I was thought of as the fair-haired boy in architecture. My mentor was, and still is, Louis Khan, even though he's thirty-eight years dead. He gave me permission to be more of myself.

I started doing books when I was twenty-six. Now I've done eighty-three books. I don't even know how many subjects they're on. Each one comes from the fact that I don't understand something and I do a book on it. One thread in my life is this compulsion to do books. It's a compulsion because I can do it by myself. I can get help on them, but

> **MY BOOKS ARE REALLY A BLOTTER PAPER OF MY EXPERIENCE FROM NOT KNOWING TO KNOWING, WHICH IS RECORDED IN A BOOK FORM.**

I publish them myself. No publisher will publish my books because I come to them being ignorant because I don't understand, say, healthcare. They don't want to publish it because they want to get a famous doctor to do it. If I do a book on Tokyo and I've never been to Tokyo, no one is going to want to support that because they want to get people who have lived in Tokyo for quite a while. My books are really a blotter paper of my experience from not knowing to knowing, which is recorded in a book form. I don't have a publisher, distributor, or publicist. I just do these different things. I'm interested in cartography so I build atlases. One of the major threads of my life is mapping. I'm still doing major mapping projects because I work with one of the largest cartography companies in the world, ESRI.

I am also launching a new project. It's an idea that I thought up called 19.20.21, doing comparative mapping for the great urban areas of the world to develop a language and methodology of how the cities can talk to each other. Each city collects and displays their information in the same manner. You would think it had been done, but it hasn't. That culminates in thirty observatories around the world. This comparative information is on flat screen and live around the world in a series of connected live small museums. That is getting underway now.

My curiosity always led me to want to speak to people who were smarter than me, so I started these conferences. I started a conference called TED. I started one called TEDMED. I just finished one called WWW, and I'm going to do one called Prophecy. I start these things and try to model what's the best way for people to gather and find out about things for myself. They're very indulgent. I invite people who I want to meet with, talk with, and ask questions of. It seems that other people like that too. I don't do it for the other people. I do it for myself. The books are basically for myself. And the maps are basically for myself. My life is really driven by trying to fill in this black hole of ignorance that I have.

I do not try to change the world. I know that if I do good work, historically, it has affected the world, but I don't try to have that effect. I am not a missionary. I don't have a mission to make a better world. I have a mission to do good work and I know that it has changed things, but I do not let that affect what I do next; not who I invite, not the topics for conferences or exhibits, not what I'm interested in. I'm not a model for other people to follow or of happiness. I feel that I'm vetting myself every day. I am in agony and anxiety every time I do a project; not knowing if I can find out about it, or if it will work, or if I'll humiliate myself, or I'm so stupid that I won't find the path. Even though, on stage, I have an air of bravado, that's the culmination of a year of agony. I don't have a committee. I don't work for anybody. I don't have a second in command. At this moment, I have no employees whatsoever. People help me with what I do. Most of the time, like Tom Sawyer painting a fence, they almost pay me money to help me because people seem to like it. It's kind of a scam, but I tell them it's a scam. I work on interesting ideas that interest other people. As most things are, it's not quite as it seems from the outside.

Lately, in the last couple of months, there have been people who recognize this hasn't been a completely stupid self-indulgent task. Well, it wasn't a stupid task, but it was pretty self-indulgent. But, it did have an effect, so the Smithsonian just gave me a lifetime achievement award. I'll get it in a couple of weeks. A week later, I get an extraordinary award from Trinity College, Dublin which is their annual gold medal which they have been giving out since 1780. It has been awarded to people like Desmond Tutu, Winston Churchill, Aung San Suu Kyi, and they're giving it to me. I'm astonished

> I DO NOT TRY TO CHANGE THE WORLD. I KNOW THAT IF I DO GOOD WORK, HISTORICALLY, IT HAS AFFECTED THE WORLD, BUT I DON'T TRY TO HAVE THAT EFFECT.

by that, but I'm going to take the medal. I can certainly be flattered into submission.

## What are the needs you are hoping to address with the WWW and Prophecy conferences. How do you hope to change the world?

I don't care about the world changing. This is about me finding out patterns. This is really key to me. I do things because I'm curious about the observation of pattern, pattern visualization. And that's why I do them. I know that they do have an effect, but I don't try for that effect. That's not my goal when I start them.

## Do you think you're more surprised by what comes out of curiosity instead of empirical study?

I'm not surprised. I've certainly embraced the fact that most everything that I've learned has turned out to be wrong. When I went to school, I was taught that all life comes from the sun through photosynthesis. Now we know that life comes from chemosynthesis. I was always told that the smallest particle is the atom. Now there's forty-two subatomic particles. Almost everything I've learned has been wrong. I learned it absolutely. Most of the health things and diet things have all flipped and turned out to be wrong. We're now learning that organic food is no better than regular food. Some of the things haven't been wrong, but most things have.

We look at patterns and think, "We're flying three, four, five hundred miles an hour, an airplane is going to be faster and faster." Well, no, it isn't. It levels off. It's a sigmoid curve. Planes really don't go any faster than they did fifty years ago. There was a moment when the Concorde was there, but now there are no more Concordes, so all the planes go about the same speed. Cars don't go any faster. It takes longer now to drive around Los Angeles because of the traffic. Certain patterns level off or go down. If Benjamin Franklin walked into your house or my house it would still look like a house.

We demand certain things that we don't demand of other things. I'm talking about very basic things. Virtually all of the food in my refrigerator is food that I didn't eat as a child. It's not because I'm wealthier now and I ate gruel as a child. It's just that when I was young, there was no such thing as an avocado that I could have in Philadelphia. There weren't the different kinds of lettuces that we eat.

A lot of things are going to change, so I accept the fact that things are going to change. I don't copyright my books. After a certain point, I destroy them and any extra copies. Things are going to change. Someone asked me if they could archive all of my work, I said, "I don't have it. I got rid of it." Change happens. It's understanding change and the change in understanding. It's both things.

## What changes do you see coming in the next fifty years?

I don't care about that. I'll mention the next couple of years and I won't look back. I don't look backwards. People at this conference told me, "Well, you must be happy. It's going so well." So I said, "Let me ask you a simple question. Did you not come here thinking it was going to be a great conference? Is it an incredible conference? Don't applaud competency. It's what you thought it was going to be. That's competent." I don't get excited about things. I try to do good work. If it's good, that's what I'm supposed to do. I think you applaud a B student that gets an A. Just do good work.

> **Who are three or so people that are doing good work today?**

There are a shitload of people that are fantastic. Ian Wilson, in his eighties, came up with a new discovery about ants. If he's right, and he says he's absolutely right, then it's revolutionary. I think he's wonderful. Jack Dangermond, who owns ESRI, is doing incredible work: GIS mapping. He's my partner in the mapping scheme. Jon Kamen runs Radical Media. Yo-Yo Ma is still just an inspiration to me. Frank Gehry is spectacular. He's going to be giving me my Lifetime Achievement Award in New York City. The people around me are incredible people. I'm just really like a pig in shit. I'm happy with the people who are in my life that I learn from.

    I'm not even bragging. It's just what I decided to do. Some people might say, "He's a starfucker." No, I'm an idea fucker. I never said that before, that's funny. I think if you ask the fifty people that know me better than others at the conference if Ricky Wurman is any different from what he was twenty-five years ago, or how he is on the stage, they'd say, "No, he's absolutely the same." I don't act different on the stage. I don't act different on the phone. I don't talk different at the dinner table. I really don't think I'm any different.

339

# MATTHEW MATTHEW

---

*Matthew Matthew is an artist and musician whose work dances at the intersection of melody, moving pictures, interaction, and storytelling.*

earscansee.com

## ON A HUMAN SCALE

The city is an instrument and we are its notes.

It hit me on a walk through the crowded streets of Shanghai with Philip Glass blasting through my headphones. Somehow the frantic combination of his relentless piano arpeggios and the countless faces popping in and out of my vision collided together and gave birth to a simple question.

What if the piano were people?

Could you craft an instrument where each key triggered a different projection of a different person from a different walk of life singing a different note? Is it possible to capture voices and faces from around the world and transform them into a playable musical installation?

I had no idea how to, only that I had to.

Before I could convince myself it wasn't possible, I hit the streets of New York City with some friends and started asking absolute strangers to sing. Reactions ran the gamut from mild apprehension to near violent opposition at the idea of singing in front of the camera. But once people let go and opened up, something changed. Singing with others is proven to chemically induce joy and trust. All of the footage has a palpable tension between fear and euphoria, people surrendering to some inexplicable bliss. This is when I realized we were on to something, and that, if nothing else, on a one-to-one level, this process was bringing a few more notes of happiness into the world.

Not everyone is Pavarotti, we learned this hard and fast. The beauty is that even the utterly tone-deaf can sing at least one good note. Because every note of *On a Human Scale* is sung by a different person, this is all we need from each participant, one good note. The magic comes not from any individual singer but when we put all of those singers' notes together. It's like an inverse *American Idol*: in the end, we all become the star.

**IT'S LIKE AN INVERSE AMERICAN IDOL: IN THE END, WE ALL BECOME THE STAR.**

I couldn't see it at first, but this notion has now become the guiding force of the work. We are all constantly confronted with human diversity, by differences, by superficial things that keep us separate: age, gender, race, religion, socio-economics, and fashion. In actuality, these differences are what make the human experience infinitely interesting. Imagining a city where everyone is exactly the same is about as compelling as listening to a song that only has one note. Not very. So instead, we embrace the differences and each of us contributes our own unique note to the scale, playing an equally important part in the greater harmonious experience—be it an instrument, a community, a symphony, or a global village.

It's important for me that the experience communicates without words. The piece has no instructions, no lyrics, and no explanation. The installation is just people, pitches, and a piano. When you hit a key you hear and see someone singing

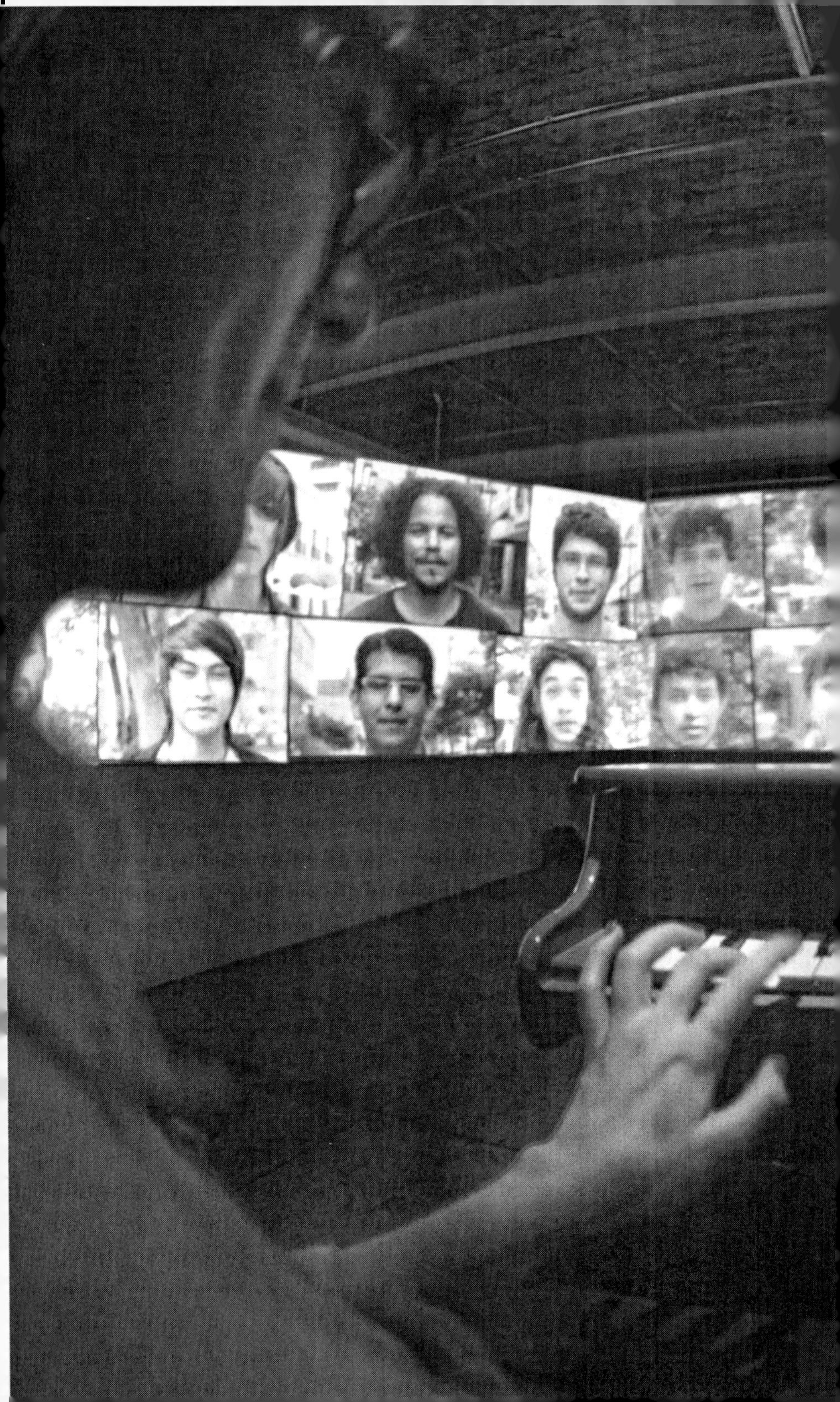

*Courtesy of Matthew Matthew*

that note. After that, it's up to you to decide how to play with it. It's kind of cheating, because music does most of the work. Music has an unfailing ability to move people—physically, emotionally, intellectually, and spiritually. Everybody is already versed in the language of music, so when used in a surprising way it can easily alter the way people imagine the world around them.

Everybody understands a piano. When you hit the keys, music comes out. It's an instant "get-ability" that lures the audience into engaging and being surprised. This notion became clear to me the first time I witnessed kids interacting with the prototype. People just want to play with the world. We expect to have control over an experience. In this case, the audience has control over an unlikely choir of everyday people that could easily be themselves. To make this possible, the installation relies heavily on technology, but what I'm really hoping for is that the purity of the interaction will render the technology invisible. When people can simply delight in playing, the conversation moves away from, "How does it work?" and towards, "How does it make us more human?"

As a creator, I believe to challenge is noble and necessary, but to delight is truly divine. So I'm aiming for the heart, not the head. True world changing is for engineers and educators, designers and diplomats, activists and inventors. The role of art is to try and lay the groundwork for change, to till society's psychic soil so new ideas and values and inventions have fertile ground to take root and sprout. It isn't about trying to make tomorrow better, it's about trying to make people better. It's about injecting a little musical wonder into the human experience with the hope it will help foster the imagination required for a brighter more harmonious future, one note at a time.

*On a Human Scale* is really only getting started, we've

> WHEN PEOPLE CAN SIMPLY DELIGHT IN PLAYING, THE CONVERSATION MOVES AWAY FROM "HOW DOES IT WORK?" AND TOWARD "HOW DOES IT MAKE US MORE HUMAN?"

filmed and exhibited small scale versions in New York City and Guadalajara, Mexico, but this is only the beginning. The piano is growing and the goal is to film, create, and stage site-specific versions of the instrument in cities around the world, one day compiling a fully playable, musical portrait of humanity.

346  AMERICAN DREAMERS

# BARATUNDE THURSTON

---

*Baratunde Thurston is a politically-active, technology-loving comedian from the future. He co-founded the black political blog,* Jack and Jill Politics *and served as Director of Digital for* The Onion *before launching the comedy/technology startup* Cultivated Wit. *He resides in Brooklyn, lives on Twitter and has over thirty years experience being black. He writes the monthly backpage column for* Fast Company, *and his first book,* How To Be Black, *is a* New York Times *best-seller.*

baratunde.com

## ON COMEDY, COMMUNITY, AND THE CREATIVE CLASS

### What is your dream for the future of America?

Less *Honey Boo Boo*. More *MythBusters*. I like to imagine an America that continues its march toward that "more perfect" union. We'd have more connected communities socially, more widespread local innovation in energy, education, and entrepreneurship. Our political system would be more accountable to more of the citizenry, and we would all walk more, listen more, and smile more, kind of like the Taylor family from *Friday Night Lights*.

***If you could really change things for the better, where would you start and how?***

It's hard to think of a single place to start because real change for the better requires parallel and coordinated effort and many great ideas are already underway, so I'm not going to have one masterful concept that is original and on its own gets the ball rolling.

That said, here's one masterful original concept to get the ball rolling: give the keys to the children, and let them drive. We know a few things about creativity and change and human development, so let's compile all that into a program that has children powering a series of community innovation hackathons. We get kids before they can be completely poisoned by the biases, shortcomings, and limitations of their parents. We know they are creative as hell, thinking about problems in ways adults don't allow themselves to. We know kids like to build things. A coordinated network of child-powered innovation labs—covering everything from community gardens to benevolent robot workers to more efficient energy production and consumption—could significantly expand our range of solutions and route around the old ideas and political gridlock of elder generations. Yeah, that sounds cool.

**GIVE THE KEYS TO THE CHILDREN, AND LET THEM DRIVE.**

***How does comedy change the world?***

Comedy changes the world by changing individuals from the inside out. Laughter causes a transformation in the person experiencing it. It loosens and opens us up. We let our guard down. We become vulnerable. Laughter helps expose who we really are, and when we're being who we really are we can see the world in a more true light. We can accept truths that in a different package, we might deny. We can find common ground with people we would swear are our enemies. Comedy can help us see the world, not just as it is, but as it might be, and that can serve as a great motivator.

## Will the world be made better through social media?

Yes. Intention is so important in determining how any tool or system affects outcomes. Television is a great potential educator and also destroyer of minds. Social media is part of a larger wave of tools that is redistributing power in a more even fashion, but its benefits are not guaranteed. We have to consciously desire and work toward using this tool as an instigator of enlightenment rather than abusing it to cause shadows and spread fear. Unlike previous generations of mass media that were based on broadcast methods, the abuse of social media can more easily be checked by participants in the system since they are an active part of it. With radio, we've seen manipulative, charismatic personalities rally forces of hatred for their own ends. In a social media context, such efforts could be effective in the short term, but over time, since the "listeners" are much more than that, other voices have a chance to counter abusive nonsense and build coalitions for good. The odds of this positive vision, however, depend on a level of education, literacy, and intention on the part of the people. If we don't know how to spot deception, if we choose not to be active, the outcome could be disastrous and would be on us.

I'd say social media (and its complementary set of power-distributing technologies and systems) have a greater potential to improve the world than any other innovation we've seen in history, but it may still lead to the spread of disinformation, discord, and nonsense if the people who comprise "social" are not vigilant in remaining conscious.

> COMEDY CHANGES THE WORLD BY CHANGING INDIVIDUALS FROM THE INSIDE OUT. LAUGHTER CAUSES A TRANSFORMATION IN THE PERSON EXPERIENCING IT. IT LOOSENS AND OPENS US UP.

## *What can we learn from blackness?*

In an American context, the most important lesson we can take from blackness is an historical recognition that blackness IS American-ness. As descendants of people brought here without choice, black Americans have had to create themselves and their culture and history on this soil and are thus co-creators and co-founders of the United States of America. Fighting, both physically and morally, to uphold and defend the values of a land that for so long refused anything approaching reciprocity is the deepest form of patriotism. All these questions and indeed all questions you may have on any subject are thoroughly answered in my book, *How To Be Black*, available in hardcover, paperback, and electrons wherever books are sold, lent, traded, or stolen.

> AS DESCENDANTS OF PEOPLE BROUGHT HERE WITHOUT CHOICE, BLACK AMERICANS HAVE HAD TO CREATE THEMSELVES AND THEIR CULTURE AND HISTORY ON THIS SOIL AND ARE THUS CO-CREATORS AND CO-FOUNDERS OF THE UNITED STATES OF AMERICA.

## *What did you learn from producing your show* Future Of*?*

I learned that I have an above average tolerance for travel, work, and talking, and I learned that there are incredibly talented and motivated people working to make and remake the world better than the condition in which they found it. Whenever I get down about the fate of humanity or some other melodramatic term to describe how we're doing as people, I think back to the brilliant people I met and how much progress they are making and the size of the ideas they are pursuing, and it makes me feel better (or at least less shitty) about our future. I also learned that the Japanese are interested in robotics to a degree that makes me uncomfortable.

I met fifty to seventy scientists, entrepreneurs, and innovators during the making of that show, and it would take too much effort to highlight everyone whose work moved or seriously impressed me, so I'll just pick one who stood out.

In Seattle, I met a scientist, Dr. Leroy Hood. I knew I would like him because I'm black, and his name is "Leroy Hood." I mean, come on. You can't make this stuff up. He's not actually black, but that doesn't matter. Look him up on Wikipedia. He's the father of what we call "molecular biology," and he's working at the intersection of computer science and biology and probably a few other disciplines I don't understand. Our interview focused on rapid diagnosis and preventive medicine brought about through a revolutionary blood test that, when paired with DNA analysis, could improve and maintain our health beyond some of our wildest dreams. Essentially, his system acts as an extremely early warning system for disease and illness. But most important to me is that he's building it out at a price point that works for the physical and economic conditions of the developing world. He's not aiming his considerable economic firepower at marginally improving the luxuries of the leisure class. He's taking on the fate of billions, and he and those he's working with could pull it off. That's some seriously inspiring shit and even now makes me feel regret for how much bandwidth I've consumed with images of my meals posted online.

## *What innovations make you excited about the future: tech, social, intellectual?*

I like the cooperative shared economy or "access economy" models of ZipCar, AirBNB, BuzzCar, Snapgoods, etc. We don't all need a unique copy of the stuff we use, especially when we only use that stuff on rare occasion. What we need is access to it, so let's build an economy around that.

I like the new hands-on tech and digital education models popping up from groups like Coder Dojo (Ireland), Decoded.co (UK), Code Academy (Internet), HackNY (NYC). We need to propagate new skills and new approaches to thinking and doing among people all across the world if we're going to make the level of difference our future demands (e.g. being able to breathe, live, work, in relative peace). Equipping people with CREATIVE digital skills is the new literacy and has the ability to radically improve the lot of communities that desperately need it.

I like those little capsules that make making coffee quite easy. It's pretty magical to just pop it in and press a button, so hooray for that.

353

# JI LEE

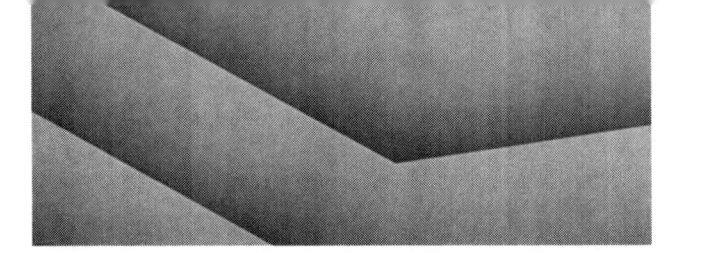

---

*Ji Lee is an artist and Creative Strategist at Facebook, who believes that ideas are nothing and doing is everything.*
pleaseenjoy.com

## OPTIMISM

Optimism is a big part of my work. The projects I get excited about are projects that involve optimism and bring a little bit of joy to people. The great thing about humor is that it knocks down the wall that people have as a defense mechanism. You know if you're smiling at someone, all the bias, preconceptions, and defense mechanisms that they may have towards you just disappear. Using humor can communicate ideas that may be difficult to communicate through criticism.

### THE BUBBLE PROJECT

*The Bubble Project* grew from my own frustration of seeing advertisements in New York subway stations. They weren't intelligent and they occupied every square inch of the city. I created bubble stickers, which invited everyone to add their comment to ads. It gave people a platform to express their opinions about advertising and about things that were nothing to do with advertising. But also, more people were looking at the ads with stickers on them—ads that they otherwise would not have looked at.

Originally, I had no idea what people would write. But we knew that if we left them empty people would write something. Many responses we got back were very intelligent. Obviously, there were a lot of responses that were sexual in nature. These were also a form of expression and I appreciated the more thoughtful responses. I love the idea of win-win situations where everyone can win with something.

Although *The Bubble Project* came out of my own frustration towards advertising, in the end, I think the bubbles enabled a link between advertisers and consumers that did not exist before. Advertisers learned some truths regarding what people really think about their ads. It's those kinds of connections that enable both parties to win.

### PIECES OF MIND

One of the things that I learned from *The Bubble Project* was to make something in a public space for anyone to enjoy for a short time. For our upcoming *Pieces of Mind* project, the idea is to make tens of thousands of miniature meditating rabbits. We give them away for free. We give these pieces to anyone who wants to participate. Then people simply put these pieces up in public space so that strangers can find them.

In ancient culture, rabbits were a symbol of fertility. I like the idea that rabbits can multiply. I like the idea of *Alice in Wonderland*'s White Rabbit, and the idea that they can take you to another world.

One thing that I observed living in a big city is, that especially when they're commuting, people mindlessly go from point A to point B listening to music, or reading books, without really paying attention to what surrounds them. Not really living in the moment. There's so much beauty that surrounds us, but we're conditioned to just go from point A to point B. Joshua Bell, one of world's best violinists, took part in an experiment where he played six Bach pieces in a D.C. subway. Very few people stopped to listen to his music. He earned thirty-two dollars. Two days before, he sold out a Boston theater where the average ticket price was one hundred dollars. People are unaware, and not in the moment, so they end up missing all the beauty that happens around them.

> **WE ARE CONDITIONED TO BE ADDICTED TO NEW FORMS.**

The meditating rabbit pieces are designed to disrupt that. They create a little piece of mystery that stops people for a few seconds and makes them wonder, "Why is this piece sitting there? Who put this piece there? What am I going to do with this piece? Am I going to leave it? Am I going to take it with me? Am I going to trash it?"

We are conditioned to be addicted to new forms. When I first came to New York City everything was so fresh, so new and exciting: the smell, the people, the sights, and the colors. As days, months, and years went by, I realized things weren't as new and fresh as before. It is the same thing with relationships. When you begin seeing someone for the first time, there is so much fascination and excitement. You just want to be with that person. The kissing and the sex; everything is incredible. Then as time goes by, you get to know him or her, and it's not as exciting anymore. What I want to do with these pieces is break that cycle of dullness, to escape the mindlessness, the getting used to stuff. These things are designed to disrupt us from taking reality for granted, by injecting little pieces of mystery, by injecting a little piece of unexpected joy to let people stop for a second. When that happens, when you are in the moment, you become an individual creative center. You ask, "Why is this piece upside down? Why is this rabbit sitting here?" That's my objective.

## PARALLEL WORLD

I'm really interested in miniatures. I lived in Korea until I was ten. One of the things I loved doing as a child was putting together plastic model pieces. A few years ago, I realized my apartment was full of stuff. Stuff was on the walls and the ground, but the ceiling was completely empty. I wondered why we had decorated our walls, our space, our furniture, but had left the ceiling empty. If you look at history, like the Victorian Age, the Middle Ages, examples like the Sistine Chapel, or French chateaux, the ceilings are decorated with moldings, paintings, and so on. With modernization at the beginning of the twentieth century, there was less ornament. People stopped thinking about ceilings. I thought it would be interesting to use that space. I decided to put a little scene on the ceiling and see how people reacted.

When people came to my apartment, most of the evening went by without people noticing. We're so conditioned not to look up. It wasn't until they were sitting on the sofa that they actually saw it, by accident. I like those moments of surprise and discovery.

## PERSONAL AND PROFESSIONAL

The balance of personal and professional projects is something that anybody can achieve. Personal projects are very simple. You do personal projects because they are fun to do. You don't know the immense pleasure of it until you start working on personal projects. It's like being a child and playing again. There are no limitations, no client, no budget. You just do this because you believe in it.

Along the way, after you graduate, your fun becomes a job. Your passion becomes a paycheck. Along the way, you forget why you are doing this. As soon as you start coming

> AFTER YOU GRADUATE, YOUR FUN BECOMES A JOB. YOUR PASSION BECOMES A PAYCHECK.

*Courtesy of Ji Lee*

back to why you are doing things and remember the things you were passionate about in school, that's when you can start professional projects.

There's an immense benefit to personal projects. Mine have connected me with many great things: people, collaboration, jobs. It's not something I predicted in the beginning. When you're doing things that you believe in and bring them to the world, great things happen.

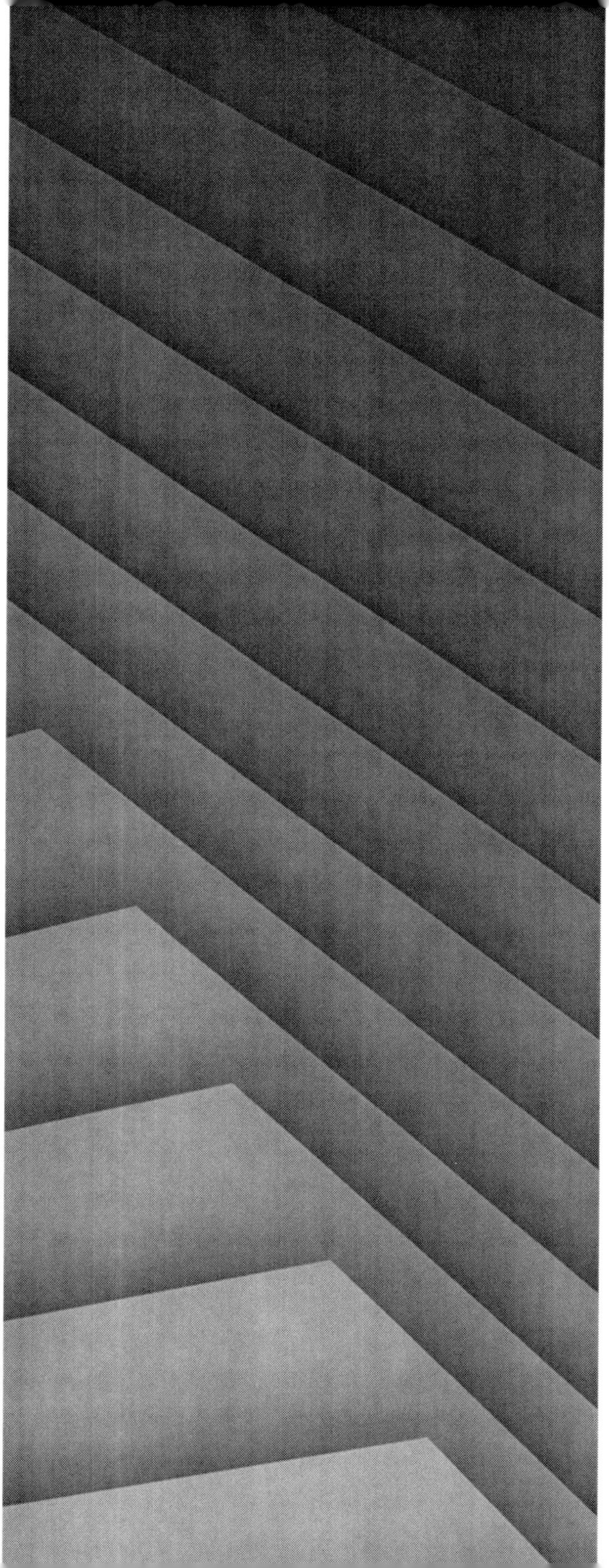

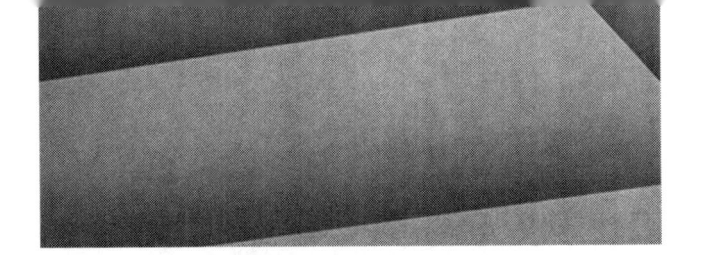

# WAYNE WHITE

Wayne White is an artist, art director, illustrator, puppeteer, and much, much more. Wayne worked as an illustrator and became a designer for the hit television show Pee-wee's Playhouse. His work was awarded with three Emmys. He also worked in the music video industry, winning Billboard and MTV Music Video Awards as an art director for seminal music videos including The Smashing Pumpkins' "Tonight, Tonight" and Peter Gabriel's "Big Time." Wayne is also the subject of the documentary Beauty is Embarrassing.

waynewhiteart.com

## "ALL THAT FAKE LAUGHIN' FOR NOTHIN'"

### What is your dream for the future?

I hope that we can eventually break down a lot of the economic class barriers that keep talented people out of the mainstream. That is one of the biggest problems of our society, the economic class war and the restraints put on people. There is a lot of talent that goes wasted because of the lack of schools, not meeting the right people, and there being no avenues for you if you are born in a certain class bracket. It is a shame because it all comes down to dollars and cents. Tons of talent gets wasted that way. I have had to struggle with that my whole life. I've struggled up a ladder out of the lower economic class brackets to get to the culture, the ideas and the resources. It is all about money. So I hope capitalism can find a way to at least give people a leg up somehow.

**How do your work, your art, and your creations help to achieve this? How does humor play a role in it?**

Humor is an invitation to everybody. Humor is a very populist idea and that is why the fine art world doesn't like it. The art world doesn't like or trust anything that smacks of populism. Even though they may have very liberal ideas of humanity, when it comes down to it they don't want to reach out to a broad audience. They want to keep the discourse on a higher plane and make things hermetically sealed so you'd have to be a real intellectual to understand. I am all for mental challenges, so-called difficult art and all that. It's fine if you want to make it an insider game. I am never gonna stop that trend in art but I use humor as an invitation to everyone. Everybody understands funny. That is my initial outreach with my art, to be funny. It is my way of being optimistic. I'm letting everybody in on the aesthetic experience. Once you have 'em laughing there are deeper levels and ideas that can open your mind up and expand it just as much as so-called intellectual art can.

Humor is my optimistic invitation for everybody to experience art and the perfect art experience opens your mind. It breaks down your preconceptions. It makes you less provincial, both in your place in the culture and as a human being. It makes you not so proud of yourself. It humbles you

> EVERYBODY UNDERSTANDS FUNNY. THAT IS MY INITIAL OUTREACH WITH MY ART, TO BE FUNNY. IT IS MY WAY OF BEING OPTIMISTIC. I'M LETTING EVERYBODY IN ON THE AESTHETIC EXPERIENCE.

364 AMERICAN DREAMERS

*Courtesy of Wayne White*

and lets you see that there are an infinite points of view, infinite amounts of wisdom, and an infinite amount of things you don't know. The art experience is about opening minds. That is what needs to be done constantly because most minds are closed. Most people are provincial. Most people act out of fear. If they had a true aesthetic experience it would break down that fear and start them thinking about the connections we all have.

> WE SHOULD NOT DISCOUNT ANYTHING AS WORTHLESS. EVERYTHING HAS A SECOND CHANCE IN LIFE. THINGS CAN BE TRANSFORMED AND THAT OPENS UP OTHER IDEAS.

My word paintings are a perfect example of this. They use humor initially. They are there for a laugh. Then after you laugh you can start thinking about the aesthetics of the painting: how I did it, what it means to recycle worthless objects, and how that can be a metaphor for life. We should not discount anything as worthless. Everything has a second chance in life. Things can be transformed and that opens up other ideas.

The word paintings use the window of humor and once you go through that window, there is a lot there to consider. There are a lot of art history references and there is a truly rich painting experience to be had. You have to laugh but the laugh breaks the ice. Say you are at a party. Do you want to hang around the guy who is funny and witty or do you want to hang around the other guy, the uptight asshole in the corner who is full of himself and talking about these really arcane art history ideas and not open to the moment, a real stick in the mud? Nobody likes a stick in the mud, but a lot of paintings come off like that, so self-serious and self-important. They all play an art history game that has nothing to do with real life. Humor has everything to do with real life. Humor is an in the moment experience. I play the art history game too, but at least I give an opening for everybody to get in there instead of coming off like a smarty pants all the time.

## Which leaders or innovators are turning things around?

I don't really believe in great leaders. I am distrustful of systems that I can't control. I am very distrustful of systematic things or programmatic things. That doesn't mean there aren't some leaders out there. I am just ignorant of them.

I look to myself to be a leader. I look to myself to lead in terms of art projects and collaborations and working with large groups of people.

It requires somebody who has lived a different life, who has seen both sides of life. I certainly have. I have lived in three very different worlds: rural Tennessee, Manhattan, and Los Angeles. I can see how they are all wrong about each other and that is the whole problem with the world, everybody is provincial. Even the most sophisticated New Yorker is provincial. I think I have a special knack for bringing people together but that doesn't mean I have risen to some powerful level.

What I look for in a leader is someone who has been around the block, through the world, and seen both sides. I do not see that in too many leaders. I see them coming up through a narrow world where they play one game but have never tried the other games. They haven't tried the other worlds.

> EVERYBODY IS PROVINCIAL. EVEN THE MOST SOPHISTICATED NEW YORKER IS PROVINCIAL.

## Do you think your attitude towards art, being an iconoclast, also comes out in these views?

Absolutely. I have an anarchic spirit. I am very much wary of the status quo. I am on the look out for it because I don't want it creeping into any of my work or thinking. I am always going to encourage people to kick against things. Don't believe in a system that tries to change human nature, you got to be flexible. You can't use the system to change human nature. Sometimes you have to fight back rather than be passive.

I have been fighting against those systems my whole life. I think things have changed a bit. People are a lot more open-minded and less rigid in their ideas. I always have to remind myself that my generation is in charge now. I am fifty-five years old. We are the bosses now and so I need to keep that in mind, to make sure I am not making the mistakes of the previous generation. We learn best from failure. Positive stuff all the time makes us think we are okay but failure shows us the problems and makes us face them. I have mainly learned from failure. I am happy now that I am going though a winning streak but most of my successes have been reacting against people like B.E. Edwards, my principal. He pulled me into his office with some of my art and said, "These are not the drawings of a red-blooded American boy." I have learned by learning what not to do. It sharpens my instincts. It is a painful process but it makes you think in a more original way. Rather than inheriting something on face value, questioning things is where its at.

**WE SHOULD FIGHT FOR THE THINGS WE LIKE AND BE HONEST ABOUT IT. FIND THINGS YOU LIKE.**

I have a painting called "All That Fake Laughin' For Nothin'." That's what a lot of people do. That's what Hollywood was for me, phony go along to get along attitudes. People were afraid they weren't gonna make money or be accepted. Most people can't be themselves. They just sit around and say they like something. That is a drag, man. We should fight for the things we like and be honest about it. Find things you like.

369

# NISHA CHITTAL

*Nisha Chittal is a digital strategist and writer living in Washington, DC. She is currently the head of social media for Travel Channel, where she oversees social media strategy, campaign development, and execution. Nisha is also a freelance writer, particularly on the topics of women's issues, media, and technology. She has contributed to* The American Prospect, Jezebel, Mediaite, Poynter, *and* Ms.

nishachittal.com

## AMERICAN WOMEN

My American Dream is that America will have a female president.

Right now, this seems like a far-fetched notion; but in fifty years, it will no longer be considered remarkable for a woman to be President of the United States. A female commander-in-chief will be perfectly common—as likely as having a male president. In the future, 50 percent of members of Congress will be female. 50 percent of Fortune 500 CEOs will be female. Women will receive the same pay as men doing the same work. Every young girl can dream that she can run for the highest office in the nation someday. And believing so is no longer considered far-fetched.

In the future, people will understand that equality for women does not mean the end of men. While there has been much hand-wringing at the moment over how the rise of women will supposedly lead to the death of masculinity, it should go without saying that the two are not mutually exclusive. Equality for women does not take away rights from men. It means that centuries-old inequalities will be rectified and both genders will have equality in opportunity, access, results, and representation. Women, starting behind, still have much ground to cover to achieve real gender equality—but this is not a zero-sum game. A world where men and women are equal is a world where both genders are happily coexisting; it is not a question of whether one or the other "rules".

**LAWMAKERS WILL STOP TRYING TO LEGISLATE WHAT A WOMAN CAN OR CAN'T DO WITH HER UTERUS.**

In politics, women will have 50 percent representation in national and state legislatures. In business, more women will serve on corporate boards. Panels at conferences and on TV news will look like the society they are supposed to represent, with people of both genders and diverse backgrounds. Women at work in technology, in politics, and in media will look around in meetings and no longer have to feel acutely aware of the fact that there is no one like them in the room.

Successful women will be judged on the basis of their work alone, not on the basis of their appearance, marital status, or maternal status—just as their male counterparts are treated. The infuriating "can women really have it all" question will no longer be an issue that follows every single successful woman around, because women—much like men— will be able to have both a loving relationship, family, and successful career if they choose to do so. And if they choose not to have children, their status as a woman will not be questioned. The tired trope of "career woman with no personal life" will have disappeared. "Work-life balance" will not solely be a woman's issue, as people of all genders balance career and family, and women doing so will not be unique to women.

Lawmakers will stop trying to legislate what a woman can or can't do with her uterus. In part, this will change because enough women will be elected to Congress that any attempt to restrict the bodily rights of women will not make it far. Lawmakers will recognize women as people who are valuable for more than their reproductive abilities; and they will focus their time in government on regulating Wall Street rather than regulating uteruses. It seems unbelievable that all of this needs to be said in 2012, but the reality is that women in 2012 are still fighting to be treated as people with full rights and equality.

> **WOMEN IN 2012 ARE STILL FIGHTING TO BE TREATED AS PEOPLE WITH FULL RIGHTS AND EQUALITY.**

## WHY IT MATTERS

Why does all of this matter? Why does it matter that more news anchors and reporters are women, that more TV shows are driven by women, that Congress is fifty precent women, that more executives and CEOs are women? Why does it make a difference if a conference speaker lineup is 50 percent women?

It matters for many reasons, not least of which is because women make up 51 percent of the population, yet hold only a tiny fraction of decision making power. Currently, 17 percent of members of Congress are women and only twelve of the Fortune 500 CEOs are women. This is abysmal, and is grossly misrepresentative of the U.S. population. More women in leadership in business and technology is simply better for business: 70 percent of household purchasing decisions are made by women, and not just things like groceries and clothes—women make decisions on big ticket items such as cars, vacations, and more. It is to the advantage of corporations to realize this and work on hiring more women at all levels, but particularly at senior levels, to bring in fresh perspective, ideas, and leadership that will help companies adapt to the changing marketplace and target the women who make purchasing decisions.

There are numerous studies that point to the business value and importance of having more women in leadership roles. A study last year found that companies with more women in senior leadership showed increased financial performance and sustainability. Moreover, the study found that when more women are in leadership, society benefits too: companies with more women leaders were likely to have more corporate social responsibility initiatives and more charitable donations. In a Credit Suisse study on corporate boards, the study found that over six years, companies with gender-diverse boards outperformed the male-only boards by 26 percent. A study by McKinsey & Company found that companies with more women on executive committees outperformed those with all-male committees by 41 percent in return on equity and 56 percent in operating results.

More women in political leadership means that issues that affect women and families are more likely to be addressed: healthcare, childcare, the economy. The vast majority of Congressional representatives are white men who too often have little understanding of the issues that affect 51 percent of the U.S. population. Those 51 percent—the women—need more women in Congress to make their voices heard and to create and support legislation that allows women more mobility, flexibility, and inevitably more success: paid maternity leave, stricter laws against sexual abuse and domestic violence, better work-life balance policies, and of course, fair pay. A study by Stanford & the University of Chicago in 2009 also found that women lawmakers are incredibly effective; they introduce more bills, find more co-sponsors, and bring home more money for their districts. So when more women are elected, all citizens benefit.

## WHAT WE'RE DOING NOW

The tide is beginning to turn, and we are witnessing it as it happens. The next wave of feminism is online feminism: harnessing social media and online communities to make women's voices heard and claim a seat at the table.

Fourth wave feminism has manifested in online networks and communities, where women are using blogs and social media to shape a new world for women in America and beyond. Networked women's communities allow like-minded women to connect with each other and form incredible online support networks. These online groups serve as a powerful organizing tool, allowing women to quickly discuss, react, organize, and support each other in the face of adversity. The Change the Ratio group, founded by Rachel Sklar, has hundreds of women who convene, discuss, and organize to advocate for women in the tech industry—and many of them have never even met in person, as social media and Google Groups enable them to do nearly everything online. Feminist bloggers have revived a movement that many thought was long gone or no longer necessary—and they're highlighting why feminism is still necessary today. Bloggers like Jessica Valenti and Jill Filipovic started two of the largest online feminist blogs, *Feministing* and *Feministe*, and paved the way for a generation of young women who found relief in an online community and support network of other women who shared their beliefs that we still have a long way to go to achieve full equality for women. Sites like Change.org have made it easier than ever to create and circulate online

> HAVING A VOICE IS NO LONGER LIMITED TO THOSE IN THE MEDIA. SOCIAL MEDIA HAS GIVEN EVERY YOUNG WOMAN A VOICE AND A PLATFORM TO FIGHT FOR THEIR RIGHTS AND DEMAND EQUALITY.

petitions. The feminist blogosphere empowered young women to start fighting back—because now, having a voice is no longer limited to those in the media. Social media has given every young woman a voice and a platform to fight for their rights and demand equality.

One needn't look far for examples of how social media has breathed new life into the women's rights movement. Each time a lawmaker says something sexist, such as Todd Akin's now infamous "legitimate rape" comment, angry Americans can inundate their lawmakers with messages via Facebook, Twitter, and blogs, until they see the consequences and apologize and retract their statements. When Facebook itself was found to have no women on its board of directors, activists turned to the very platform Mark Zuckerberg created to tell him that he needed at least one woman representing Facebook's millions of female users, on its board. And eventually, Facebook acquiesced and added COO Sheryl Sandberg to their board. When the Susan G. Komen Foundation announced it would withdraw its funding of Planned Parenthood, frustrated citizens created a days-long furor on Twitter until the Komen Foundation recanted and agreed to continue its funding of Planned Parenthood. When Daniel Tosh made a rape "joke" about an audience member, women (and men) were in uproar and took to Twitter and blogs to criticize Tosh, quickly forcing him to apologize. When TechCrunch Disrupt, a leading technology industry conference, was found to have very few women speakers, women in tech created an organized response online to TechCrunch head Michael Arrington, who finally instituted more women speakers and a "women in tech" panel event at the conference. While social networking sites at the individual level may seem insignificant, when used in large numbers, they have powerful effects—they have proven effectiveness at grabbing the attention of leaders and making them take action.

Groups like the Women's Campaign Forum, the White House Project, and EMILY's List have dedicated themselves to the mission of getting more women elected to office. From encouraging women to run, to endorsing, training, supporting, and assisting with fundraising, these organizations are providing the crucial support necessary for many women to take the daunting first step of deciding to run for political office. Studies show that women are often less likely to run for office because of feelings of self-doubt, because they are often discouraged, because they often face more opponents, and because women face more difficulty fundraising.

These organizations are taking the crucial step of recruiting more women to run for office, encouraging them to believe that they really can run for office, and supporting them through the process. One woman at a time, they're helping to change the gender makeup of America's political leadership. Online women's communities are creating a grassroots movement to fight for equality in every aspect of public life: business, technology, media, politics, and more. No act of misogyny goes unnoticed in the era of online feminism, where every woman has a platform to find support and amplify their collective voices.

The women's rights movement has seen a major and necessary resurgence in the last few years, and it is largely in part due to the democratizing effects of social media. In my American Dream, gender equality is no longer something we talk about—it's a reality.

> NO ACT OF MISOGYNY GOES UNNOTICED IN THE ERA OF ONLINE FEMINISM.

377

# JASON POLLOCK

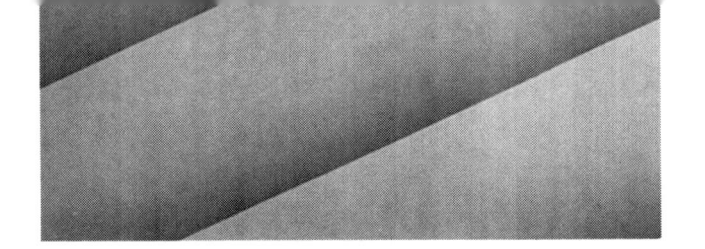

*Jason Pollock is a filmmaker, writer and activist. His first film,* The Youngest Candidate, *followed teenagers running for political office.* Undroppable *is currently in production.*

undroppable.com

## UNDROPPABLE

There's a bad guy, a Darth Vader, in every movie. In *Undroppable*, society is the bad guy. We are the ones that are responsible for this. I'm not going to point the finger at anybody. I'm going to point the finger at everybody. Education is an issue that is not as high up on the list as it should be. We like to invest in quick scores, quick wins. Education is not a quick win. It's the only way to win. The world will be better off when we make smarter people.

A lot of recent education content either attacks a political issue or tries to right something that isn't working. Instead of doing that, I want to shine a light on the amazing students and teachers who are in these "dropout factories", the fifteen hundred schools in America with the highest dropout rates. The way to get it higher is to put a human face to it.

We say that every student deserves the same education in America. But kids that come to school with so much less can't get the same education as the kids that come to school with everything. They have to get more. Kids who come from these areas deserve more to make it fair because they carry so much extra weight on their shoulders.

When I walk into a school on the first day with my camera, the secretary's face often looks worried because she's come to expect that if a man with a camera comes in, something bad has happened. We're trying to change that. We're trying to show these schools and these districts that there are people in the world with cameras in the media who want to show the positive things that are going on in these schools.

I was Michael Moore's assistant for three years. I made *Fahrenheit 911* with him and I helped produce his tours, books, and films. That inspired me to make content that matters and to use the model from *Fahrenheit 911*; creating content in an election cycle and using that content to push a conversation during the presidential election cycle.

When I left Michael Moore in 2006 I wanted to work in the youth education area and create that model around a nonpartisan topic. So, I created *The Youngest Candidate*, a film about teenagers who run for political offices in America. It's a story about four teens running for real positions in their city. I've been using that as a tool to get the youth word out as well as to show high school students and college students the kind of power they have in the political system. Most kids don't realize that they can even run when they are eighteen years old.

For the last two and a half years I've been working on getting this education project off the ground. Originally, I saw the project as two things. I was going to run a social media campaign on education and I was going to make a feature documentary on education. But I realized what I was really trying to do was make a documentary using social

> WE SAY THAT EVERY STUDENT DESERVES THE SAME EDUCATION IN AMERICA. BUT KIDS THAT COME TO SCHOOL WITH SO MUCH LESS CAN'T GET THE SAME EDUCATION AS THE KIDS THAT COME TO SCHOOL WITH EVERYTHING.

media. I was going to run a social media campaign and at the same time, run my documentary production and wrap the two together.

In the summer of 2011, I started pitching my project as the first-ever social media documentary. I wanted the campaign to influence the film. A week after Labor Day, Adam McKay, director of *Anchor Man* and *Anchor Man II*, signed on as producer of my project. That was a dream come true. Then we partnered with Get Schooled, which is a project of Viacom and the Gates Foundation and works with 230 schools. I'm now embedded in six high schools. Each of the schools has their own network. Each student and teacher has his or her own page.

I hope *Undroppable* can help schools understand and learn how to use social media more effectively. I've worked as a social media consultant for celebrities, brands, and nonprofits. Now I want to be a social media consultant for education to help schools and kids who don't usually have the resources.

Every producer has already dedicated their backend to charity. So, I'm changing the way we make a documentary, and changing the communication around education. I'm sharing stories of students who have similar horrible experiences to many at-risk kids who come from poverty, but these kids have shown extreme resilience and are making it through.

It's all about poverty. It's all about how poverty affects youth, the different ways it affects these kids. It pushes school down to the lowest level. Life has to become the highest priority. Survival has to become the priority. When survival is your priority, school is not your priority. A lot of these kids are so smart. If you grow up in these areas, from the very beginning, you have to learn different skills and you have to wear a different suit of armor than kids who don't have to deal with these things.

At a very early age, you have to be more with it. You have to deal with more real life issues. There are different issues that poverty brings to the table. Parents love their kids but they can't be there because they have to work all the time. Because they can't be there, the kid is home alone a lot, so they have to take care of themselves. If they are the older sibling and their parents have to work late, they become the parent.

If you are poor and your life is really rough, you build up aggression. The more aggression you have inside you, like any human being, you have to let it out. When we see things like drugs, violence, or gangs, it's a human response to having so much built up aggression. It's a very human response. People in poverty are not any different from anybody else. They've just been pushed to the limit by the realities of their lives.

I talked to many students. I want to mention two of them: Darius P. from Massachusetts and Cynthia G. from Des Moines. Cynthia is Mexican. Her mother immigrated to America. She has her papers. When she was seven, the cops raided her apartment. Her father was sentenced to jail for fourteen years for drug dealing. She's only seen her father one time since then. She has two older sisters and one older brother. All of them dropped out of high school. When the father went to jail, the mother moved around, sometimes multiple times a month. When Cynthia was sixteen, she fell in love with a guy that was in a gang. She got pregnant. They kept the baby. She stayed in high school with the baby and graduated in May. Cynthia's video is so powerful and heartbreaking. It shows how much she had to go through to get to graduation day. After we posted her film, Justin Bieber tweeted it and it now has seventy five thousand views.

Darius' story is another one of incredible strength. Darius' father is a life long alcoholic. His mother was a crackhead. He didn't know his mother until he was four because she lost custody of him. He was reunited with his mother and went to live with her. His father went to jail regularly. His mother would call the police on his father all the time. His father is in jail right now. He has all these things he has to deal with. He was going to get his GED, but didn't because the day he went to take the test, he got hit by a truck. He got a girl pregnant when he was a senior. They had the baby. He graduated this year. He's a mentor in New Bedford now.

Many of these kids are just dangling by a thread. Somehow they figure out a way to pull themselves back up. I see them as superheroes. Going through what they've been through, then graduating high school is just mind-boggling. They deserve so much more credit, respect, and love than what they are getting right now. I think the best way to get that for them is not to attack the systems that need to help them, but to just show the system what's happening.

Making this film, I sat in a room with kids for weeks at a time. Laughed and cried with them. Some of the kids that came into the room had confidence already, but many of the kids didn't. It gave them confidence. They have seen the power of their story.

*Undroppable* helps students understand that they are valuable. A student who is fifteen or sixteen years old is easily pushed in one direction or the other. If you show them the right way, you open a door for them. If you show them they can do it, then they do it. If you don't show them the right way, then they don't do it.

The main message of *Undroppable* is that education needs to be more of an important issue in our society. If we're ever going to fix this economic funk the world is in, we need to fix our education system. Some people see education as an expense. It's an investment. You may have to wait ten years to see a return which is why we don't like to invest in it.

> SOME PEOPLE SEE EDUCATION AS AN EXPENSE. IT'S AN INVESTMENT.

There are two things I'd like to see change. I want to see political change and private business change. I want to see more money going to more education programs and legislative bills being passed around America where we say we're not cutting education anymore.

I want to remind people that education is undroppable.

384  AMERICAN DREAMERS

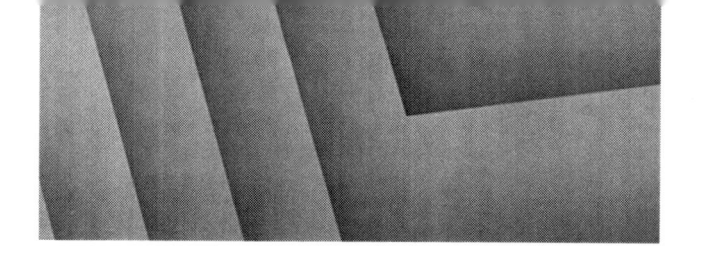

# NAOMI POMEROY

---

*Naomi and her sous chef Mika Paredes first welcomed customers to Beast on September 27, 2007. Accolades and awards have followed.* Bon Appètit *named Naomi as one of the top six of a new generation of female chefs in September 2008.* Food and Wine Magazine *recognized her as one of the Ten Best New Chefs in America in 2009. She has been twice nominated as a finalist by the James Beard Foundation for best Chef in the Pacific Northwest. In 2010, Naomi was awarded top honors for women in business from both* Oprah Magazine *and* Marie Claire. *Naomi also appeared as a contestant on* Top Chef Masters, *and more recently, served as a judge for the tenth season of* Top Chef.

## ANALOG FOOD

My restaurant, Beast, was started with fifty thousand dollars. That is what the whole thing cost to build. It was sustainable because I didn't take out a huge loan. The space was really small. Beast was going to be a play on the word bistro. Our plan was to do small tables and French-y bistro food. After we got our kitchen equipment, which was one electric convection oven, two electric convention burners (which we used for three years), and two little refrigerators, we realized it wouldn't work. If someone came in and spent twenty-five dollars but spent three hours talking to friends, we would not stay in business. We needed more tables. The first thing about a business is that it has to be sustainable.

My biggest passion in the world is everybody doing what they want for a living. Ultimately, that is what saves the planet. Everyone would be happy. I had an incredible opportunity to do what I wanted to do in the restaurant but it was being dictated by the space. So I let the space talk to me. It was hard for me to say, "Put two big tables in here and charge more money." That way we didn't have to do as many covers to be sustainable.

I had already been doing that model but had been doing it in my backyard. I used to run an underground supper club out of my house. After I had sold my other restaurant and left other jobs, I started doing these backyard dinners. It was always a viral marketing thing. We emailed people the menu and they could reply with a RSVP. It was me and my sous chef, who is now my chef de cuisine, and we did them in the yard because we didn't have anything else to do. We didn't have a space and we didn't have money but things fell into place. We took the concept and kept it going at Beast because it was good. We could survive on doing sixteen people a night. It didn't matter if it was full all the time because it was just the two of us. What is sustainable about the model is that we grew intentionally and carefully. In the beginning we didn't have a dishwasher. It was me, my sous chef, and two servers. That was it. No other employees for the first whole year.

What that meant was we were working one hundred hours a week, always. It was totally insane but we were willing to put the time in. That is something missing in today's culture. We think, "Hey, where's mine?" We need to bust that up, the idea that anything other than really hard work makes things happen. It is easy to work hard when you are super passionate. It is all about finding what you want to do. So the restaurant evolved, grew, we got busy, and recognized. We love what we do.

**You mentioned your passion is getting people to do what the love to do, what are the benefits of that? What does a world look like when we do that?**

I talk to people who can't wait to retire. They count the minutes until the weekend and live two lives. We have a customer that comes in all the time, sits at the chef's counter and tells me, "I have always hated going to work." He is in his sixties. I have heard all those ads that say, "You spend a third of your life sleeping so you should have a good mattress." You spend two-thirds of your life working so love what you do! It is interesting when people have the thing they begrudgingly have to do and then think they can separate from it as they recreate on the weekends. It is really backwards and carries over. It has to, right? You can't not bring it home.

When I go into work I am excited. I could stay until two o'clock in the morning if I have to because I love what I do. It does get hard and sometimes I have to remind myself that I love it.

When people are joyfully working the work is better. If people were truly passionate about coffee you would never have a bad cup of coffee. Portland is a great example because there are a lot of people who are truly passionate about coffee. We have so much good coffee here. There is so much great food here and incredible wine.

> WHEN PEOPLE ARE JOYFULLY WORKING THE WORK IS BETTER. IF PEOPLE WERE TRULY PASSIONATE ABOUT COFFEE YOU WOULD NEVER HAVE A BAD CUP OF COFFEE.

### *What are the values you put into your food?*

Mika, my chef de cuisine, and I always talk about our food as analog. We are not digital. If you listen to a recording on CD you get a pristine version of a recording. No scratches and every sound is crystal clear, but I would rather listen to a record, one hundred times over. It is about the idea that things in the world are not perfect. I find beauty in the imperfection of things. Not to say I don't want my food to be perfect but it is perfect in the imperfections. I constantly tell my staff not to strain the stock three times because it is okay to have a little cloudiness, that is the flavor. Our digital age tries to strain that out of people.

After my wedding, my parents came over and saw how many records my husband and I have and asked, "What are all these old records?" They asked why we would want them but my husband didn't answer. He just put on a record and my dad could hear all the scratches and pops. It is nostalgic and real. I always think about my food like that. We are not trying to reinvent something here or create something new. We just try to serve food that is something you want to eat in a refined and graceful way. I hate to call it high-level comfort food or any other weird buzz words. I just try to stay in harmony with things.

Everyone always asks how I make a menu. I make it different every time. Sometimes I just make one Sunday afternoon. Other times I go to the farmer's market and see something. A whole menu grows out of the these dark purple heirloom carrots that I saw. There is always a center point. I am always intentional. The meal is like a symphony with a beginning, middle, and an end. It is done with intention. We think about how the soup goes with the entree and what the dessert should be like because of that.

A lot of people are used to getting what they want. "How come you don't have salmon on the menu?" I am not trying to

> I FIND BEAUTY IN THE IMPERFECTION OF THINGS. NOT TO SAY I DON'T WANT MY FOOD TO BE PERFECT BUT IT IS PERFECT IN THE IMPERFECTIONS.

be arrogant, but if I go to a music producer's house I am not going to tell them what album to put on. I am gonna let the DJ be the DJ. For me, it is the same thing at my restaurant. Let me do what I do. If someone gets a salmon entree and then chocolate pudding for desert, that grosses me out. There is really nothing wrong with wanting that, but in my mind those things do not go together. It is about the start to finish as a larger picture.

It is really fun for me and so wonderful when people get the wine pairings. We are able to introduce people to things they would never get. It connects back to people being passionate about what they do. I got my wedding dress from Adam Arnold. He is passionate about what he does. He has done every dress I have ever worn to anything. I told him, "Just make me something awesome." My dad made my wedding ring. I didn't see it until it went on my hand. I like to give the trust I want people to give to me. The passion is what forms the end result.

If we did what we love we would have a lot more time. Can you imagine if you just trusted your landscaper to come and put in your backyard for you? You wouldn't have to figure things out because he would be so excited to be be doing it.

It would be more community oriented because we would be talking to each other more. Can you imagine how frustrating it is to be a mechanic and have people not trust you? People bring their car to you but always ask, "What are you doing? What is that?" I can see it when people come to Beast and don't know what to expect. If there was that trust and people trusted each other there would be a responsibility. You would have to take care of people on a really high level. I desperately want everyone who comes to be really happy, and I want to pass that on to them.

> I LIKE TO GIVE THE TRUST I WANT PEOPLE TO GIVE TO ME. THE PASSION IS WHAT FORMS THE END RESULT.

390 AMERICAN DREAMERS

# JESSIE ZAPOTECHNE

---

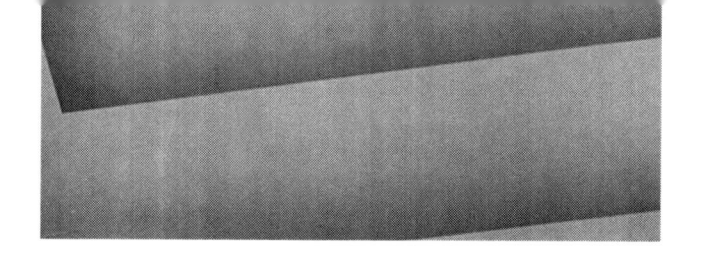

*Jessie Zapotechne has been running and leading runners with NYC BRIDGERUNNERS since 2005. She resides in Brooklyn and prefers to run and cycle for a streets-eye view of life in New York. As a Creative Arts Therapist with extensive experience working with youth in the juvenile and criminal justice systems in Detroit and NYC, Jessie is dedicated to at-risk youth and young adults with a focus on experiential learning, public art, and social justice.*

nycbridgerunners.com

## I WANT TO TALK ABOUT RUNNING

I want to talk about running.

I want to talk about why I chose and continue to choose to help others run. I want to talk about the Bridge Runners and how they embody what I love about running. I want to talk about why running is a gift. To do this, I must first talk about how I found running and how running found me.

I found running the same way that I have found most everything I love in life. Pure accident.

I remember the day so vividly. I was in the sixth grade and it was the last day of school. It was the (ugh) middle school track and field day. For some reason my parents came. This was unusual because I was the oldest of eight children and they were most often too consumed to notice much of what I was doing. That day was the kind of day where you just wanted to be in the class tug-o-war and then get your hot dog and say goodbye to school. I was never that lucky. When I arrived at the high school field that day, I found my name handwritten onto a paper for the 4x100 meter relay. I had never set foot on a track before and I was scared. I can remember the feeling of my stomach tightening, feeling that for certain I must have had to pee, tingling legs, hands, and fingertips. I was the third leg of the relay. All I knew was that my job was to grab the stick out of the other person's hand and go. When the time came and I had the baton in my hand, I ran my little heart out. I had never experienced such a feeling before in my life. It was the feeling of flying. I felt so free. Later, my mother told me that my father leaned over to her and said, "Hey look at that girl, she is really fast," and my mother said, "That girl is your daughter."

I found running again the same way I have found many things I needed in life. It found me.

Many years went by. I had gone to college, pursued a passion to study art and had found love. In my post-college adult world, life had gotten in the way and I believed at that time that being an athlete had come and gone. I had forgotten running. I had picked up some bad habits and a less than healthy lifestyle. The drawn out painful ending of a long emotionally abusive relationship coupled with a damaged courage to pursue an art career pushed me to pack everything up. I moved home to regroup. I remember telling my mother,

"When I get there, Mom, I'm going to be really depressed. I don't want you to worry. I just want you to know." I got myself there, and when I did, a close friend was waiting. She was home for the summer on the way to graduate school. She had picked up running. She called me on our landline and said, "Jessie, you want to go for a run? You can tell me about what's going on in your life." Almost every day, in between my early morning job and my night shift bartending, we would find the time to jog a mile or so super slow and spill our guts about everything. I started to get strong again.

I ran away from running and it caught up to me.

In my process of regrouping, I began to rebuild myself as a person. I had lost a lot of the former me. I wasn't healed, and knew that I wasn't going to be at my old home. I decided to get out of there. I left and came to New York with the little bit of cash I had saved up bartending. I had gotten myself into graduate school and with a lot of luck and perfect timing, landed a bartending gig downtown that covered the rent. School was going well but it was hard. I was pursuing my passion of working with adolescents through art, making and working seven days a week at night. Physical and emotional burnout started creeping in. So did some unsavory characters and bad habits that I had cultivated for coping previously. For as tough as I thought I was, I was struggling and vulnerable. Nightlife was an easy out but daytime was getting increasingly harder. I kept running into the same mysterious guy. It seemed like I would always bump into him on a dark street or he would pop up from around a corner. A couple of times he would say something to me about running. I didn't know what he was talking about.

A few months went by. This guy again... a running

group... just show up... the Chinatown track. It was fuzzy as to why I decided to give running with a group of people at night in Chinatown a try. But for whatever reason I went. I didn't have running shoes or clothes so I wore something crazy and showed up. There were a couple of guys there and me and my friend. I will never forget it. We ran over the Manhattan Bridge, into Brooklyn and made our way to the Brooklyn Bridge. I had no concept of pace, or form, or breath. I just tried to keep up. I remember the beauty of seeing the skyline from the crest of the Brooklyn Bridge for the first time, mixed with the searing pain in my lungs and stomach and the racing thought, "Don't throw up in front of these dudes and don't stop." I made it through that first run with what I later came to know as the Bridge Runners. It was my longest run ever. I remember feeling sick and proud. Most of all it re-opened something inside of me that I had felt long ago. I felt free.

**I FELL IN LOVE WITH RUNNING AND IT SET ME FREE.**

I fell in love with running and it set me free.

So what happened next was that I never stopped running. This love affair, obsession, addiction with running was awakened that night with Bridge Runners roughly around 2005 or 2006. I remember my friend saying to me, "Jess, I think you are addicted to this running," and I thought, "Yeah, but it's good right?" I wasn't really thinking about being healthy at that point. I was addicted. There was something so powerful about pushing beyond how far you had ever run before, or running a new bridge, or even running without feeling like throwing up. I was growing and I saw the limits that my mind had set, or the walls that I had imagined begin to break down. It started to be that running was helping me to understand why roadblocks in my life were self-constructed. I started to see possibilities beyond where I had imagined. I appreciated the pain of pushing myself to a limit and pushing past that limit. I also started to see the parallels between life and running. What was unique about Bridge Runners was that they accepted me. They took me in with my crazy non- running clothes, with my ignorance of long-distance running, and my kind of wild lifestyle. I never once felt judged or that I was in the wrong place. The reality was, I was becoming a part of a group of non-runners who wanted to run. We were learning together. And the message was that, "You should never have to run alone." No one told me not to run a half marathon because I had only ever run five miles. They told me, "You have to run this half marathon, of course you can do it." Blind faith, pure intentions, plus sheer determination equaled the Bridge Runners. Three marathons and thousands of miles later, I/we push on.

Giving the gift of running to others brings much fulfillment.

Over the years, my commitment to being a Bridge Runner led me into a place of leadership and mentorship by helping other new runners. I would pass on the tips that other runners, my mentors and coaches, taught me. "Lean forward on a downhill and enjoy your recovery. Let gravity do the work. Don't let other people change your pace—find yours. Let others push you. Work together. Never forget to take in the view." Most important is to share with others what you have learned. I knew that if I could share my experience of running with others, that it could bring the same feelings of empowerment, freedom, and strength. I hoped that I could help other non-runners like me learn to love running.

> I KNEW THAT IF I COULD SHARE MY EXPERIENCE OF RUNNING WITH OTHERS THAT IT COULD BRING THE SAME FEELINGS OF EMPOWERMENT, FREEDOM, AND STRENGTH.

Empowering others is essential to creating a better future.

Running any distance for the first time is a triumphant and powerful experience. It is the realization that "I can," and then the next thought is, "What else can I do?" Helping others set goals and work towards them is incredibly exciting, and inspiring even when you have been running for a while. Somehow it doesn't get old when you share a running experience with someone else. Each runner shows up to the run for different reasons. Sometimes they might share why they are running today, or what they want to get out of it. Sometimes we share private talks, hopes, dreams, and challenges while we run.

Today we are here and it is marathon season. I have been working with the team of Bridge Runners over the past few months to build up a base of miles that will prepare them for whatever races they may have in the coming weeks. Many of the runners are new to running this year, or in the past year or two. In addition, many of these runners are doubling or tripling their longest miles ever run. Some of them have never raced or trained for one. I am excited for them. It pushes me. I think about a new runner who pushed herself to her limit, and then with a little nudging pushed on past that. It feels good to know that soon she will run beyond me.

397

# CHRIS ANDERSON

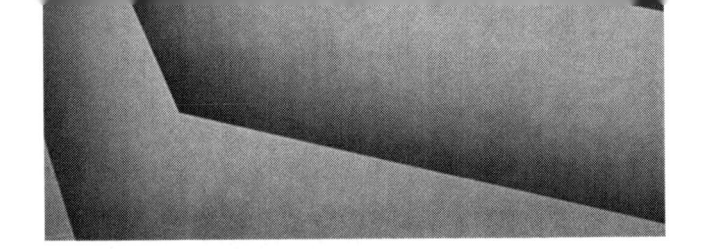

Chris Anderson is the curator of the TED Conference, a conference that explores the power of ideas to make a difference in the world. Under his stewardship, over one thousand TED talks have been released free online to a global audience. He oversaw introduction of the TED Prize, the TED Fellows Program, the TED open translation program, the TED-ED initiative, and the TEDx program that allows hundreds of independently organized TED-like events to be held around the world.

ted.com

## ARCHITECTS OF THE FUTURE

*This dream for the future is an excerpt from a speech given at the 2011 Harvard School of Architecture Graduation Ceremony.*

There is a talent that is unique to our species. I'm not talking about intelligence, fine breeding, good looks, dress sense, or compelling social skills. I am talking about the talent which some would call... imagination or invention or innovation. It is the remarkable ability first of all to model some aspect of the external world inside our heads... and secondly to play with that mental model until suddenly—bingo! You find a way to rearrange it so that it's actually better. This is the amazing engine that underpins both technology, the 'T' of TED, and design, the 'D' of TED. It is this skill that has made possible the human progress of the last fifty thousand years.

It's really astonishing that we can do this. For almost the entire period of life on earth, the appearance of design has been driven differently, by random trial and error. Like a drunkard lumbering through a dark maze of passages, life has lurched its way forward. For every evolutionary step forward there have been countless dead ends. In a single lifetime, change was not detectable. It happened slowly, painfully over millions of years. Somehow in our species the light came on. We actually found a way to model the future before lumbering into it.

> LIKE A DRUNKARD LUMBERING THROUGH A DARK MAZE OF PASSAGES, LIFE HAS LURCHED ITS WAY FORWARD.

That.

Changed.

Everything.

Viewed from a different perspective, you could say our brains became the ecosystems for a new kind of life, a life that replicated and transformed itself at a rate hitherto unknown in our corner of the universe. The thrilling life of the world of ideas. TED is devoted to nurturing this life form. We at TED nurture ideas by putting free talks up on the Internet, you will be not just dreaming them but turning them into reality so that thousands or millions of other people will be impacted by them. And that is why I'm so excited by this group brain scan I'm holding here in my hand. It's the future right here.

Wait! I think I can make out something, albeit it's a little fuzzy. Espoused in a mind over here, I think I can just about make out... a gorgeous building, full of natural light whose bio-inspired curves evoke wonder and delight in everyone who sees it. Over there I can see a once barren industrial wasteland converted into a glorious city park where people gather, mill, walk, play, and dream. And emanating from a mind on this side... Oh, wow! Here is a spectacular city of the future. One in which cars are replaced by intelligent, next-generation transport systems, and human-scale meeting places where people naturally mingle and connect. A city which breathes and adjusts and interacts with its citizens like a living system.

When you sum up all the visions contained here, I have to tell you, the future looks pretty enticing. And the most thrilling part? A significant proportion of those dreams will within the next decade or two become real. Why? Because you will make it so. Like few other people on earth, you have the skills and the resources to truly change the world.

But here's the rub. What will determine which of the dreams present here today see the light of day, and which will languish unfunded, forgotten, ignored?

> ONE OF THE MOST TRAGIC THINGS IN THE WORLD IS A POWERFUL IDEA STUCK INSIDE THE HEAD OF SOMEONE WHO CAN'T ACTUALLY EXPLAIN IT TO ANYONE ELSE.

Usually a single person can't make a big idea come true (unless they have extremely rich parents). In almost every case an idea needs multiple backers. So it must first spread from one brain to many, spreading excitement as it goes. So what makes THAT happen? It certainly helps if the idea itself is powerful. By which I mean some combination of beautiful, ingenious, and... affordable. But there's something else. It needs to be communicated with power. One of the most tragic things in the world is a powerful idea stuck inside the head of someone who can't actually explain it to anyone else. At TED, over the years, we've had a lot of architects come and share their visions with us, and a good number of them have been absolutely... awful. How can that be? They have the most compelling subject matter imaginable. Giant designs at a scale that impacts thousands or millions of people. Yet, when it comes to articulating them, they descend into gibberish—the abstract, over-intellectual language of architectural criticism that makes an audience's eyes glaze over and their brains numb. This is an utter tragedy! Whatever else you do in the coming years of your life, I beg you, I truly beg you to find a way of sharing your dreams in a way that truly reveals the excitement and passion and possibility behind them.

Today, slowly, gingerly, it's become possible once again to use language the rest of us can understand. I think it's even okay to use that B word again. Beauty. Not as a proxy for arrogant artistic self-expression, but as a quest to tap into something that can resonate deeply in millions of souls around the world. I'm happy to report that in the last couple years at TED we've been wowed by a new generation of architects: Joshua Prince-Ramus, Bjarke Ingels, Liz Diller, Thomas Heatherwick and others, as they've shared with us—in plain English—their passion, their dreams, and yes, the beauty of what they're created. When Thomas Heatherwick shared his vision for a stunning, new residential complex in Kuala Lumpur, curved out from narrow bases like a bed of tulips, I had just one thought. I wish I had been born in the future.

I suppose an architect might have dreamt of such a development thirty years ago... but it could never have been built. And that brings us to the second trend. Technology is changing the rules of what's possible. The astounding power of computer-assisted design and new construction techniques are giving us the ability to actually build what before could only have been a whimsical doodle on a sketchpad. Suddenly the fractals and curves of Mother Nature are a legitimate part of the architectural lexicon. And around the world, as people watch these new buildings arise, instead of muttering "monstrosity", their jaws are dropping, their eyes moistening.

And finally, perhaps most important of all, we're at a moment in history where the world is paying attention to you like never before. As leading designers of scale, you, more than anyone else, hold in your hands the answers to the most important question we all face. Namely this: can the coming world of ten billion people survive and flourish without consuming itself in the process? The answers if they are to be found—and I think they will—will come from... design. Better ways to pattern our lives. There is nothing written into our nature that says that the only path to a wonderful, rich, meaningful life is to own two cars and a McMansion in the suburbs.

It is becoming urgent for the world to start to see a compelling alternative vision. Probably it's going to come down to re-imagining what a city can be, and making it so wonderful, that few people would want to live anywhere else. If there are to be ten billion of us, we will have to, for the most part, live close to each other—if only to give the rest of nature a chance. Indeed more than half the world already lives in cities and the best of them offer so much to the world: richer culture, a greater sense of community, a far lower carbon footprint per person, and the collision of ideas that nurtures innovation. And the future cities you will help create need not feel claustrophobic or soulless. By sculpting beautiful new forms into the city's structures and landscapes; by incorporating light, plants, trees, water; by imagining new ways to connect with each other and work with each other, you will allow the coming crowd to live more richly, more meaningfully, than has ever been possible in history—and to do so without sacrificing your grandchildren.

The architect Moshe Safdie ended his TED talk a few years ago with this poem.

> **PURSUE KNOWLEDGE. BE RELENTLESSLY CURIOUS. LISTEN, LEARN. YOUR LEARNING CANNOT EVER, EVER BE ALLOWED TO STOP.**

*He who seeks truth shall find beauty.*
*He who seeks beauty shall find vanity.*
*He who seeks order, shall find gratification.*

*He who seeks gratification, shall be disappointed.*

*He who considers himself the servant of his fellow beings shall find the joy of self-expression.*

*He who seeks self-expression, shall fall into the pit of arrogance.*

*Arrogance is incompatible with nature.*

*Through nature, the nature of the universe and the nature of man, we shall seek truth.*

*If we seek truth, we shall find beauty.*

You've been told again and again to "follow your passion." But my advice would be... *Don't* pursue your passion directly. At least not yet. Instead, pursue the things that will empower you. Pursue knowledge. Be relentlessly curious. Listen, learn. Your learning cannot ever, ever be allowed to stop.

Pursue discipline. It's an old-fashioned word, but it's never been more important. Today's world is full of an impossible number of distractions. The world-changers are those who find a way of ignoring most of them.

Above all, pursue generosity. Not just because it will add meaning to your life—though it will do that—but because your future is going to be built on great ideas and in the future you are entering, great ideas HAVE to be given away. They do. The world is more interconnected than ever. The rules of what you give and what you hold on to have changed forever. If you hold on to your best ideas, maybe you can for a moment grab some short-term personal commercial gain. But if you let them roam free, they can spread like wildfire, earning you a global reputation. They can be reshaped and improved by others. They can achieve impact and influence in the world far greater than if you were to champion them alone. If we've discovered anything at TED these past few years, it's that radical openness pays. We gave away our talks on the web, and far from killing demand for the conference, it massively increased it, turning TED from something which

> **TODAY'S WORLD IS FULL OF AN IMPOSSIBLE NUMBER OF DISTRACTIONS. THE WORLD-CHANGERS ARE THOSE WHO FIND A WAY OF IGNORING MOST OF THEM.**

reached eight hundred people once a year to something which reached half a million people every day. We gave away our brand in the form of TEDx, and far from diluting TED, it democratized it, and multiplied its footprint a thousand fold.

Knowledge, discipline, generosity. If you pursue those with all the determination you possess, one day before too long, without your even knowing it, the chance to realize your most spectacular dreams will come gently tap you on the shoulder and whisper... "Let's go!" And you'll be ready.

That is how you're going to help shape a better future for all of us.

No pressure or anything, but we're counting on you.

To explore more American dreams and to learn more about Sharp Stuff visit makesharpstuff.com or talk with us on Twitter at @MakeSharpStuff

CPSIA information can be obtained at www.ICGtesting.com
Printed in the USA
BVOW012341210413

318708BV00007B/17/P